T0326460

Job Insecurity and Union Membership

European Unions in the Wake of Flexible Production

P.I.E.-Peter Lang

Bruxelles · Bern · Berlin · Frankfurt am Main · New York · Oxford · Wien

SALTSA
A Joint Programme for Working Life Research in Europe

SALTSA is a programme for research on European working life run in close co-operation by the Swedish National Institute for Working Life (NIWL/ALI) and the Swedish Confederations of Trade Unions (LO), Professional Employees (TCO) and Professional Associations (SACO).

The aim of SALTSA is to generate applicable research results of a high academic standard and practical relevance. Research is largely project-based.
Research is carried out in three areas:
- labour market and employment
- work organisation
- work environment and health

The Work Environment & Health Programme

Research on work environment and health focuses instruments and methods for healthier working conditions, the effects of certain risks in current working life as well as the conditions of selected groups of workers. Projects are designed with the ambition to contribute to the political debate and decision-making, applied occupational health and work environment management as well as participatory processes involving social partners in European working life.

Chairman of the Programme Committee for Work Environment and Health is Professor Per Malmberg.

website: www.niwl.se/saltsa

Magnus SVERKE, Johnny HELLGREN, Katharina NÄSWALL,
Antonio CHIRUMBOLO, Hans DE WITTE & Sjoerd GOSLINGA

Job Insecurity and Union Membership

European Unions in the Wake of Flexible Production

Arbetslivsinstitutet

lo TCO SACO

SALTSA — JOINT PROGRAMME
FOR WORKING LIFE RESEARCH IN EUROPE
The National Institute for Working Life and The Swedish Trade Unions in Co-operation

"Work & Society"
No.42

The research project, which was initialized in order to examine the role of unions in contemporary working life, was funded by the Swedish National Institute for Working Life (NIWL) through the Joint Programme for Working Life Research in Europe (SALTSA). We would also like to acknowledge the financial support that made possible our data collections: in Belgium, the Christian Labour Union (ACV) and the Hoger Instituut Voor de Arbeid (HIVA) at K.U. Leuven; in Italy, CGIL-Nazionale; in the Netherlands, the National Christian Trade Union Federation (CNV).

© P.I.E.-Peter Lang s.a.
Presses Interuniversitaires Européennes
Brussels, 2004
1 avenue Maurice, 1050 Brussels, Belgium
info@peterlang.com; www.peterlang.net

ISSN 1376-0955
ISBN 90-5201-202-4
US ISBN 0-8204-6622-0
D/2004/5678/22
Printed in Germany

Bibliographic information published by "Die Deutsche Bibliothek"

"Die Deutsche Bibliothek" lists this publication in the "Deutsche Nationalbibliografie"; detailed bibliographic data is available in the Internet at <http://dnb.ddb.de>.

CIP available from the British Library, GB
and the Library of Congress, USA.

Table of Contents

Preface

In Europe, as well as in other industrialized economies all over the world, employment relations have undergone profound transformations over the last decades. Large numbers of workers have been displaced, involuntarily part-time employed, or hired on temporary employment contracts. The increasing flexibility in the staffing of organizations is experienced, by many employees, as a threat to the continuation of their employment relationships. A growing body of research suggests that such job insecurity can be of fundamental importance from the occupational health perspective as well as the managerial, due to its effects on employees' work attitudes and well-being.

This book addresses the nature of job insecurity and investigates its consequences for individuals, the organizations they work for, as well as their labor unions. It also examines whether factors associated with union membership help employees to cope with employment uncertainty. The book is based on a European comparative project involving Belgium, Italy, the Netherlands, and Sweden.

Our work with the book would not have been possible without the support of various actors. The research project, which was initialized in order to examine the role of unions in contemporary working life, was funded by the Swedish National Institute for Working Life (NIWL) through the Joint Programme for Working Life Research in Europe (SALTSA). A special thanks to Anders Schaerström, Ph.D. and Secretary in the SALTSA Work Environment & Health Committee, for his encouraging support. We would also like to acknowledge the financial support that made possible our data collections: in Belgium, the Christian Labour Union (ACV) and the Hoger Instituut Voor de Arbeid (HIVA) at K.U. Leuven; in Italy, CGIL-Nazionale; in the Netherlands, the National Christian Trade Union Federation (CNV); and, in Sweden, the Swedish Council for Work Life Research. Finally, we are grateful to David Speeckaert and Hanna Stillström for their proofreading and work with the language.

Magnus Sverke   *Johnny Hellgren*   *Katharina Näswall*
Antonio Chirumbolo   *Hans De Witte*   *Sjoerd Goslinga*

CHAPTER 1

Introduction

Job insecurity is a perceptual phenomenon [and] in situations where objectively all jobs are equally at risk, employees are likely to differ in the amount of job insecurity experienced. (Jacobson, 1991a, p. 31)
Workers react to job insecurity, and their reactions have consequences for organizational effectiveness. (Greenhalgh & Rosenblatt, 1984, p. 438)
The relationship between trade unions and job insecurity has been strangely neglected. (Bender & Sloane, 1999, p. 123)
Unions may reduce both job insecurity and the stress associated with job insecurity. (Barling, Fullagar & Kelloway, 1992, p. 187)

These quotes communicate four critical observations concerning job insecurity and union membership. First of all, Jacobson (1991a) makes the important remark that job insecurity is a subjective phenomenon, based on the individual's perceptions and interpretations of the immediate work environment. Secondly, in their article – indeed one of the first systematic accounts of job insecurity and its consequences – Greenhalgh and Rosenblatt (1984) note that this stressor is not only burdensome for employees who worry about losing their jobs, but that it may also be of detriment to the organizations they work for.

The third observation is that research on job insecurity, as noted by Bender and Sloane (1999), typically has been reluctant to take labor unions into account. For instance, in comparison to the amount of effort that has gone into understanding how employees and companies are affected by feelings of employment uncertainty, the consequences for the unions have received only limited attention (e.g., Hartley, 1991). Despite this imbalance, there is research that suggests unions may also suffer the negative consequences of job insecurity (e.g., Armstrong-Stassen, 1993). Finally, it is also important to recognize that unions are relevant objects of study – since they may help protect members from job insecurity. Indeed, as Barling et al. (1992) state: "Because unions affect organizational functioning, it is simply impossible to obtain a comprehensive understanding of organizational behavior while simultaneously ignoring the role of unions" (p. 6).

The general aim of this book is to contribute to the understanding of the nature of job insecurity, its consequences, and the role of labor unions. The book is the result of a European research project – involving Belgium, Italy, the Netherlands, and Sweden – which was designed to shed light on job insecurity and union membership. The four themes outlined above will be subject to detailed scrutiny throughout the book. Initially, however, we would like to give some brief background information on why job insecurity is becoming an increasingly important problem in working life.

The Trend toward Escalating Employment Uncertainty

Several factors have contributed to employment relations gradually becoming more uncertain in the last decades. In Europe, as well as in other industrialized economies all over the world, organizations have had to adjust to the pressures imposed by an intensified global competition. For instance, the increasing internationalization has forced companies and organizations to reduce their production costs, which in turn has resulted in extensive organizational changes and more flexible and temporary terms of employment. Along with this, the strong belief in a market-driven economy has changed national policies and relaxed employment legislation in many countries. Furthermore, new technology has enabled production to become less labor intensive and reduced alternative employment options for unskilled labor. The rapid transformation from manufacturing centered industry to service production has resulted in major redistributions of the workforce and induced many employees to question their employers' stability within the labor market (Gallie, White, Cheng & Tomlinson, 1998; Jacobson & Hartley, 1991; Heery & Salmon, 2000; Howard, 1995; Sverke & Hellgren, 2002; Tetrick & Barling, 1995; Van Ruysseveldt, Huiskamp & van Hoof, 1995).

As briefly indicated above, transformations in the economic, social, and political spheres have forced organizations to undertake a variety of adaptive strategies in order to remain competitive in an increasingly flexible labor market. Such organizational responses are realized in actions such as outsourcings, privatizations, mergers, and acquisitions, and often occur in combination with personnel reductions through lay-offs, offers of early retirement, and the increased utilization of subcontracted workers (Burke & Cooper, 2000; Burke & Nelson, 1998; Pfeffer, 1998). Indeed, downsizing – or, as it is sometimes called, "rightsizing" – has become highly characteristic of contemporary working life, and the industrialized world has witnessed an increase in large-scale reductions that subject millions of workers to redundancies, involuntary part-time work, and fixed-term employment contracts (Cascio, 1995). For example, during the 1980s and 1990s, more than three million white-collar jobs were eliminated in the United States alone, and the situation in Asia and Europe is not much different (Rifkin, 1995).

Downsizing is a deliberate attempt to improve organizational effectiveness through workforce reductions (Cameron, Freeman & Mishra, 1991), and organizations engaged in downsizing often expect positive effects such as lower overhead costs, decreased bureaucracy, faster decision-making processes, smoother communication, increased productivity, and better earnings (Kets de Vries & Balazs, 1997). However, several studies have come to the conclusion that the postulated benefits of organizational downsizing are seldom achieved and that the negative side effects have severe consequences for the organization's vitality and competitive ability. For those who remain in the organization, the "downsizing survivors", the workload typically increases and uncertainty over task performance is likely to be prevalent (*e.g.*, Burchell, 2002; Burke & Nelson, 1998; Cameron *et al.*, 1991; Cascio, 1995, 1998; Kets de Vries & Balazs, 1997; Kozlowski, Chao, Smith & Hedlund, 1993; Pfeffer, 1998). Official statistics confirm this depiction of work intensification. For instance, every fourth employee (24.3 percent) within the European Union has declared that they are working at a very high speed all the time or almost all of the time, and almost one-third (29.4 percent) state that their job involves working with tight deadlines (European Foundation, 2001).

A key feature of the recent developments is that they have brought about changes in management practices and led to an increased emphasis on flexibility in the staffing of organizations (Cappelli, 1999; Gallie *et al.*, 1998; Pfeffer, 1998; Sparrow, 2000). Indeed, in an attempt to increase efficiency, organizations in most industrialized countries are currently involved in a phase of continuous restructuring that is increasingly geared towards greater numerical and functional flexibility (Purcell & Purcell, 1998; Sparrow & Marchington, 1998). It is important to note that employment relations have undergone profound transformations in connection with the rise in "atypical" employment arrangements, even though the sheer number of part-time jobs, temporary contracts, and different types of flexible work that deviate from "traditional" employment raises the question of whether such atypical employment arrangements are indeed so very atypical (Goslinga & Sverke, 2003; Van Ruysseveldt, 1995). Despite the fact that the unemployment rate within the European Union decreased at the end of the 1990s – from 10.7 percent in 1995 to 8.2 percent in 2000 – part-time work increased from 16.0 to 17.7 percent over the same period, and the proportion of temporary contractual arrangements rose from 10.0 to 11.4 percent (European Commission, 2001). Even if there exists various forms of temporary work (McLean Parks, Kidder & Gallagher, 1998), the deregulation of employment legislation in recent years has resulted in a substantial increase in temporary agency work (OECD, 1999). In terms of numbers, there were 2.2 million workers in this sector within the European Union in 1998 (CIETT, 2000). The gradual increase in temporary employment contracts takes on further significance given the fact that approximately one-third of all temporary workers in the European Union report that they involuntarily hold temporary jobs (European Commission, 2001).

Job Insecurity and Its Consequences

The transformation of working life, discussed in the previous section, has brought the topic of insecure working conditions to the forefront, and a growing number of scholars and practitioners are addressing the issue of job insecurity. A report from the OECD (1997), for instance, shows that media references to job (in)security increased substantially within the G7 countries in the 1980s and 1990s. The same OECD Employment Outlook report shows that there was an increase in the number of individuals who perceived their employment as insecure in the 1990s. Data from workers in all OECD countries show, for example, that the proportion stating that they were satisfied with their job security dropped from 61 to 56 percent between 1992 and 1996. The figures for 1996 ranged from 31 percent reporting unsatisfactory levels of job security, in Norway, to 50 percent or more in France, Japan, the United Kingdom, and the United States (OECD, 1997). The labor force also shows actual signs of being affected by these changing circumstances. Data from the third European survey on working conditions show that 60 percent of the workers in the European Union countries are of the opinion that their job affects their health in some way, while 27 percent even believe that their health and safety are at risk because of their job (Fagan & Burchell, 2002). The spread of work-related anxiety makes it all the more important to try and understand the various reasons why employees report lower well-being at work than they used to.

These data indicate that feelings of job insecurity are of vital importance in modern working life. A growing number of employees face the risk of losing their jobs as a consequence of organizational restructuring and layoffs. In the new labor market, keeping a job for any desired length of time is thus no longer a certainty. Several commentators have observed that long-term relationships based on mutual dependence between employer and employee have gradually given way to short-term employment relations based on flexibility (Hartley, 1995; Sparrow, 2000; Sverke & Hellgren, 2002; Van Ruysseveldt, 1995). There are researchers that go so far as to suggest that job insecurity will be a permanent ingredient in working life, that employees have to accept a certain degree of job insecurity, and that lifetime employment, along with a guaranteed standard of living, is no longer realistic (*e.g.*, Burke & Nelson, 1998; Pfeffer, 1998; Roskies & Louis-Guerin, 1990). It has even been claimed that we live in an "age of insecurity" (Elliott & Atkinson, 1998).

We will provide a more detailed account of the nature of job insecurity in subsequent chapters. At the moment, suffice it to say that job insecurity here is defined as a perceptual phenomenon, reflecting the fear of involuntary job loss. Job insecurity thus represents an individual's perception of the employment situation as more insecure than he or she desires. In the psychological research tradition, the experience of job insecurity is regarded as a stressor (Barling & Kelloway, 1996; Klandermans, Van Vuuren & Jacobson, 1991). According to stress theories, a stressor results in some type of strain reaction, with consequences for the health and well-being of the individual as well as for his/her work-related attitudes and behavior. Along these lines, it has even been remarked that "it would be strange indeed if the fear of unemployment had no implications for the way in which the employees experienced their work" (Gallie *et al.*, 1998, p. 21). However, job insecurity is likely to have more far-reaching consequences. In discussing the potential consequences of insecure employment, Heery and Salmon (2000) noted that:

> Insecurity is damaging to long-term economic performance, through its promotion of an employment relationship founded on opportunism, mistrust and low commitment; and [...] the emergence of an insecure workforce imposes severe costs on both individuals and the wider society. (Heery & Salmon, 2000, p. 1)

A growing body of research suggests that job insecurity may have important consequences for both the individual and the organization (for a review and meta-analysis of job insecurity and its consequences, see Sverke, Hellgren & Näswall, 2002). Empirical studies have shown that job insecurity is associated with mental and physical ill-health, as well as biological stress reactions (*e.g.*, Ashford, Lee & Bobko, 1989; Domenighetti, D'Avanso & Bisig, 2000; De Witte, 1999; McDonough, 2000). Previous research has also identified negative effects of job insecurity on organizational attitudes and behaviors directed towards the organization (*e.g.*, Ashford *et al.*, 1989; Davy, Kinicki & Scheck, 1997; Hellgren, Sverke & Isaksson, 1999). Other studies indicate that job insecurity may have effects such as setting off a resistance to change (Noer, 1993) and instigating a lack of compliance with safety regulations (Probst & Brubaker, 2001). One striking characteristic of previous research, however, is that it has generated only limited interest in trying to unravel what the effects of job insecurity are on labor unions.

Job Insecurity and Labor Unions

As we have seen above, it appears that job insecurity may have detrimental consequences for the employees as well as their organizations. Hence, the identification of factors that may reduce such negative effects certainly represents an important area for research. One could say that employees' reactions to uncertainties in a given organizational context are of fundamental importance from both the occupational health and managerial perspectives (Matteson & Ivancevich, 1987). The identification of moderators of the detrimental impact of job insecurity therefore takes on a twofold importance. From the occupational health perspective, it becomes crucial to understand how the negative consequences of job insecurity for employee well-being and work attitudes can be buffered. From the managerial perspective, it is obvious that a workforce plagued with stress reactions and impaired well-being cannot reverse organizational decline and make their organization more effective (Greenhalgh & Sutton, 1991; Sverke *et al.*, 2002).

The protecting of workers from the stress associated with job insecurity is definitely a matter of union interest. Not surprisingly, job insecurity appears to be a strong motive for joining unions (Bender & Sloane, 1999; Crocket & Hall, 1987). However, despite the fact that job insecurity is an important factor in unionized as well as non-unionized workplaces, only a few studies have actually focused on the role of unions. In the literature on labor unions there are studies that have examined the reasons for joining unions, the relationship between membership attitudes and participation, and how the unions may have an influence on salary, productivity, and employee attitudes (*e.g.*, Barling *et al.*, 1992; Freeman & Medoff, 1984; Gallagher & Strauss, 1991; Klandermans, 1986; Sverke & Kuruvilla, 1995; Wheeler & McClendon, 1991). Very little research, however, has focused on whether union membership may be related to job insecurity and its postulated outcomes (Bender & Sloane, 1999; Sverke & Hellgren, 2002).

Although the role of unions has often been overlooked in research on job insecurity, there are theoretical reasons suggesting that labor unions may be of importance for the understanding of work stress and strain. It has been suggested that "in addition to the well advertised effects on wages, unions alter nearly every other measurable aspect of the operation of workplaces and enterprises" (Freeman & Medoff, 1984, p. 19). One of the major benefits of unionization is indeed the protecting of workers from arbitrary treatment (Kochan, 1980). Union representation involves institutionalized forms for collective bargaining and formal procedures for protection of members' interests (Barling *et al.*, 1992). By providing the workers with a collective voice in turbulent situations, and through the negotiation of issues such as seniority systems and employment contract terms, "unions boost an individual's power to resist threats to overall job continuity or to job features" (Johnson, Bobko & Hartenian, 1992, p. 48). However, if the union is not successful in protecting members from job insecurity, serious backlashes may result. For instance, it has been shown that job insecurity is associated with dissatisfaction with the union (Johnson *et al.*, 1992), and that members who attribute uncertain employment conditions to the union respond with impaired loyalty to the union (Mellor, 1992). The determination of which support strategies are most effective for the membership would therefore, from the union perspective, appear to be of great importance.

Plan of the Book

The overall aim of this book is to increase the understanding of job insecurity and its consequences by focusing on the role of labor unions in an increasingly unpredictable labor market. Figure 1, which provides a schematic representation of the model underlying our research in this book, illustrates that this involves a number of different tasks. First, given that relatively little research has examined the predictors of job insecurity, an important issue is to identify some of the demographic characteristics that can make employees more vulnerable to the perception of job insecurity. An additional objective concerns the outcomes of job insecurity. While there is a growing body of literature on its consequences for the individual and the organization, we extend the understanding of job insecurity by also investigating how the union may be affected. Thirdly, since only a limited amount of research attention has been directed at uncovering how unionization affects employees' reactions to job insecurity, the book also aims to shed light on the labor unions' roles in addressing the consequences of the intensified flexibilization of the labor market. An important issue, in respect to this, concerns how union members evaluate the collective support that is provided through union membership, and to what extent such support affects the consequences of job insecurity for the individual, the organization, and the union.

Our discussion of job insecurity, its consequences, and the role played by the union is accompanied by a set of empirical tests. Whereas most research is based on data from a single sample, we use survey data

17

from employees in four European countries – Belgium, Italy, the Netherlands, and Sweden. The selection of countries guarantees sufficient heterogeneity concerning labor market contexts and industrial relations characteristics (*e.g.*, Ferner & Hyman, 1998; Visser, 1996; Waddington & Hoffmann, 2000), which implies that the results of the analyses may be meaningful within a European context. In this book, we are especially interested in the robustness of the empirical associations. It is beyond the scope of this analysis, therefore, to make detailed comparisons between countries, although differences will of course be discussed. Rather, the use of data from four European countries allows for the investigating of to what extent the results generalize across cultural settings.

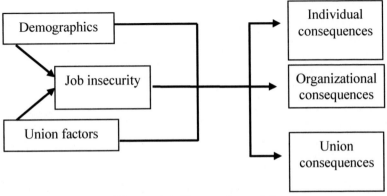

Figure 1.1. Research model

Chapter 2 describes the context of our study of job insecurity and its consequences. The sketching of similarities and differences in labor market characteristics and industrial relations climates between the four countries involved in the project provides a background against which to interpret the empirical findings. The chapter also describes the samples used in the different countries. This description is supplemented by an Appendix, which offers a more detailed account of our measures of the variables of interest.

The theoretical background of the book is described in Chapter 3, in which previous theory and research on job insecurity is discussed. It provides a description and definition of job insecurity and different aspects of the phenomenon. We relate the concept to stress theory and theories on psychological contracts between employee and employer. These theories, both of which emphasize the subjective nature of job insecurity, add to the understanding of job insecurity and its consequences by supplementing each other. The chapter is also dedicated to a discussion of how perceived job insecurity differs from unemployment and holding temporary employment contracts.

In Chapter 4, we describe how previous research has operationalized and measured job insecurity. Although various instruments for assessing the construct are available, measurement properties in terms of reliability, factor structure, and predictive validity are far from clear. In order to allow for meaningful comparisons of results across countries, the chapter contains a description and validation of the measure of job insecurity used in the present project.

Chapter 5 investigates the characteristics of individuals experiencing job insecurity. To shed light on this matter, we discuss various factors affecting the individual's experiencing of the situation as a threat to continued employment. These factors can be divided into two main groups. The first group of factors is mainly attributed to the individual and concerns personal characteristics such as age, sex, and different personality dispositions. The second domain deals with factors related to the organization and the social environment. Examples of these factors are employment contract and union membership. The theoretical discussion is accompanied by empirical tests of how different factors interact to shape the experience of job insecurity.

The consequences of job insecurity are the focus of Chapter 6. We give an account of the results pertaining to the consequences of job insecurity for employees' health and well-being, as well as for their attitudes relating to the job and the organization. The fear of losing one's job can, for example, result in feelings of anxiety and discomfort. This can have negative health effects, or involve decreased commitment to one's employer, possibly to the point where one wants to resign. The chapter also investigates how experiences of job insecurity relate to attitudes toward the union.

Chapter 7 investigates how factors associated with union membership relate to the consequences discussed in Chapter 6. Of particular interest is whether such factors can mitigate the negative effects of job insecurity. We discuss the role of the labor unions in this context and, more specifically, whether union membership and the collective support provided to members can help employees tackle the negative consequences associated with job insecurity perceptions. Given that the individual's work environment and well-being at work represent traditional issues on the union agenda, it becomes especially important to investigate to what extent union membership and perceptions of union support can reduce the negative consequences of job insecurity for the individual, the organization, and the union.

Chapter 8, the concluding chapter, discusses the major empirical findings of the book and integrates them with the theories used. In addition, various factors that may have affected the conclusions are also discussed, such as the characteristics of the countries included in the study and methodological issues relating to our questionnaire studies. The chapter outlines the theoretical implications of our results for future research on job insecurity as well as the practical implications for contemporary working life.

CHAPTER 2

Four European Countries

This book focuses on four countries, Belgium, Italy, the Netherlands, and Sweden. The use of four different countries provides a greater scope of information on job insecurity and the unions than studies that only focus on a single country. The empirical material is typically based on secondary data that had been collected for other purposes within each country, which we then reanalyzed focusing specifically on unions and job insecurity. Due to this, the information available in the different data sets differs somewhat from country to country. However, most of the variables analyzed appear in all countries, providing a broad foundation for our research issues. This chapter serves to describe the different countries appearing in the book, providing the reader with a contextual framework. We believe it is important to offer some background information regarding the context of the employment and the unions in the different countries. It is reasonable to suppose that four countries, in different parts of Europe, will differ somewhat in respect to labor market characteristics and union traditions. Also, since our data originated from four different data collections, we have included descriptions of the procedures that were used in the different countries.

Labor Market Characteristics

The four countries, which the results and discussion presented in this book are based on, differ from each other in a number of different areas. This section presents how these countries stand when it comes to labor market characteristics such as unemployment levels, different types of employment contracts, satisfaction with employment security, work pace and work-related injury. The objective of this presentation is not to compare these countries with each other but rather to provide a background for the contexts in which the respondents of the four countries work.

In general, data from the Office for Economic Cooperation and Development (OECD, 2002b) show that, over the last 20-year period, the proportion of service workers has risen, in all four countries, primarily at the expense of the agriculture sector but also at the expense of the industrial sector. Regarding the service sector, increases were shown in the proportion of the total civilian labor force in the period 1980–2000: from 62 percent to 74 percent in Belgium, from 48 to 62 percent in Italy, from 64 to 76 percent in the Netherlands, and from 62 to 73 percent in Sweden. This means that the service sector employed over 70 percent of the civilian labor force in three of the countries investigated, and over 60 percent in Italy.

Table 2.1 provides the employment rates for the year 2000 for individuals in the four countries that were between the ages of 15 and 64. Based on the table, it can be seen that the Netherlands and Sweden had the highest rate of employment – a little over 70 percent had some form of employment in the year 2000. The corresponding figure was approximately 60 percent for Belgium and 53 percent for Italy. These figures reveal that Italy and Belgium had the lowest proportion of employed persons between 15 and 64.

Table 2.1. Employment, 2000

	Belgium	Italy	The Netherlands	Sweden
Employment rate[a]	60.5	53.5	73.2	73.0
Women's employment rate[a]	51.5	39.6	63.7	71.0
Unemployment rate	7.0	10.5	2.7	5.9

[a] Employed persons as proportion of all individuals in age 15–64.
Source: European Commission (2001).

The higher employment rates in the Netherlands and Sweden can be explained by the fact that women are working to a greater extent in these countries. The table also indicates that Italy had the lowest proportion of women in the labor force for the year 2000. In Italy, the proportion of employed women between the ages of 15 and 64 was approximately 40 percent. The corresponding figures for Belgium and the Netherlands were around 52 and 64 percent, respectively. In Sweden, the proportion of women in the labor force was 71 percent. It can therefore be claimed that Sweden has the highest proportion of female participation in the labor market and Italy the lowest.

In regard to the proportion of unemployed persons, the table shows that Italy had the highest level of unemployment for the year 2000, at around 10 percent, while the figures for Belgium and Sweden were around 7 and 6 percent, respectively, for that same year. The lowest unemployment rate was found in the Netherlands, with less than 3 percent. These figures, following the same pattern as those earlier, indicate that Italy and Belgium have the lowest proportions of individuals in the labor force between the ages of 15 and 64, as well as the lowest proportion of employed women. These two countries also boast the highest unemployment levels for the year 2000.

Another interesting area that pertains to the labor market characteristics of the participating countries has to do with the proportions of the civilian labor force that are employed on different types of employment contracts. Over the last few decades, we have seen a rise in the use of various types of temporary employment (McLean Parks *et al.*, 1998; Purcell & Purcell, 1998; Sherer, 1996) that can naturally have an effect on an individual's sense of security and position in the labor market. Table 2.2 shows the percentage of part-time, fixed-term, and temporary agency contracts as well as the proportion of self-employed in relation to the entire labor forces of the four countries.

Table 2.2. Employment contracts, in percent

	Belgium	Italy	The Netherlands	Sweden
Part-time employment, 2000[a]	20.8	8.4	41.1	22.6
Fixed-term employment contracts, 2000[a]	7.5	7.5	11.9	13.1
Temporary agency work, 1999[a]	1.6	0.2	4.0	0.8
Self-employment, 1996[a]	15.4	24.8	11.2	11.7

[a] As share of total employment.
Sources: European Commission (2001); Gold & Weiss (1998); Storrie (2002).

When it comes to part-time employment, we find the highest percentage in the Netherlands where around 40 percent of the labor force is employed under part-time contracts. The corresponding figures for Belgium and Sweden are around 20 percent. Italy has the lowest proportion of part-time employees at around 8.5 percent. The highest proportions of people employed under fixed-term contracts can be seen in Sweden, at 13 percent, and in the Netherlands, at 12 percent, while both Belgium and Italy have 7.5 percent of their labor forces in fixed-term employment contracts in 2000. Regarding individuals working for temporary agencies, the figures show that the Netherlands had the highest proportion, 4.0 percent of the total labor force during 1999. The corresponding figure was 1.6 percent for Belgium and 0.8 percent for Sweden. The lowest figure amongst our countries was Italy's with 0.2 percent of its labor force working for temporary employment agencies in 1999. The proportion of self-employed workers in 1996 was highest in Italy where one fourth of the labor force was self-employed, while the corresponding figure for Belgium was around 15 percent. In the Netherlands and Sweden, the proportion of self-employed workers was around 11 percent for that same period.

It appears, then, that the highest proportions of the labor force that hold part-time or temporary employment contracts are to be found in the Netherlands and Sweden. The Netherlands also has the highest proportion of its labor force in temporary employment agencies. It could also be said that the highest proportion of self-employed is to be found in Italy.

A gradual shift to more temporary employment forms also brings with it a rise in uncertainty over the future and not least of all in regard to an individual's ability to keep the current job. Temporary employment is one of the factors that could be expected to generate an increase in the worry that large sections of the workforce sense in relation to their employment. Table 2.3 shows the proportion of workers who do not regard their employment as being completely secure as well as the proportion who are satisfied with their employment security (the reader may be alerted that this operationalization of job insecurity may make the estimate seem rather large). There is an indication that the tempo of working life has increased which can carry with it an increase in the number of work-related injuries. Table 2.3 also shows the proportion of serious work-related injuries occurring per 100,000 workers for each of the countries. Additionally, the table reveals how large of a proportion of their GDPs the public sectors of these countries each spend on health, labor market programs and labor market training.

If we consider those workers who in 1996 did not believe their employment was secure, we find the largest proportion in Sweden (73.3 percent), followed by Belgium (71.5 percent), Italy (69.6 percent) and lastly the Netherlands (60.3 percent). A similar pattern can also be seen when we examine the proportion who are satisfied with their employment security, where Sweden shows the lowest proportion of satisfied workers (49 percent), followed by Italy (55 percent). For Belgium and the Netherlands, it was 60 and 61 percent, respectively, who reported they were satisfied with their employment security. The percentages are based on the norm level of employment security and are calculated as the average of the percentage reporting favorable answers to four questions concerning the level of job insecurity perceived (for details, see OECD, 1997).

Table 2.3. Work intensification

	Belgium	Italy	The Netherlands	Sweden
Insecure job, 1996 (%)[a]	71.5	69.6	60.3	73.3
Satisfied with job security, 1996 (%)	60.0	55.0	61.0	49.0
Working at very high speed, 2000 (%)[b]	18.3	22.6	32.0	35.5
Fatal occupational injuries/100,000 workers, 1996	5.4	7.0	–	2.3
Public expenditure on health (% of GDP)	6.7	5.3	6.2	7.2
Public expenditure on labor market programs (% of GDP)	3.5	–	3.4	2.3
Public expenditure on labor market training (% of GDP)	0.2	0.1	0.8	0.3

[a] Proportion of workers not strongly agreeing to the statement "My job is secure".
[b] Proportion reporting working at very high speed all the time or almost all of the time.
– No data available.
Sources: European Commission (2001); ILO (2000); OECD (1997, 2002a); World Bank (2000).

The proportion of employees to report that they work at a very high tempo all the time or at least nearly all the time is highest in Sweden (35.5 percent) and the Netherlands (32.0 percent), while both Italy (22.6 percent) and Belgium (18.3) report a lower proportion working at a high tempo for the year 2000. Regarding the occurrence of work-related injuries per 100,000 workers, we find the highest proportion in Italy, where 7 out of every 100,000 suffered serious injury at work in 1996. The corresponding figures for Belgium and Sweden were, respectively, 5.4 and 2.3 per 100,000 workers. The data on the number of serious work-related injuries for the Netherlands is missing. Lastly, we can observe that it is Sweden that spends the highest proportion of its GDP on public health (7.2 percent), followed by Belgium (6.7 percent) and the Netherlands (6.2 percent). The country to spend the lowest proportion of its GDP on public health in this study is Italy (5.3 percent). When it comes to the proportion of GDP that goes towards labor market programs, the figures are 3.5 percent for Belgium, 3.4 for the Netherlands and 2.3 percent for Sweden (information on the proportion of GDP that goes towards labor market programs is lacking for Italy). Of the proportions going towards labor market programs, each of these countries dedicates a percentage to the financing of labor market training: 0.2 percent in Belgium, 0.1 percent in Italy, 0.8 percent in the Netherlands and 0.3 percent in Sweden.

These data indicate that a large portion of the labor force in the participating countries does not feel that they enjoy secure employment and that many of these employees are also dissatisfied with their job security. It can furthermore be observed that between 20 and 30 percent of the workforce works at a very high tempo for all or nearly all of the workday. In this context it can also be of interest to see how the proportion of overtime hours worked is distributed among the countries of this study. According to Smulders and Klein Hesselink (1997), the amount of overtime for 1996 was 1.7 hours per week for both Belgium and Italy, 1.4 hours for the Netherlands and 1.2 hours per week for Sweden.

Industrial Relations Characteristics

In this section, we describe several factors that characterize the labor movements of Belgium, Italy, the Netherlands, and Sweden. Just as there are a number of labor market characteristics that distinguish these countries from one another, differences also exist regarding the characteristics of their industrial relations. Likewise, alongside certain common trends and phenomena existing in labor market conditions, there are also a number of labor movement features that these countries have in common. Once again, our primary aim is still to supply a background for the contexts in which the data were collected and not to conduct a comparative analysis of the differences between these countries. Nor does this section attempt to provide a comprehensive description of the industrial relations climates in the four countries. For such information, the interested reader should refer to those edited volumes that, for most European countries, provide a thorough account of the history of the union movements, including detailed analyses of the change in unionization rates and rich descriptions of the relations between the various actors in the labor market (*e.g.*, Ebbinghaus & Visser, 2000; Ferner & Hyman, 1998; Waddington & Hoffman, 2000).

One area where there exist considerable differences between the countries concerns the unionization rate. Table 2.4 shows the proportion of workers that belonged to trade unions in the mid-1990s. In 1995, the proportion of unionized workers in Sweden (85 percent) stood in contrast to the rather low union density rates of the Netherlands (23 percent) and Italy (32 percent), with Belgium (60 percent) in an intermediate position (Ebbinghaus & Visser, 2000; Kjellberg, 2001; figures including unemployed workers). It is interesting to note that in Sweden, Italy, and the Netherlands (the data was not available for Belgium) the proportion of union members is higher in the public sector than in the private (Boeri, Brugiavini & Calmfors, 2001).

Table 2.4. Union membership, mid-1990s

	Belgium	Italy	The Netherlands	Sweden
Overall union density	60	32	23	85
Private sector union density	–	36	19	77
Public sector union density	–	43	45	93

Sources: Boeri *et al.* (2001); Ebbinghaus & Visser (2000); Kjellberg (2001).
– Data not available.

Despite the considerable fluctuations that have occurred in the rates of unionization in all four countries over the years, the current figures reflect a relatively consistent trend. In Italy, for instance, union density sank from 51 percent in 1950 to 30 percent in 1969, then gradually rose to nearly 50 percent again over the next ten year period, before sinking once again (Regini & Regalia, 2000). In contrast, the proportion of union membership in Sweden, with only a few exceptions, has steadily increased during the post-war era (Kjellberg, 1998, 2001). By only examining the development of the union density rates from the mid-1980s through the mid-1990s, we can observe that rather dramatic declines occurred in Italy and the Netherlands (-7.5 percent and -11.0 percent, respectively); in contrast, the level of unionization held stable in Belgium (-0.2 percent) and increased in Sweden (+8.7 percent) over that same period (Gold & Weiss, 1998).

The differences in unionization rates amongst the countries are naturally a reflection of the ability of the unions to attract and organize different categories of employees. One of the key reasons that Sweden, in an international comparison, has a very high unionization rate is because the Swedish labor unions have long since made it a practice to organize groups of employees who, in other countries, are not involved in unions to such a large degree. If we consider, for example, the rise in the participation of women in the workforce, such a development should, among other things, be reflected by a corresponding influx of women into the unions, but what we find is that the proportion of female members varies considerably between the countries (Lovenduski, 1986). And, while the level of unionization among females in Sweden (90 percent) exceeds that of the males (83 percent), the situation in the Netherlands is the opposite (33 percent for males, 20 percent for females) (Boeri *et al.*, 2001). Today's figures reflect the strong rise in female union density occurring in Sweden from the 1960s through the 1980s (+42.5 percent), as compared to countries such as the Netherlands (-1.5 percent) (Curtin, 1997). Another example concerns the rate of unionization among younger employees. Despite the fact that the younger generation, due to the processes of individualization, is less interested in joining a union (Allvin & Sverke, 2000; Valkenburg, 1996), major differences exist between the countries. In the Netherlands, for instance, less than 14 percent of young employees (16–24 years) belong to unions (Valkenburg & Coenen, 2000), while the corresponding figure for Italy, in the same age category, is around one third (Regalia & Regini, 1998), and nearly 50 percent for both Belgium (Van Gyes, De Witte & van der Hallen, 2000) and Sweden (Kjellberg, 2000). A further example concerns the organization of white-collar employees in the private sector, as it is an area where Swedish unions, in contrast to most other countries, have been successful in organizing this segment of the workforce (Kjellberg, 2001).

Another distinguishing characteristic has to do with the organization of part-time and temporary workers, whose rate of unionization, in general, is clearly lower than that of employees with traditional forms of employment. One reason for this is that employees with "atypical" employment contracts are often regarded, by the unions, as being more difficult to organize (Gallagher & Sverke, 2000; Goslinga & Sverke, 2003). Another reason for the lower union density rates among atypical workers might be that many unions have been reluctant to accept new employment types. In the same way that the union movements of many countries initially opposed part-time employment, there has also been an opposition to the spread of temporary employment since such employment forms provide less employment security (Barling & Gallagher, 1996; Delsen, 1995). It is also worth noting that even though union membership among workers holding temporary or part-time contracts is lower than among their full-time and permanently employed counterparts, these differences are less pronounced in countries with extremely high unionization rates, such as Sweden and Finland (Barling & Gallagher, 1996; Delsen, 1995).

There are of course a number of different reasons for the variations in the levels of unionization amongst the countries. One often mentioned reason has to do with the administration of the unemployment insurance system. The majority of European countries introduced some type of publicly supported unemployment insurance protection program before World War II. This was either a compulsory system directed by government agencies or a voluntary, but state supported, system that was administered by the union, the so-called Ghent system (Rothstein,

1992). In Sweden, the unemployment insurance funds are administered by the unions, which results in many unemployed individuals retaining their memberships in order to benefit from the unemployment insurance (Kjellberg, 2001). In Belgium, unemployment insurance was placed under state control after World War II, but the unions managed to retain an important part in the administration of the system and even received state support that enabled them to do it (Vilrokx & Van Leemput, 1998). In the Netherlands, the use of unionized unemployment funds was discontinued in 1952 and was followed by a state administered unemployment insurance system – which is often given as a reason for the strongly declining unionization rate in recent decades (Western, 1997). The difference between the Ghent system and the state system can, in part, provide an explanation for the differences in unionization that exist between Belgium and the Netherlands, as well as between Norway (that has the state system) and the other Scandinavian countries (Ebbinghaus & Visser, 2000).

Another reason for the differences in unionization rates has to do with the degree of union representation at the workplace. In both Belgium and Sweden there are union organizations that fulfill important functions directly at the workplace, as they provide members with somewhere to turn when they have questions (Kjellberg, 2001). Local organizing of this nature not only means that members can more easily see to that their work-related interests are met and quickly receive help with their problems, but also that the union gains a higher visibility. In both of these countries, there is a combination of local organization and strongly centralized union activity. A characteristic of the Swedish model of interest representation, which has long served as a source of inspiration for union officials as well as industrial relations researchers, is this very combining of broad centralization with decentralization through strong organizations at the workplace (Kjellberg, 1998). In contrast to Belgium and Sweden, there is a lack of union organizations at the workplace in the Netherlands. The picture is more complex for Italy. Periods of centralization and decentralization have succeeded each other in this country, but since the middle of the 1980s, Italy has been characterized by company-level decentralized action through local unions and works councils (Regini & Regalia, 2000).

There are also interesting differences between the countries regarding trade union structures and the division of the labor movement into confederations. As Table 2.5 shows, by the end of the 1990s, there were three confederations in each of Belgium, Italy, and Sweden, while there were four in the Netherlands. What makes this interesting is the principle used for the distribution of unions and members between these confederations. The federations are divided along political as well as religious lines in Belgium (Van Gyes *et al.*, 2000) and according to occupational status and religion in the Netherlands (Valkenburg & Coenen, 2000), whereas the Italian union movement is divided on political grounds (Regini & Regalia, 2000), and Sweden has separate confederations for blue-collar workers, white-collar employees, and professionals (Kjellberg, 2000). The number of unions, as well as the number of members, varies between these confederations (Visser, 1995).

In Belgium, the trade union movement is divided into three major organizations – the catholic *Algemeen Christelijk Vakverbond/Confédération des Syndicats Chrétiens* (ACV-CSC), the social democratic *Algemeen Belgisch Vakverbond/Fédération Générale du Travail de Belgique* (ABVV-FGTB), and the liberal *Algemene Centrale der Liberale Vakbonden van België/Confédération Générale des Syndicats Libéraux de Belgique* (ACLVB-CGSLB) (Van Gyes *et al.*, 2000). The catholic ACV-CSC is the largest confederation and organizes approximately half of all union members in the country, while the socialist ABVV-FGTB has about one third of the union members, and the liberal ACLVB-CGSLB organizes about 10 percent of all union members in Belgium. While the ACV-CSC and the ABVV-FGTB include approximately 20 and 10 member organizations respectively, the ACLVB-CGSLB is an organization without unions (Visser, 1995). As Table 2.5 shows, 90 percent of all workers in Belgium are covered by the collective bargaining agreements that are met by employers and union organizations (Boeri *et al.*, 2001).

In contrast to Belgium, the union movement in Italy is divided exclusively according to political preference. The *Confederazione Generale Italiana del Lavoro* (CGIL) can be characterized as communist/social democrat, the *Confederazione italiana sindacati dei lavoratori* (CISL) as catholic/social democrat, and the *Unione Italiana del Lavoro* (UIL) as social democrat (Regalia & Regini, 1998). Both CGIL, which organizes approximately 50 percent of all unionized workers in Italy, and CISL, organizing around a third of all members, had 17 member unions in the 1990s. The smallest confederation – UIL – with around 10 percent of all unionized Italian workers, was the most fragmented with 27 member unions (Visser, 1995). In Italy, around 70 percent of all workers are covered by some collective bargaining agreement (Boeri *et al.*, 2001).

In the Netherlands, the relatively weak union movement (with regard to membership numbers) is also divided into confederations. In the middle of the 1990s, the largest confederation – the social democratic/catholic *Federatie Nederlandse Vakbeweging* (FNV) – had almost

60 percent of the membership with 19 affiliates. The Christian federation *Christelijk Nationaal Vakverbond* (CNV) had 15 member unions and organized around 20 percent of all union members. The *Verbond van Hoger en Middelbaar Personeel* (VHP), organizing professional employees, had 3 affiliates, whereas the *Algemene Vakcentrale* (AVC), organizing workers in the public sector and crafts workers, had more than 20 member unions (Visser, 1995, 1998). The proportions of union members organized by both the VHP and the AVC were small. However, in 1998 the AVC was incorporated into the FNV. The collective bargaining coverage includes around 70 percent of all Dutch employees (Boeri *et al.*, 2001).

In Sweden, the structure of the union movement is based on different occupational groups. *Landsorganisationen* (LO) organizes blue-collar workers, *Tjänstemännens Centralorganisation* (TCO) organizes white-collar employees, whereas professional employees with university degrees are organized by *Sveriges Akademikers Centralorganisation* (SACO). In 2002, these confederations had 16, 19, and 25 unions, respectively. The LO has always been the largest confederation, even if differences in membership numbers between the confederations have diminished gradually. In 2001, the LO organized 53 percent of all Swedish union members, the TCO 33 percent, and the SACO 12, whereas 3 percent belonged to independent unions not affiliated with any of the three confederations (Kjellberg, 2002). In the mid-1990s, 83 percent of all Swedish workers were covered by the collective agreements between employers and unions (Boeri *et al.*, 2001).

Table 2.5. Structure of union movement, 1990s

	Belgium	Italy	The Netherlands	Sweden
Number of confederations	3	3	3	3
Cleavage[a]	Religion/ political	Political	Collarline/ religion	Collarline
Main level of collective bargaining	National/ sector	Sector	Sector	Sector
Collective bargaining coverage (% of employees)	90	70	81	83

Sources: Boeri *et al.* (2001); Van Gyes *et al.* (2000); Visser, (1995)
[a] Cleavage for structuring the union movement into federations: religion, political, collarline (white- *vs.* blue-collar).

Still another area where there are differences between the four countries concerns industrial conflicts (*i.e.*, the number of strikes and lockouts). Italy, like a number of other southern European countries, is known for having a relatively unstable industrial relations climate, where industrial conflicts are a daily event (Regini & Regalia, 2000). In contrast to this, Sweden has a reputation for being a country characterized by peaceful labor relations, which can, in part, be attributed to the stable power balance existing between employers and the unions, which is itself a consequence of the high unionization rate and the well established framework for resolution of conflicts of interest. The Netherlands are also known for having a cooperation-friendly climate amongst the various parties in the labor market despite their considerably lower level of union membership. Belgium falls in the middle since it has clearly had fewer strikes and lockouts than Italy, yet generally more than both the Netherlands and Sweden. Data from the International Labour Office (ILO, 2000) essentially confirm this picture and show that the frequency of industrial conflicts in Italy (typically around a thousand per year) clearly outnumbered that of the Netherlands and Sweden (normally between 10 and 20 per year) in the 1990s, whereas the number of industrial conflicts in Belgium varied considerably more (*e.g.*, 17 in 1997 and 484 in 1998). It becomes evident that even though the strike frequency has decreased considerably in Belgium since the 1970s (Vilrokx & Van Leemput, 1998), it is still higher than in both the Netherlands and Sweden.

Table 2.6. Industrial conflicts, 1996

	Belgium	Italy	The Nether-lands	Sweden
Number of strikes/lockouts	60	904	12	9
Workers involved	19,971	1,689,400	8,126	9,137
Percent of workforce involved	0.5	7.5	0.1	0.2
Days not worked	146,256	1,930,000	7,394	61,348
Rate of days not worked (per 1,000 employees)	34	85	1	14

Sources: ILO (2000); OECD (2002a).

Table 2.6 presents the data regarding industrial conflicts in the four countries for 1996. In total, there were 904 strikes and lockouts in Italy for this year, which affected nearly 1.7 million employees (ILO, 2000). This means that, on average, 7.5 percent of the civilian workforce was involved in some sort of industrial conflict during 1996. The Netherlands and Sweden had, in contrast to this, only around ten or so such conflicts that in each country affected fewer than ten thousand workers, resulting in only 0.1 percent (the Netherlands) and 0.2 percent (Sweden) of their respective labor forces being affected. In Belgium, there occurred a total of 60 strikes and lockouts for this year, affecting nearly 20,000 employees, which indicates that about one half of a percent of its civilian workforce was involved in some sort of industrial conflict. When the number of days not worked because of industrial conflicts is set in relation to the total civilian workforce, we arrive at the proportion of days lost per thousand employees; this figure was highest for Italy (85) and lowest for the Netherlands (1) with Belgium (34) and Sweden (14) coming in between.

The Samples Used in This Book

The analyses reported in this book are typically based on secondary data, assembled from different countries in order to address our research questions. Each country is thereby represented by one data set, described below. However, for some of the analyses, we have used alternative data sets from Belgium and Sweden, since the standard data sets lacked information on some central variables. Therefore, we have also included brief descriptions of these alternative data sets below. Table 2.7 supplies information on sample sizes and response rates, and Table 2.8 reports basic demographic information for each sample. Measurement charac-teristics for the variables used in subsequent chapters are reported in the Appendix.

Data Collection

The Belgian data were collected by means of a postal survey in No-vember and December of 1998. The target population came from the three different parts of Belgium (Flanders, Brussels, Wallonia), which necessitated the use of two languages: Flemish and French. This data collection was part of a larger study focusing on health and repetitive strain injuries. The sampling was done in two stages. First, a representa-tive sample of Belgian companies with at least five employees was selected. The personnel manager of each of these companies was con-tacted and asked whether he or she was willing to distribute question-naires among the employees. The questionnaires were randomly distrib-uted in those cases where the staff exceeded 60 persons – otherwise, the entire personnel received the questionnaire. Of the 439 companies con-tacted, only 116 personnel managers could be reached, with some among them not wishing to participate. Among those who did agree to participate, a total of 3,003 questionnaires were sent out. Despite the difficulties in assessing how many actually reached the employees, a total of 1,120 questionnaires were returned, which makes the lowest possible response rate 37 percent.

Table 2.7. Sample sizes and response rates

	Belgium	Italy	The Netherlands	Sweden
Sampling frame	3,003	865	1,590	2,564
Respondents	1,120	476	799	1,923
Response rate (%)	37	55	50	75

Since the standard Belgian data set did not include information on union attitudes, it was supplemented with an alternative data set. These data were collected in the spring of 1998, from a sample representative of the Belgian population in size and province. In this case, telephone interviews were used instead of postal questionnaires. A specific sample consisting of 23,912 persons was selected to be contacted by telephone (the unemployed and other non-actives in the labor market were excluded). Of these, 25 percent could not be contacted, 25 percent refused to participate, and 44 percent were found not to fit the criteria. Only 1,487 of the original selected sample fit the criteria and agreed to be interviewed. Thus, the response rate reached approximately 11 percent.

In contrast to Belgium, the Italian data were collected after the start of the project, and the data collection could thereby be tailored to fit the research questions. Data were collected from May to July of 2000 among a sample recruited mainly from the northern and central areas of the country among persons primarily employed in the private sector. A total of 865 workers received the questionnaires, which were chiefly distributed among small groups at the workplaces of the respondents. The response rate reached 55 percent, as 476 usable questionnaires were returned.

The data from the Netherlands were taken from a large longitudinal panel-survey among members of the largest trade unions affiliated with the National Christian Trade Union Federation, the CNV. Accordingly, all respondents were union members. For this panel survey, which started in 1992, randomly selected union members are interviewed via telephone at each instance of data collection. Members are asked to participate in three telephone surveys and are then replaced by fellow members. The interviews, on average, take about 25 minutes. Before the first interview, the members receive a letter from their union with some information on the procedure and goal of the study, along with a request to participate. Prior to a second or third interview, members who have already participated once or twice receive a similar letter from the researchers. The data used in this book were collected in the thirteenth wave of the panel study. The participants consisted of 799 members out of a sample of 1,590 (response rate 50 percent).

Data for Sweden were collected in a national sample of blue-collar workers from the Swedish Municipal Workers Union (Kommunal) that is affiliated with the Swedish Trade Union Confederation (LO). The respondents were randomly selected from a total population of 370,590 members. Questionnaires were sent out to the home addresses of 2,564 workers. Those returned yielded 1,923 usable questionnaires for a response rate of 75 percent.

The standard Swedish data set was supplemented with an alternative data set that included data on education, occupational status, and personality. The alternative Swedish data were collected among the staff of two emergency hospitals in Wave 3 of a longitudinal study investigating the effects of ownership changes in healthcare. Questionnaires were mailed to the home addresses of all 2,455 employees at the two hospitals. A total of 1,501 usable questionnaires were returned to the research team, resulting in a response rate of 61 percent.

Sample Characteristics

Table 2.8 reports general demographic information on the four countries. The majority (65 percent) of the respondents in the standard Belgian data set were men, with a mean age of 37 years (ranging between 18 and 62). A third of the sample had completed a higher-level education of some type. Approximately a third of the sample reported that they were employed in some type of blue-collar work, and the same proportion reported that they worked in some kind of white-collar work. The average length of employment with the organization was 14 years. Most of the respondents worked full-time and held permanent contracts. Approximately half of the respondents were members of a union.

The respondents in the alternative Belgian data set exhibited demographics similar to those in the standard data set. The mean age was 39 years, with a range of between 20 and 65 years. The majority of respondents were male (58 percent). The social class of the respondents varied; about a third of the respondents reported that they were blue-collar workers, and another third indicated they were white-collar workers. Almost half of the respondents (45 percent) had completed some sort of higher education. Most of the respondents reported working full-time (82 percent) and in permanent positions (92 percent). Slightly more than half (59 percent) of the participants were union members.

The majority of the Italian respondents were men (68 percent), and their mean age was 39 years (ranging between 19 and 64). A little less than half of the respondents (42 percent) had completed high school.

35

About one third of the respondents reported they were blue-collar workers, and an even larger proportion (46 percent) reported that they were white-collar workers. The average organizational tenure was 13 years, and the majority worked full-time, holding permanent positions. About two thirds of the Italian respondents were union members. Of the respondents, 65 percent were living with a partner, and 57 percent were responsible for the care of at least one child.

As was the case in both the Belgian and Italian data sets, the majority of the Dutch respondents were men (75 percent). Their age ranged between 16 and 85 (for a mean age of 48 years). Since the sampling was based on union membership, as opposed to employment, some respondents (23 percent) were unemployed, on disability leave, or retired. The majority (80 percent) of the members with paid employment had a full-time job. Most of the employed persons held permanent positions, and here only a small proportion (8 percent) worked in white-collar type jobs. The rest were fairly evenly divided amongst blue-collar or professional employment, and 40 percent had completed high school. The majority of the Dutch respondents were married or living with someone, and approximately half of the respondents had children living with them. All participants were union members, with an average union tenure of 18 years.

Contrary to the previous data sets from the other countries, women made up the majority (78 percent) of the participants in the standard Swedish data set. The average age of the respondents was 45, ranging between 19 and 75 years of age. Most of the employees (93 percent) were permanently employed, but less than half (47 percent) worked full-time. The average length of employment was 14 years. All participants were members of a union for blue-collar workers.

The alternative Swedish data set contained more explicit information on demographics. As in the standard data set, the majority (83 percent) of the respondents were women, with an average age of 43 years. Half of the participants reported themselves to be white-collar employees, and about one third blue-collar. A majority (83 percent) were permanently employed, and 60 percent worked full-time. The average organizational tenure was 12 years. Two thirds of these respondents were living with a partner, and one third hade children living at home. The proportion of union members was 92 percent.

Table 2.8. Sample characteristics

	Belgium	Italy	The Netherlands	Sweden
Personal demographics				
Mean age (years)	37	39	48	45
Gender (% women)	38	32	25	78
Married/cohabitating (%)	–	65	84	–
Children at home (%)	–	57	55	–
Highest level of education				
Compulsory school (%)	23	31	55	–
High school (%)	42	58	40	–
University (%)	35	11	5	–
Work-related demographics				
Average organizational tenure (years)	14	13	–	14
Part-time work (%)	9	7	20	53
Temporary employment contract (%)	6	11	10	7
Social class				
Blue-collar (%)	36	29	47	–
White-collar (%)	36	46	8	–
Professional (%)	28	25	45	–
Union-related demographics				
Union members (%)	49	63	100	100
Average union tenure (years)	–	13	18	16

– Not measured in the standard sample (for details concerning the alternative data sets used for Belgium and Sweden, see descriptions in the text).

Concluding Remarks

In light of the above presentation, we can see that there are a number of similarities between Belgium, Italy, the Netherlands, and Sweden when it comes to trends and developments within the labor market and the industrial relations areas. There are also of course a number of differences to be found between these four countries in regard to their labor market characteristics and the factors related to trade unionism. Certain differences can also be found regarding the respondents and the sample characteristics of the various data sets underlying this book's empirical material, particularly in the areas of sampling, data collection methods, and response rates. The individuals of these countries also differ somewhat when it comes to the demographic variables of average age, gender, education, and union tenure. These differences and similarities will be important to remember when we take a look at job insecurity and union membership in the four countries in subsequent chapters. Although the aim of this book is not to compare countries with each other, it is still important to keep the characteristics that are specific to certain countries in mind when the results are interpreted and discussed, since they have a bearing on the results presented.

CHAPTER 3

The Nature of Job Insecurity

The uncertain and unpredictable conditions prevailing in the labor market have extensive consequences. One of these consequences is the experience of job insecurity, which has been associated with stress reactions among individual employees. Job insecurity can be described briefly as the difference between an individual's preferred level of job security and his or her perception of the actual security of the employment. If the future of the employment is perceived to be more insecure than is desired, in that the individual feels that there is a risk of losing a job he/she wants to keep, then this results in the experience of job insecurity. This chapter presents a theoretical framework for understanding job insecurity and its consequences. The chapter argues in favor of a subjective definition of job insecurity, and discusses how job insecurity can be understood by using a stress theoretical framework as well as theories relating to the notion of the psychological contract.

Definition

Job insecurity refers to worries related to the continuation of the present job (De Witte, 1999; Sverke & Hellgren, 2002). The concept is described as the subjective perception of a threat to the future of the job (*e.g.*, Greenhalgh & Rosenblatt, 1984). To emphasize the subjective nature of job insecurity, it has been described as a "perceptual phenomenon" (Jacobson, 1991a, p. 31). A perceptual phenomenon allows for the subjective experience of a situation to differ from its actual objective nature. A perceptual definition of job insecurity focuses on the discrepancy between the desired job security and the actual experience of security, based on interpretations of the work environment. Such a discrepancy would lead to feelings of job insecurity in the case of experienced risk of involuntary job loss (Greenhalgh & Rosenblatt, 1984).

Among the definitions of job insecurity we may discern a common denominator, namely that job insecurity is a stressor with potentially negative consequences for well-being and work-related attitudes (De Witte, 1999; Klandermans *et al.*, 1991; Sverke & Hellgren, 2002). Most definitions used in the social and behavioral sciences, especially in the field of psychology, emphasize the importance of the subjective experience. Some authors also include involuntariness in their definition of the job insecurity construct. Based on this, a number of somewhat similar definitions have been presented in the literature. Job insecurity has, for example, been described as:

- "one's expectations about continuity in a job situation" (Davy *et al.*, 1997, p. 323);
- "powerlessness to maintain desired continuity in a threatened job situation" (Greenhalgh & Rosenblatt, 1984, p. 438);
- "an overall concern about the future existence of the job" (Rosenblatt & Ruvio, 1996, p. 587);
- "an employee's perception of a potential threat to continuity in his or her current job" (Heaney, Israel & House, 1994, p. 1431);
- "a discrepancy between the level of security a person experiences and the level she or he might prefer" (Jacobson & Hartley, 1991, p. 7);
- "the subjectively experienced anticipation of a fundamental and involuntary event" (Sverke *et al.*, 2002, p. 243).

It should, in this context, be pointed out that certain researchers in the behavioral sciences, although perhaps more extensively in other scientific disciplines, use definitions of job insecurity that are largely "objective". These definitions are based on the assumption that job insecurity occurs as a contextual phenomenon independent of the individual's experiences and interpretation of the situation. An example of this is Pearce (1998), who defined temporary employment as an objective type of job insecurity that is characterized by "an independently determined probability that workers will have the same job in the foreseeable future" (p. 34). Others have classified entire organizations or workplaces as being more or less marked by job insecurity (*e.g.*, Büssing, 1999; Ferrie, Shipley, Marmot, Stansfeld & Smith, 1998). Still others evaluate the employees' experiences of job insecurity by using job tenure as a proxy, suggesting that labor markets characterized by shorter job tenure have more job insecurity than labor markets with longer job tenure (*e.g.*, Heery & Salmon, 2000). There are also researchers who base their definitions of job insecurity on the level of unemployment in society, which means that a rise in unemployment can be interpreted as a rise in general job insecurity (*e.g.*, Gallie *et al.*, 1998). The basic assumption in these objective definitions is that individuals who find themselves in temporary types of employment, have short organizational tenure, and/or work in organizations that are classified as insecure have a higher amount of job insecurity than is the case with individuals who hold a "safer" type of employment contract or work for one of the organizations deemed as safe.

One distinguishing feature about the definition of job insecurity is that it is concerned with an uncertainty regarding future events. The employees do not know whether they will be able to keep their jobs or not (Van Vuuren, 1990). This can be compared with employees who have already been informed that they will lose their jobs. These employees already know that they will have to deal with job loss, which enables them to take action. Those employees who do not yet know the future status of their jobs cannot clearly formulate a line of action to deal with the sense of threat, or adequately prepare for unpleasant experiences, since they do not know what will happen. Even if job loss is traumatic, being informed about the future relieves the stress of uncertainty.

Given the distinctions between the *objective* and *subjective* definitions of job insecurity discussed above, we argue in line with De Witte and Näswall (2003), thus suggesting that job insecurity should be regarded as a subjective experience generated from the evaluation and interpretation of the individual's current situation in the organization. By defining job insecurity as a subjective and perceptual phenomenon, we also assume that different people in the same objective situation may interpret it differently. Some will feel a threat to the future of the job; others in the same situation will not worry about losing their job. This difference in the experience of job insecurity may also arise when there is an objective threat to the present employment, for example, in terms of organizational restructuring and cutbacks in personnel (Greenhalgh & Rosenblatt, 1984; Jacobson, 1991b).

Accordingly, in this book, we define job insecurity as the fear or worry that arises in connection with the subjectively perceived possibility of loss of a present job, and that this situation is undesired by the individual.

Dimensions of Job Insecurity

Although most researchers agree at least on the basic aspects of job insecurity, theorists differ from one another when it comes to the notion of whether job insecurity is a unidimensional or a multidimensional concept. Different writers focus on different facets of the concept, and the various measures used in their research also differ from one another. Below, we discuss the different dimensions of job insecurity used in theory and research.

Anxiety and Probability

The definitions discussed above emphasize that job insecurity entails a *fear* or *worry* over losing one's job. This worry has been regarded as one of two dimensions of job insecurity by some researchers (Borg & Elizur, 1992; Jacobson, 1991a). Fear and worry about the future is a feeling and constitutes the affective dimension of job insecurity. The other dimension constitutes the perceived *probability* of the threat being realized, that is, actually losing one's job. This has been labeled the cognitive dimension. These dimensions interact to form the level of perceived job insecurity, which is a combination of the fear or worry over losing one's job and the perceived probability of this event really occurring.

Merely asking individuals whether or not they *think* they are going to lose their jobs does not yield any information on how they *feel* about the situation. It does not reveal whether job insecurity is considered a problem or, for example, whether it poses difficulties or is unpleasant. This, on the contrary, is the purpose of the dimension that aims to assess individuals' levels of *anxiety* over potential job loss. The dimension focusing on anxiety gives an indication of how the perception of the probability of losing one's job affects the employees. According to Borg and Elizur (1992), both these dimensions are necessary in order to get a true picture of the employees' experiences of job insecurity.

Thus, the perceived probability of future job loss does not capture the feeling of fear or worry individuals may experience when they perceive their future position in the organization as threatened. Therefore, it is possible that individuals may consider the probability of job loss to be high, but not necessarily react with feelings of fear or worry regarding the future (Sverke *et al.*, 2002). This may be due to individual characteristics and coping strategies as well as perceived employability and how important the present employment is for the individual. Consequently, it has been argued that the fear or worry aspect of job insecurity is the most important one, especially when job insecurity is defined as an involuntary and stressful event that may generate unpleasant or even harmful feelings in the individual (Sverke & Hellgren, 2002; Sverke *et al.*, 2002).

The Strength and Importance of the Threat

Another distinction that has been made is the one between the perceived strength of the threat against the present employment and how important this threat is for the individual. For example, Greenhalgh and Rosenblatt (1984) discuss the perceived strength – or severity – of the threat as an important aspect of job insecurity. This, in combination with the individual's feelings of powerlessness, represents the basis for the level of experienced job insecurity, according to Greenhalgh and Rosenblatt. The evaluation of a threat as having severe consequences that cannot be counteracted by the individual will thus result in intense feelings of job insecurity.

The severity of the threat is based on the individual's evaluation of the situation. When faced with a threat, the individual tries to determine whether the realization of this threat would involve a temporary or permanent job loss, and whether the threat involves a loss of employment or just a deterioration of working conditions (Greenhalgh & Rosenblatt, 1984). Another determining factor for the severity of the threat is the subjectively evaluated likelihood that the threat actually will be realized. This evaluation is shaped by the sources of information that are available to the individual. The reliability and type of information are important here. Examples of the main sources of information are, according to Greenhalgh and Rosenblatt (1984), signs of organizational decline and reorganizations. Such events give the employees the impression that the organization is unstable, and that there may be a risk of personnel reductions, and this impression may then bring about perceptions of job insecurity if the individual perceives his/her job to be at risk.

Whether or not the individual feels that the threat can be counteracted is also important in determining the perceived strength of the threat. A sense of powerlessness is, according to Greenhalgh and Rosenblatt (1984), founded in the individual's perception of four factors. The first factor is a perceived lack of protection, in terms of, for example, unions, legislation, or the contents of the employment contract. In addition, the individual has various expectations on what any changes will entail; the sense of powerlessness increases if these expectations are unclear. The culture of the organization also plays a part; an organization with an open culture where the employees' opinions matter may reduce the sense of powerlessness. A final determining factor influencing the sense of powerlessness is the individual's perception of the company's course of action during changes and cutbacks; to have the perception that the organization is making sure to act in a fair manner may reduce an individual's experience of powerlessness and thereby increase the feeling of control in the situation (Barling & Kelloway, 1996). Perceptions of fairness and justice may also affect the experiencing of job insecurity in the future as well as the attitudes and behaviors of personnel who survive a re-organization involving personnel layoffs (Brockner, 1990; Brockner, DeWitt, Grover & Reed, 1990; Brockner & Greenberg, 1990; Brockner, Grover & Blonder, 1988; Brockner, Grover,

Reed & DeWitt, 1992; Brockner, Grover, Reed, DeWitt & O'Malley, 1987).

Several researchers have used the dimensions put forward by Green-halgh and Rosenblatt (1984) as a starting-point (*e.g.*, Ashford *et al.*, 1989; Barling & Kelloway, 1996; Klandermans *et al.*, 1991), and subsequently expanded the description of them and how they are related to each other. Job insecurity is thus described as resulting from the combination of a perceived sense of powerlessness and the strength/importance of the threat. The strength of the threat is in turn the outcome of the probability of the loss of one's job or altered working conditions, and how this loss is evaluated (Klandermans *et al.*, 1991). The consequence of defining job insecurity as such a product is that high levels in all factors are required for the experience of job insecurity to be strong. Accordingly, a strong sense of powerlessness without a strong sense of threat does not result in job insecurity, or vice versa. This definition of job insecurity is thus multiplicative.

The Loss of One's Job or Changing Work Conditions

The most common feature of job insecurity is the threat of future job loss, and one aspect of this is the fear of involuntarily being given notice by the organization. This constitutes one dimension of job insecurity. Apart from this threat to the future of the employment, a threat against other aspects of the job may create perceptions of insecurity for the individual; this constitutes a second dimension of job insecurity. Replacement, degrading, less attractive work content, loss of colleagues through downsizing, and deterioration of the salary trend are examples of such aspects. Generally speaking, they are the features of the job that the individual values and perceives as important and meaningful to the present work situation. It might also be that the individual, upon entering the employment situation, experienced promises regarding certain features of the work, and if these expectations are not fulfilled the individual may feel betrayed by the organization (*cf.* psychological contract theories). Greenhalgh and Rosenblatt (1984) were among the first researchers to emphasize the importance of broadening the view of job insecurity to include different aspects of the job. They pointed out that these aspects are important and often underestimated in job insecurity research. Consequently, the experience of job insecurity does not necessarily just concern the employment itself, but also various qualities involved in the work situation. It is thus not only the anxiety over the prospect of a possible loss of the *job itself* that comprises the concept of job insecurity – but, in addition, any perceived threats against *the nature and content of the job* should also be included.

Based on this line of argument, several researchers have broadened the concept of job insecurity, and consequently, job insecurity can entail both worry about the loss of the job itself and concern about deteriorated terms of employment and work conditions (Sverke, Hellgren & Näswall, 2001; Sverke & Hellgren, 2002). The concept of job insecurity has been divided into categories, where one concerns job loss as a whole, and the other concerns anxiety over future career and growth opportunities (Burchell, 2002; Davy *et al.*, 1997; Roskies & Louis-Guerin, 1990). Other researchers have expounded the dividing of job insecurity into two main dimensions, named quantitative and qualitative insecurity (Hellgren *et al.*, 1999). Quantitative insecurity applies to the insecurity that arises in connection with one's future employment as a whole. The qualitative dimension, on the other hand, applies to insecurity over important aspects of the job, such as the opportunity for career development, job content, and salary trends.

Given the definitions presented above, job insecurity can be regarded as a classic work stressor (Barling & Kelloway, 1996) that reflects the individual's experienced fear or worry regarding the future existence of the present employment as well as the existence and nature of various work features that are important to the individual.

Job Insecurity from a Stress Perspective

Stress is often described with the help of a model, and various researchers have presented several stress models. Many of these models include similar factors while focusing on different aspects of the phenomenon. Some of the stress models presented in the literature and previous research will be discussed in this chapter. We have chosen those models that helped guide our own research in order to illustrate the phenomenon of job insecurity. These models are well suited for describing the circumstances relating to job insecurity and facilitate the understanding of this phenomenon.

The first model to be discussed is the ISR Model (from the Institute for Social Research at the University of Michigan), developed by Katz and Kahn (1978). It has served as a basis for many subsequent theories. This model is characterized by the notion of stress as a process, originating in the interaction between the individual and the environment (see Figure 3.1).

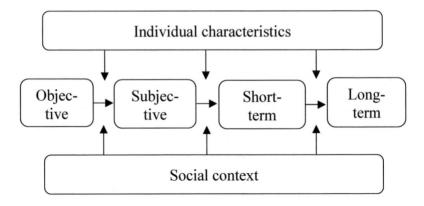

**Figure 3.1. The stress process
(based on the Katz and Kahn (1978) model)**

The model describes the stress process as one in which the individual creates a subjective or psychological conception of the objective reality, and it is this subjective interpretation which then triggers reactions – of a physiological, psychological, and behavioral nature – that finally, in the last stage of this process, result in the development of mental and physical health complaints. Moreover, the model also describes the stress process as being influenced by both individual characteristics and the environment, and it is these aspects together that affect an individual's stress experiences and stress reactions. The model therefore makes it clear that individual characteristics (such as one's self-adjudged employability), or demands in the environment (such as needing to provide support for others or having to handle bank loans), together affect how seriously an individual looks at and interprets objective threats to the security of employment.

Katz and Kahn's (1978) model supposes variation between individuals in their evaluation of the situation and their immediate reactions to the situation. Such variations arise because the evaluation and reaction partly depend on individual features such as gender, age and personality, and in part depend on the social relations between the individual and important people and groups in his or her environment. This model emphasizes the differences in both evaluations and reactions between individuals in similar actual situations.

Along this line of reasoning, Lazarus and Folkman (1984) have developed a theoretical framework that focuses more explicitly on the individual's affective and cognitive reactions and behaviors during stress experiences. Lazarus and Folkman also describe reactions to stress as being part of a process, originating from the individual's appraisal of the situation. When evaluating a situation, the individual tries to establish whether it is irrelevant, positive, or stressful to him/her. Harmful situations can be divided into three groups: the damage has already been done, there is a threat of future harm, or the situation is seen as a challenge. Individuals cannot counteract damages or losses that already have occurred (such as the loss of one's job); instead, they have to try to deal with the consequences. Threat entails the perception of a risk of a negative event occurring in the future, for example, a perceived risk of being given notice. An important difference between a challenge and a threat is that a challenge has the potential of positive outcomes. Nevertheless, threats and challenges share similarities since they both allow the individual the possibility of changing the situation. However, while a threat only has negative connotations, a challenge may bring about positive feelings such as a fighting spirit or hopefulness.

According to Lazarus and Folkman (1984), it is also necessary to differentiate between primary and secondary appraisal. Primary appraisal is an evaluation of the type of threat or challenge the individual is exposed to, and of its strength and importance for the individual. Secondary appraisal entails an evaluation of the possibilities the individual has for counteracting the threat, and how effective these counteractive methods are expected to be. Secondary appraisal also involves assessing the expectations of the results and the expectations of the individual's own capabilities (Bandura, 1982). Expectations of the results involve to what extent the individual believes that certain actions lead to a desired outcome. Such expectations concerning one's own capabilities involve how the individual judges his or her own ability to perform the actions leading to the desired outcome. The individual's attempt to determine the consequences of potential strategies, given both personal and external factors, is also included in the secondary appraisal (Lazarus & Folkman, 1984). The experiencing of stress occurs when the individual, after the secondary appraisal, feels that the strategies and resources available are not sufficient to counteract the negative components of the situation.

As we described earlier, a stressor is considered to arise when an individual experiences signals in the environment that indicate the presence of a threat. The perceived risk of losing one's job can be such a threat, which the individual interprets as something negative and thus tries to counteract. An examination and evaluation is made of the resources and viable strategies available for the counteracting of this threat. It may turn out that individuals feel that they do not have access to the necessary resources, or that they are not able to utilize these resources in a way that would eliminate the threat to employment. If that is the outcome of the evaluation, the individual will experience stress which, in this case, is in the form of job insecurity (Greenhalgh & Rosenblatt, 1984). Just as the term suggests, job insecurity implies a great deal of uncertainty. Lazarus and Folkman (1984) explain that it is indeed the uncertainty over whether a threat will be realized (in this case, whether one becomes unemployed) that constitutes a great source of stress for many people. To be in a state of uncertainty about the future may evoke anxiety and lower well-being (Ganster & Fusilier, 1989; Spector, 1986). In accordance with this, many researchers argue that stressors are especially harmful when they are combined with a low sense of control (Bishop, 1994; Elsass & Veiga, 1997; Karasek & Theorell, 1990; Lundberg & Frankenhaeuser, 1978; Peterson & Stunkard, 1989; Thompson, 1981). It has also been suggested that having the ability to exert control over the work or the situation helps the individual in coping with stressful events (Frankenhaeuser & Johansson, 1986). Given this, it is also important to note that it is not necessarily control, in an objective sense, that may have an effect on the situation, but rather the subjective feeling of having control that is important (Bishop, 1994; Thompson, 1981).

It has also been suggested (Furda & Meijman, 1992) that the predictability and controllability of the situation are important factors. Job insecurity, by its uncertain nature, implies unpredictability. An uncertain future makes it difficult to foresee what will happen, and subsequently how to act upon this. One does not know what – if anything – should be done. The other factor related to this is uncontrollability. Job insecurity implies, as we have seen earlier, a sense of powerlessness in maintaining the employment (Dekker & Schaufeli, 1995; Greenhalgh & Rosenblatt, 1984). It is out of the employee's control whether he/she is allowed to keep the job or not. Previous research on stress illustrates that a recurrent feeling of lack of control is more detrimental to well-being than the more serious but rare incidents are, such as the actual loss of the job (Dekker & Schaufeli, 1995; Furda & Meijman, 1992).

The phenomenon of control can be roughly divided into two different types: behavioral control and cognitive control (Bishop, 1994; Thompson, 1981). Individuals with a perceived sense of behavioral control consider themselves to have access to one or more behavioral responses generating control over the situation. Such responses can be simply switching off or removing the source of the problem, or mentally minimizing the effects of the problem. The other type of control is called cognitive control because it relates to the individual's ability to handle a situation cognitively and thus reduce its impact. This form of control can be exerted by the individual focusing on positive aspects of the situation, or simply by mentally shutting oneself off from the situation (Bishop, 1994). Accordingly, this type of control focuses on the individual's cognitive ability to handle the situation.

In order to improve the understanding of how stress arises, and hence the understanding of the phenomenon of job insecurity, we also build upon a stress model developed by Siegrist (1996) which emphasizes the comparison individuals make between their efforts and the rewards they get from the same efforts – the Effort–Reward Imbalance Model. This model also emphasizes the importance of keeping or restoring vital social roles in order to maintain a sense of mastery and control over the life situation. Siegrist refers to these social roles as status control.

The model presupposes that individuals put a certain amount of effort into their work in order to be rewarded accordingly. The amount of effort a person puts into the work partly depends on external factors such as organizational demands, and partly on individual factors such as commitment. According to Siegrist (1996), important rewards for balancing effort are money (salary), self-esteem, and secure employment, of which the latter would be the most interesting reward in this context. The perception of imbalance between efforts spent and rewards received is supposed to be particularly stressful when it concerns important domains of social life (Siegrist, 1996, 2000). In the model, this domain is referred to as status control and incorporates those aspects of working life that threaten a person's self-regulatory functions and sense of mastery and esteem – which evoke negative emotions such as fear, anger, or irritation. Threats against self-regulatory functions are particularly likely to arise in a situation where the continuity of critical social roles is interrupted or lost (Siegrist, 1996, p. 30).

Siegrist (1996) also makes the arguments that occupational position is one such critical social role, that fragmented job careers and job instability are social roles associated with low status control, and that lack of status control may override the importance of task control. Furthermore, he maintains that high-cost/low-gain conditions are likely to be present when the employee perceives a low level of occupational status control, due to the fact that work and occupation hold a central role in modern society (Siegrist, 1996, 2000). Thus, according to the model, experiences of job insecurity are likely to produce sustained emotional distress since important social roles connected with the job are threatened. This line of argument is also followed by De Witte (1999), who suggests that the social role associated with unemployment is less legitimate than that of permanent employment, especially for persons between 30 and 50 years of age with family responsibilities or other economic or social engagements. Hence, insecure terms of employment, in spite of hard work, would bring about the experience of stress and its consequences.

Many researchers have identified job insecurity as an important work stressor (*e.g.*, Ashford *et al.*, 1989; Barling & Kelloway, 1996; Mauno, Leskinen & Kinnunen, 2001; Sverke *et al.*, 2002) that involves an uncertainty over the future and often lasts for an extended period of time. The sensing of a threat to future employment or valued aspects of it can thus be assumed to have negative consequences for the individual and thereby for the organization as well. In accordance with stress theories, it is also believed that individuals who live with the threat of a negative event occurring sometime in the future experience the negative effects of uncertainty as intensely, or even more intensely, than if the event had actually happened (Dekker & Schaufeli, 1995; Latack & Dozier, 1986; Lazarus & Folkman, 1984). Experiences of job insecurity involve, by definition, an unpredictability over the future. This makes it difficult for individuals to manage job insecurity since it is unclear whether they will lose their jobs or not.

Many researchers have similar ideas, that is, they believe that the lack of control or the experiencing of powerlessness over a situation, along with how that situation is to be dealt with, together, constitute a key dimension of the construct of job insecurity (Ashford *et al.*, 1989; Dekker & Schaufeli, 1995; Greenhalgh & Rosenblatt, 1984). It seems, therefore, that the unpredictability and uncontrollability brought on by job insecurity is central to the phenomenon and intimately connected with an individual's experiencing of stress and discomfort in a situation (see also Lundberg & Frankenhaeuser, 1978).

Job Insecurity and the Psychological Contract

The framework utilized in research on psychological contracts may be used to further explain and understand the phenomenon of job insecurity. The psychological contract is described as the perceived mutual obligations between two parties, in our case the employee and the employer (*e.g.*, Robinson, Kraatz & Rousseau, 1994; Rousseau, 1989). Rousseau (1989) distinguished between three types of contracts that exist between the individual and the organization – the formal contract, the implied contract, and the psychological contract. The formal contract is characterized by the existence of a written agreement between the interested parties. The implied contract has more to do with the norms and values that are established through the recurring interaction of the parties. The psychological contract consists of the duties and commitments the employee perceives to have in the employment relationship. These duties and commitments have arisen as a response to those rewards employees expect to gain for the fulfillment of their duties and for being loyal to the employer (Rousseau, 1989). In our context, an example of one such reward is job security in exchange for loyalty and good work.

Figure 3.2 shows a schematic representation of the process that is believed to underlie the psychological contract. The figure illustrates that the individual and the organization place expectations on each other regarding opportunities and behaviors, and that these expectations lead to demands from both the individual's and the organization's side. This implies that the individual expects to receive something from the organization parallel to the organization placing demands on the individual. According to the model, the perception of a breach in the reciprocal relationship between organization and individual thus represents a breach of the psychological contract, either from the individual's or from the organization's side. In terms of employment uncertainty, the experience of job insecurity would thus constitute a feeling of a broken psychological contract; the employee feels the contract has been breached (Davy *et al.*, 1997; King, 2000).

The psychological contract is based on mutual trust between parties, an understanding by both parties of mutual responsibilities. A valid contract results in an exchange between two parties who are satisfied with what they get in comparison to what they give. The employee expects the employer to act in a way that is favorable, or at least not unfavorable, to him/her. This trust affects how the employer's actions are perceived and interpreted by the employee, as well as his or her reactions to these interpretations (Robinson, 1996). The psychological contract is not discussed between parties, and may appear different depending on who is asked to describe it (Rousseau, 1989). Nevertheless, it is important to point out that the psychological contract is based on one party's (*e.g.*, the employee's) belief that the other party (*e.g.*, the organization) has promised certain positive outcomes in exchange for certain behaviors (Robinson, 1996). Because this is a subjective notion, it is possible that the employer does not even consider this promise to be given, at the same time as the employee might take it for granted.

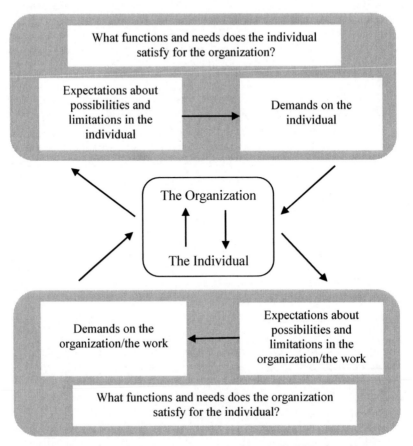

Figure 3.2. The exchange process underlying the psychological contract between the individual and the organization

When the employee feels that expectations on the employer are not fulfilled, the psychological contract is perceived to be breached (Robinson & Morrison, 2000). An individual's reaction to a breach of contract involves intense feelings of disappointment and anger towards the party who is seen as responsible for the perceived breach (Rousseau, 1989). These intense feelings, and the sense of a broken trust, can seriously damage the relationship between the parties (Robinson *et al.*, 1994). The employee's trust in the employer decreases and his/her sense of duty to perform certain tasks might diminish. As a consequence, the individual might cease to make that extra effort that was important to the business and the employer (Robinson *et al.*, 1994).

Failing to give an expected pay raise is one example of the employer retracting a promise, and thereby not fulfilling it. There may be several reasons for this. For one, the organization may not be able to afford any pay increases, and therefore *cannot* do what the employee has been implied. Altered financial circumstances make it impossible for the organization to live up to the individual's expectations of the psychological contract (Robinson & Morrison, 2000). A promise can also be retracted when the organization does not *want* to fulfill its part of the contract, either because it has never intended to do so, or because it believes the employee is not fulfilling his/her part of the contract (Robinson & Morrison, 2000). Reactions to a breach of contract vary depending on the reasons attributed to the breach. One possibility is that the employee reacts more negatively in situations where management seems to be ignoring its part of the perceived agreement. In this case, the employer appears to be unscrupulous and unreliable, and the employee's trust in the organization is seriously damaged.

Job insecurity can be described as a breach of the psychological con-tract, given that the individual regards secure employment terms as a part of his or her implied agreement with the employer. Individuals who experience a threat to their terms of employment, when expecting tenure in exchange for their work and loyalty to the organization, are likely to feel let down. Instead of being rewarded for their loyalty and work, the employees may feel that the employer does not fulfill its part of the psychological contract, by announcing notices or allowing takeovers (Martin, Staines & Pate, 1998).

A breach of the psychological contract may give rise to strong reactions by the party experiencing the breach (Rousseau, 1989) and seriously impair the relationship between the parties (Robinson *et al.*, 1994). These strong reactions have been called violations and consist of a strong negative emotional response towards the party who is seen as being responsible for the breach (Morrison & Robinson, 1997; Robinson, 1996). The trust in the employer that used to prevail has been damaged. It can, however, be restored if the organization takes measures to prevent the same situation from happening again (Greenhalgh, 1991), in other words, by making efforts to avoid another breach of the psychological contract.

Furthermore, conceptualizing stress as an imbalance between effort and reward can be compared with a breach of the psychological con-tract. According to Siegrist's (1996, 2000) Effort–Reward Imbalance Model, an imbalance between the estimation of one's worth (given the effort one has put into work) and what one is rewarded may result in the feeling of betrayal or unfair treatment. According to the model, this may result in stress reactions. In this, we thus find a connection between stress theory and theories of psychological contracts. When an individual feels he/she has not received what has been promised from the organization, there will be an imbalance between effort and outcome which can generate both stress (Siegrist, 1996) and the feeling that the psychological agreement existing between the individual and the organization has been breached (Robinson & Morrison, 2000; Robinson & Rousseau, 1994).

Various studies investigating the consequences of psychological contract breach have reported its effects on both work- and organization-related attitudes and behavior. Robinson and Morrison (1995), for example, reported that violations of psychological contracts were negatively related to trust in management, which in turn was found to be negatively related to organizational citizenship behavior (civic virtue; see Organ, 1988; Podsakoff, MacKenzie, Moorman & Fetter, 1990). Robinson (1995, 1996) also noticed the negative effects of psychological contract breach on outcome variables such as job satisfaction, civic virtue, organizational commitment, trust, intention to remain in the organization, and self-rated performance. Another study, by Lester, Turnley, Bloodgood, and Bolino (2002), found psychological contract breach to be negatively related to affective organizational commitment among subordinates but not among supervisors. This study also reported that contract breach was unrelated to self-rated performance but instead was associated with supervisor-rated performance. These results thus show that employees who perceived the psychological contract as breached did not deem their own performance to be diminished – the supervisors, however, found employee performance to be lower than before.

Studies have also shown that psychological contract breach, in terms of broken promises, relates negatively to an individual's everyday mood and emotional reactions (Conway & Briner, 2002). In a longitudinal study examining reactions after a downsizing, Allen, Freeman, Russell, Reizenstein, and Rentz (2001) stated that organizational commitment and job involvement, for those who retained their jobs (the survivors), were the attitudes most difficult to restore to their original levels. These authors suggest that in order for the management to succeed in this, it must forge a new psychological contract to replace the former that is perceived as breached – and that one of the key dimensions to this work involves reestablishing a sense of job security.

We can conclude that a breach of the psychological contract carries with it consequences for the individual as well as the organization, and that the perception of job security is one of the central aspects essential to the psychological contract.

Job Insecurity Is Not Unemployment

When discussing the consequences of job insecurity, we must also point out that there is a difference between the experience of job insecurity and actually losing one's job. Holding a job can be described as a step in an individual's development (Winefield, 1996). This description is based on Erik Erikson's (1959) stage theory of personality development, which asserts that individuals go through different stages in their development. Each of these stages contains conflicts that have to be resolved, and getting a job is one of the ways to resolve conflicts in the latter stages (*e.g.*, identity *vs.* role confusion). According to this theory, unemployment is a great obstacle to the resolution of this developmental conflict (Winefield, 1996).

There are several differences between job insecurity and actually losing one's job (Jacobson, 1991a). One of the main theoretical differences is that the actual loss entails exchanging one role for another, while job insecurity involves a change within the same role. In losing a job, a new role needs to be developed, which could be easier to handle than having to reassess the same role. Job insecurity often involves feeling that the change is for the worse. There is also a difference in time between the two phenomena (Jacobson, 1991a). The loss of a job is immediate and can be subsequently tackled in various ways. Job insecurity, on the other hand, is often a prolonged experience, which adds to the fact that it might have more negative consequences than actual job loss has.

Previous studies have also identified differences between the consequences of job insecurity and those of unemployment. In a study by Dekker and Schaufeli (1995), two groups of employees were surveyed before they were given notice. At this point the groups reported job insecurity and psychological problems to the same extent. At a later time of measurement, when one group had been laid off, the remaining group of employees reported higher levels of job insecurity and psychological problems than the employees who lost their jobs. This can be explained by the aspect of uncertainty involved in the job insecurity experience. Such uncertainty increases the stress since the individuals do not know what strategies to use in order to handle the problem, or what will take place in the future. When the loss of a job is an actual fact, then at least the uncertainty is gone, and the individual can move on by mourning the loss and looking for a new job.

Job Insecurity Is Not Temporary Work

As we have already described, job insecurity refers to the subjective experience of a threat to the present job (Jacobson, 1991a; Sverke & Hellgren, 2002). It is important to emphasize that this subjective threat may be experienced even if there appear to be no objective threats to the employment (Rosenblatt & Ruvio, 1996). There are also situations where actual threats to the employment can be observed but no job insecurity perceived among the employees. Temporary employment is sometimes referred to as such an objective threat (*e.g.*, Pearce, 1998). This type of employment does not provide the employee with certainty over the future, which makes it similar to job insecurity. However, it is important to distinguish between these two types of uncertainty.

Temporary employment has been defined as "precarious employment" (*e.g.*, Letourneux, 1998), "non-standard employment" (*e.g.*, Jenkins, 1998), and "contingent work" (*e.g.*, McLean Parks *et al.*, 1998; Sverke, Gallagher & Hellgren, 2000). Many authors describe this type of employment arrangement as a means to achieving and maintaining numerical flexibility since it allows the number of employees to fluctuate without layoffs or downsizing. Many temporary employees are not directly hired by the organization they work for, but by a temporary agency that also bears the responsibility for them (*e.g.*, Klein Hesselink & Van Vuuren, 1999; Reilly, 1998). Usually, a distinction is made between three main types of contracts: fixed term contracts, contracts for temporary work, and temporary agency contracts. However, the literature makes an even further differentiation between the different types of contracts (*e.g.*, Aronsson, 1999; McLean Parks *et al.*, 1998; Sverke *et al.*, 2000). Common to the "flexible" contracts is that the employment relationships formed through them are temporary. These contracts are considered to constitute *objective* forms of job insecurity (Pearce, 1998) in that they, to some extent, involve an implied likelihood of job loss in the near future. The need for this flexibility in employment contracts is prompted by augmented demands for flexibility (De Witte & Näswall, 2003; Purcell & Purcell, 1998). The increasingly competitive climate highlights the need among organizations to be able to round up, or get rid of, the necessary number of employees within a short period of time. Temporary contracts limit the commitment of the employers to the employees, and allow adjustments to sudden changes in demand, for example, by quickly having access to a large number of employees to fulfill the demands of increased production.

Since temporary employment implies some uncertainty about the future, it seems reasonable to assume that this type of employment will be associated with the subjective experience of job insecurity. This link has been made explicit in previous literature. Pearce (1998) considers the possibility of job loss to be central to temporary employment, which is in agreement with Beard and Edwards (1995) who describe expected job discontinuity as a distinguishing feature of contingent (temporary) work. Also, empirical studies investigating the link between temporary work and subjectively experienced job insecurity have shown that temporary workers report more uncertainty regarding the future of their job (*e.g.*, Klein Hesselink & Van Vuuren, 1999; Näswall & De Witte, 2003; Sverke *et al.*, 2000; Vandoorne & De Witte, 2002). The association between type of contract and the experience of job insecurity typically remains after demographic characteristics are being controlled for (*e.g.*, Vandoorne & De Witte, 2002). Kinnunen and Nätti (1994) showed that temporary employment was the second strongest predictor of feelings of job insecurity (the most important predictor was previous experience of job insecurity).

The relation between temporary contracts and subjective job insecurity has also been exhibited on an aggregate organizational level. Goudswaard and De Nanteuil (2000) showed that the percentage of reported job insecurity increased in more than two thirds of the workforce after forms of numerical flexibility were introduced. Nevertheless, this association is not perfect, since about one quarter of those holding temporary contracts still consider their jobs "secure" (Letourneux, 1998). In a study comparing objective and subjective types of job insecurity, De Witte and Näswall (2003) found that, among those experiencing a high degree of job insecurity, it was the permanent rather than the temporary employees who reported lower levels of both job satisfaction and organizational commitment in comparison with the temporary employees. These authors went on to argue that job insecurity cannot only be defined from characteristics of the situation but should contain an element of subjectivity. Again, this may be taken as evidence for why it is important to recognize the subjective nature of the job insecurity experience.

Another important way to differentiate between objective uncertainty (temporary employment) and subjective job insecurity is to consider the consequences of the different phenomena. In previous studies, temporary employment has not been associated with the reductions in job satisfaction and organizational commitment expected to result from job insecurity. However, the subjective experience of job insecurity has been consistently associated with lower levels of both these work-related attitudes. Such an inconsistency (*i.e.*, a lack of association between temporary work and negative work attitudes) can be explained by the fact that subjective job insecurity is an addition to objective insecurity. The negative effects of objective uncertainty only appear if employees actually make the subjective assessment that their jobs are in danger, that is, if they experience job insecurity (*cf.* De Witte & Näswall, 2003; Klandermans & Van Vuuren, 1999). Investigating subjective job insecurity thus leads to a more complete explanation of changes in work-related attitudes than merely studying objective uncertainty.

Concluding Remarks

This general overview of theories describing stress, psychological contracts, and job insecurity was intended as a background to the following, more empirically focused, chapters. We have described job insecurity as a subjective experience that may occur in any given work situation, regardless of the objective uncertainty. We have also described this phenomenon as the perception of a threat of future job loss. This threat can only result in job insecurity if job loss is involuntary; by our definition, having positive feelings about being unemployed is incompatible with the experiencing of job insecurity. We have also emphasized the possibility of broadening the concept of job insecurity to also include perceived threats towards important aspects of the job, such as career opportunities, salary increases, and the content and nature of the job as a whole.

Both stress theories and theories on the psychological contract have been used to present job insecurity as a negative experience, with negative effects for both the individual and the organization. The experience of job insecurity is assumed to generate feelings of reduced control and unpredictability regarding one's future in the present organization, which, according to stress theories, may generate or trigger stress experiences. The chapter has also addressed the issue of job insecurity perceptions as a breach of the psychological contract, or agreement, that exists between the individual and the employing organization, and how these experiences may result in negative consequences for both the individual and the organization.

In this chapter, we have clarified that job insecurity is different from unemployment. Unemployment may be objectively observed, whereas job insecurity is a subjective uncertainty regarding future job loss. This uncertainty is in many cases more negative than the knowledge that one is about to lose one's job. Not knowing what to expect is a stressor in itself. We have also distinguished between job insecurity and temporary work. Temporary work can be a form of objective uncertainty, in that it presents the individual with uncertainty regarding the continuation of employment. However, we argue that job insecurity arises through individual perceptions and is by nature a subjective phenomenon, and that job insecurity experiences may arise in situations characterized by stability as well as those more turbulent.

We have based our further investigations of job insecurity on the theoretical background described here. We believe that the empirical research presented in the following chapters will add to the theoretical knowledge of job insecurity, as well as illustrate the phenomenon of job insecurity and its relation to outcomes in a European context.

CHAPTER 4

The Measurement of Job Insecurity

In the previous chapter we defined and described the job insecurity phenomenon. As we saw there, job insecurity can be described as a uni- or a multidimensional construct. The different descriptions of the construct's dimensionality have also contributed to the development of different measures. Several operationalizations have been used to assess job insecurity among employees. In this chapter, we review some of the measures that have been developed to reflect different operationalizations, and relate them to the theoretical definitions of job insecurity. We put special focus on the measure used to assess job insecurity in the empirical tests in this book. This measure captures a unidimensional operationalization of job insecurity that mainly reflects a sense of worry about the future of the job. In our four samples, we present and compare the levels of job insecurity, as well as offer a validation of this measure by investigating its factor structure and reliability.

Measures of Job Insecurity

Initially, job insecurity was measured as its reverse – job security – and included in inventories assessing broader aspects of job satisfaction and work climate (*e.g.*, Hackman & Oldham, 1975; Ivancevich, 1974; Rizzo, House & Lirtzman, 1970). In these inventories, respondents indicated their satisfaction with features of the job, and one factor among these features was job security. Job security was assessed as one of several motivators in these indices and not specifically targeted in theoretical discussions. One of the first studies addressing the issue of job insecurity, as an important factor, is the one conducted by Caplan, Cobb, French, Van Harrison, and Pinneau (1975). This study was pioneering in two important respects. First, in contrast to previous studies which had treated the opposite of job insecurity (*i.e.*, job security) as a motivating factor, the Caplan *et al.* study used a measure of job insecurity where it was conceptualized as a stressor. Second, whereas previous studies typically assessed job insecurity with just a single item, Caplan *et al.* used a multi-item measure.

However, it was not until Greenhalgh and Rosenblatt's (1984) seminal work that job insecurity became the focus of more systematic research, and measures with a stronger theoretical basis were developed. Still, there is a lack of general consensus on how to measure job insecurity, and the use of a single-item indicator remains common as well as the utilization of job insecurity scales developed for specific research studies (Mauno *et al.*, 2001; Sverke & Hellgren, 2002; Sverke *et al.*, 2002).

Global Measures

It is important to make a distinction between global and multidimensional job insecurity scales. A global scale is intended to assess the overall level of concern over the future of the job, in general. These global scales assess perceptions of threat regarding imminent job loss. Such one-dimensional measures often focus on either the perceived probability (*e.g.*, Mohr, 2000; Van Vuuren, 1990) or the fear of job loss (*e.g.*, Johnson, Messe & Crano, 1984). Some global measures are single-item indicators, such as those assessing the probability of job loss. One example of such a measure is the one used by Mohr (2000), which simply asks "How do you assess the probability of losing your job in the near future?". Other global measures use multiple items and may, in comparison with single items, be typically formulated as "The thought of getting fired really scares me" (Johnson *et al.*, 1984). Not many studies have compared the different types of job insecurity scales; however, it has been shown by a meta-analysis that single-item measures tend to underestimate the relation between job insecurity and its outcomes (Sverke *et al.*, 2002). In addition, multiple-item indicators have traditionally been considered to be more accurate and reliable measures of those concepts that are not easy to measure objectively (Gorsuch, 1997; Spector, 1992). With multiple items it becomes possible to tap into a certain concept in more than one way, thereby increasing the content validity of the measure. It is also possible to estimate the reliability of measures with more than one or two items (Nunnally, 1978). A study conducted by Mauno *et al.* (2001) compared global and multidimensional scales and found global scales measuring fear of job loss to be stable over time, in terms of factor structure, validity, and reliability. This indicates that global scales may be used for the assessment of job insecurity. Another study comparing global and multidimensional scales found that the global scales (focusing on fear of job loss) explained more variance than multidimensional measures in outcomes such as organizational commitment and trust (Reisel & Banai, 2002).

Multidimensional Measures

The multidimensional scales, on the other hand, are developed to capture threats against valued job features in addition to the threat of job loss (Ashford *et al.*, 1989; Greenhalgh & Rosenblatt, 1984; Hartley & Klandermans, 1986; Hellgren *et al.*, 1999; Roskies & Louis-Guerin, 1990). The multidimensional instruments are typically designed to reflect the conceptual distinctions between dimensions of job insecurity, such as worry and probability, the strength and severity of the threat, or the worry of losing the job altogether and concern over the deterioration of important job features.

Ashford *et al.* (1989) published one of the most popular multidimensional scales, and the entire scale, or subsections of it, is still being used. This scale consists of 57 items forming five dimensions, corresponding to those dimensions identified in the definition proposed by Greenhalgh and Rosenblatt in 1984 (*i.e.*, threats to the job itself, importance of total job, threats to valued job features, importance of valued job features, and a feeling of powerlessness to counteract these threats). The five dimensions are utilized in order to obtain as broad a representation of the experience of job insecurity as possible. However, these dimensions are most commonly combined into a global measure, rather than being used to capture the effect of each dimension. To achieve this, a multiplicative formula is applied to the measure in order to assess the perceived overall job insecurity among employees. However, this measure is also rather lengthy for use in questionnaires measuring other concepts as well. Therefore, it is of interest to try to develop measures that capture as much of the phenomenon as possible in a relatively short form, and some researchers use only one or a few of the subscales of the Ashford *et al.* (1989) scale (*e.g.*, Kinnunen, Mauno, Nätti & Happonen, 1999; Mauno *et al.*, 2001; Sverke *et al.*, 2000; Sverke & Hellgren, 2001).

Mauno *et al.* (2001), in their comparison of different measures of job insecurity, caution against the combining of importance, powerlessness, and probability scales into one composite scale, since they partly reflect different aspects of job insecurity. Moreover, some of the dimensions comprising the multidimensional scales were found to be less stable than others. The authors discuss that the use of multidimensional scales must be done carefully and by taking the different scales into account (Mauno *et al.*, 2001).

Another set of multidimensional measures focus on the threat itself, without taking into account any feeling of powerlessness. One such measure assesses the affective and cognitive dimensions of job insecurity (Borg & Elizur, 1992). The affective dimension is concerned with how worried individuals are about losing their job. The cognitive dimension focuses on whether a threat is perceived or not, regardless of how worried the respondents are about this threat.

Still other researchers focus on the distinction between threats to the job *per se*, and threats to job features. Hellgren and his colleagues (1999) present one example of this in a study distinguishing between quantitative (worries about losing the job itself) and qualitative (worries about losing important job features) job insecurity. Nonetheless, besides those mentioned above, many researchers have their own preferred scales (*e.g.*, Barling & Kelloway, 1996; Roskies & Louis-Guerin, 1990; see also Sverke & Hellgren, 2002, for a review of the different measures used in the job insecurity research).

This review, although brief, reveals that job insecurity is often measured in an *ad hoc* manner. Although scales have been developed to measure different dimensions of job insecurity in questionnaires (see *e.g.*, Ashford *et al.*, 1989; Hellgren *et al.*, 1999; Roskies & Louis-Guerin, 1990), the measurement quality of these scales is far from consistent. Despite this fact, most operationalizations of job insecurity reflect the same underlying features, that is, a feeling of worry about the future of one's job, or a perceived likelihood of job loss in the near future. The measure used in the empirical investigations of this book largely corresponds to this underlying feature, focusing on the worry over imminent job loss by using a multiple-item indicator. Still, it is of importance to validate and investigate the measurement properties of the scale used, relating it to the theoretical basis of the construct.

Evaluating Our Measure of Job Insecurity

In this section, we turn our attention to an actual measure of job insecurity, used within the present research project. Using the data described in Chapter 2, we evaluate the measurement properties of the global scale used in each of the four European countries participating in the project (Belgium, Italy, the Netherlands, and Sweden). The scale consists of five items, which are based on items previously developed by Ashford *et al.* (1989), Hellgren *et al.* (1999), and De Witte (2000). All responses to the items were assessed using a five-point Likert scale anchored by 1 (strongly disagree) and 5 (strongly agree). The use of four different samples allows us to obtain a picture of how the scale works in different settings, and to specifically test whether our measure has similar properties in different countries. Table 4.1 lists the five items along with their mean values and standard deviations for the four countries.

**Table 4.1. Means (and standard deviations)
for the job insecurity items**

Item	Belgium	Italy	The Netherlands	Sweden
I am afraid I will get fired	2.10	2.30	1.76	2.00
	(1.18)	(1.24)	(0.76)	(1.30)
I worry about keeping my job	2.40	3.23	1.85	2.03
	(1.09)	(1.29)	(0.85)	(1.30)
I fear I will lose my job	2.27	2.51	1.83	1.92
	(1.06)	(1.27)	(0.83)	(1.24)
I think I might get fired in the near future	2.00	2.36	1.75	1.85
	(0.91)	(1.21)	(0.73)	(1.20)
I am sure I can keep my job (R)	2.55	2.65	2.08	2.63
	(1.09)	(1.13)	(0.89)	(1.34)
Total	2.26	2.61	1.85	2.09
	(0.89)	(0.87)	(0.69)	(1.06)

(R) indicates reverse-scored item.

Examining the measurement properties of the five-item job insecurity scale is necessary in order to evaluate its construct validity. By construct validity we are referring to the degree of correspondence between a theoretical construct and the measure designed to capture the construct, which gives an approximation of the similarities between the theoretical and empirical levels of a phenomenon (Bagozzi, 1978; Bollen, 1989; Cook & Campbell, 1979). There are a number of suggested methods for assessing construct validity in scales (*e.g.*, Angoff, 1988; Bagozzi, Yi & Phillips, 1991; Cook & Campbell, 1979; Campbell & Fiske, 1959; Cronbach & Meehl, 1955; Messick, 1975; *Standards for Educational and Psychological Testing*, 1985). In this chapter, we focus on evaluating the measure's factor structure and reliability, as well as on looking at the mean levels of job insecurity in each sample.

Factor Structure

A given measure of a certain construct may be viewed as merely one of many potential indicators of the same construct (Cronbach & Meehl, 1955). Our job insecurity scale is thus just one out of many. When empirical results display similar conclusions, it demonstrates that the different scales have a commonality, and this may indicate that an underlying construct is being measured (Messick, 1995). Similar results also lend more support to the hypotheses tested, and allow for the ruling out of alternative hypotheses (Messick, 1995). Measures that are developed based on theoretical assumptions are testable, in the sense that the hypothesized factor structure may be compared to the actual structure of the measure, using confirmatory approaches (Bollen, 1989; Nunnally, 1978). In this chapter, we present a test that is designed to examine the extent to which the job insecurity scale can be said to represent a single dimension in the four countries participating in the study. We also test, perhaps somewhat conservatively, wether the measurement characteristics are stable across countries, indicating that the measure captures job insecurity in exactly the same way, independent of the cultural context (*cf.* Mulaik, 1988). Below, we test whether our assumption that the factor model parameters, such as factor loadings, factor variances, and measurement errors, are the same in the four samples.

In order to empirically test the assumption of a unidimensional job insecurity scale in all four countries, we used the multi-group confirmatory factor analysis procedure (maximum likelihood estimation) of Lisrel 8 (Jöreskog & Sörbom, 1996). Here we test the plausibility of a one-factor solution, that is, that the measure is unidimensional. Table 4.2 shows standardized factor loadings for the five job insecurity items in the respective countries. Here we see that all factor loadings were significant ($p<.05$), with magnitudes ranging from .72 to .86 (Belgium), from .43 to .81 (Italy), from .67 to .90 (the Netherlands), and from .52 to .92 (Sweden).

In order to test the similarity of the measurement properties over the four countries, we conducted a test that was divided into a series of steps. The first step involved comparing a model to data where there were equal factor variances in all samples. In the next step, we added the restriction of invariant factor loadings to the model. This tests whether the magnitude of the loading of each item is the same in all countries, at the same time as the factor variances are the same. In the last step, which is also the most restrictive test, the error variances were also constrained to be of the same magnitude across samples, along with the factor variance and factor loadings.

In order to assess how well the measurement model actually corresponded to the data, we utilized a number of tests of model fit. The first indicator is the traditional and most commonly used chi-square test. This test indicates whether the proposed model fits the actual data perfectly. A significant chi-square value would indicate that the proposed model does not exactly fit the data that it has been compared to (Jöreskog & Sörbom, 1996). As a complement to this test, we also used the root mean square error of approximation (RMSEA; Browne & Cudeck, 1993). In contrast to the chi-square test, the RMSEA fit indicator is considered to be less sensitive to the degrees of freedom in the model and provides an indication of close fit rather than exact fit of how the model corresponds to the data it is tested on. Browne and Cudeck (1993) argue that RMSEA values of .08 or less indicate a reasonable fit of model to data. For descriptive purposes, we present the standardized root mean square residual (SRMR; Jöreskog & Sörbom, 1996), which describes how much the proposed model differs from actual data. With this measure, we get a sense of whether the proposed model underestimates or overestimates the extent to which the variables in the model are related. The SRMR ranges from 0 to 1, where the closer to 0 the number is, the better the model fits to the data. We also evaluate differences between nested models with the chi-square difference test. By observing the change in chi-square value for each model compared to data, this test allows us to see which model fits to the data better than other comparable models. In addition to this, we compare the Akaike value (AIC; Akaike, 1987) for each model, where lower values indicate a better fit of model to data.

Table 4.2. Freely estimated factor loadings for job insecurity items (standardized) and factor variances (unstandardized)

Item	Belgium	Italy	The Netherlands	Sweden
I am afraid I will get fired	.79	.67	.90	.85
I worry about keeping my job	.84	.43	.84	.90
I fear I will lose my job	.86	.81	.89	.92
I think I might get fired in the near future	.77	.65	.84	.73
I am sure I can keep my job (R)	.72	.57	.67	.52
Factor variance	.88	.69	.56	1.21

All factor loadings significant ($p<.05$).
(R) indicates reverse-scored item.

The results of the different steps of the confirmatory factor analysis test are presented in Table 4.3. The chi-square test turned out significant for all models, indicating that the model tested did not exactly fit the structure of the data. However, the additional fit indices, which give an idea of how closely the model fit the data, show that the one-factor model, where no parameters are proposed to be equal across countries (Model 2), was the best representation of our data. The RMSEA value indicated a reasonable error of approximation, and the other fit indices also showed reasonable estimations, suggesting that this model provided a decent representation of our data. The subsequent models fitted less well to data; model fit was noticeably impaired for Model 3 (where we tested equal factor variances in all countries) and even more for Model 5 (where all model parameters were constrained to be equal across countries). The results support our hypothesis that the five items capture one dimension of job insecurity in all participating countries. We did not receive support, however, for the suggestion that the measurement model parameters (factor variance, factor loadings, and error variances) are of the same magnitude across countries.

In general, these results suggest that the job insecurity measure used in the project is psychometrically sound. We received support for one underlying dimension of job insecurity in all samples, since all items loaded significantly on one factor, and found that this model fitted the data reasonably well in all participating countries. When we expanded the model to test whether the factor variances were equal, the model did not fit as well to the data, however. Moreover, the model fit was impaired when factor loadings and error terms were constrained to be of equal magnitude across samples. The last step in our model test is conservative; it is difficult to obtain a reasonable model fit in multi-sample analyses that include several countries. Therefore, we take the results as an indication that the measure assesses only one single dimension in all countries despite the lack of absolute similarity of the measurement model parameters (*i.e.*, factor variances, loadings, and error terms) across samples.

Table 4.3. Test for equality of factor structure of the job insecurity measure across countries

Model	df	χ^2	Δdf	$\Delta \chi^2$	RMSEA	SRMR	AIC
1. Null model; no relations	40	15605.57	–	–	.62	.52	15645.57
2. One dimension; freely estimated parameters	20	129.67	20	15475.90	.07	.02	209.67
3. Equal factor variance	23	218.90	3	89.23	.09	.12	292.90
4. Equal factor variance and loadings	35	335.18	12	116.28	.09	.16	385.18
5. Equal factor variance, loadings and errors	50	2244.05	15	1908.87	.21	.18	2264.05

All chi-square values significant ($p < .05$).
– Not applicable.

Reliability

The internal structure of items intended to capture a suggested construct may also be an indication of construct validity (Cronbach & Meehl, 1955). The internal structure, or reliability, of a measure indicates that the items of a scale measure the same concept. A homogenous measure, with high reliability, consists of items that tap into the same underlying construct. The issue of acceptable internal consistency is also important to the assessment of validity, since less reliable measures tend to affect the empirical results and increase the risk of the observed relationships being due to chance, rather than to actual association (Campbell & Fiske, 1959; Sjöberg & Sverke, 2001). One indication of internal consistency is that the items included in a scale are highly correlated. There are, however, several other indicators of reliability. In this study, we investigated the internal consistency of the job insecurity measure by computing Cronbach's alpha (α; Cronbach, 1951). This measure considers the correlation between items, but also takes into account the number of items included in the scale. Carmines and Zeller (1979) have argued that "reliabilities should not be below .80 for widely used scales" (p. 51). However, other researchers, such as Nunnally (1978, p. 245), suggest that a Cronbach alpha of .70 is acceptable in early stages of research and tests of measures. Since the items of our scale were combined to measure job insecurity for the purpose of the present project (our study may also be considered, in part, a test of our measure), we consider .70 to be a sufficient criterion for reliability.

Table 4.4 shows the Cronbach alpha reliability estimates for the measure of job insecurity in each country. These estimates of internal consistency were of satisfactory standard in all participating countries. The reliability estimates surpassed the .70 criterion in all four countries (and exceeded .80 in three). This implies that the job insecurity scale can be used to reliably assess the phenomenon of job insecurity in the different countries. Satisfactory internal consistency, and homogeneity, lends further credibility to the measurement properties of the job insecurity scale.

Table 4.4. Reliability estimates for the job insecurity measure

Country	Alpha
Belgium	.90
Italy	.76
The Netherlands	.91
Sweden	.89

Mean Levels of Job Insecurity

The results presented above suggest that our measure is reliable, and that it taps into a similar construct in all four countries. Given a unidimensional and reliable scale, and the knowledge that the factor structure is similar in all samples, the mean levels of job insecurity can now be considered. Even if the mean scores, shown in Table 4.1, were fairly low, there were significant differences between the four samples ($F_{[3,4081]}$=64.889, p<.001). The Dutch sample reported scores below 2 on the five-point scale (1.85), while respondents in the other three countries were to report job insecurity levels above 2. In Italy, the score reported (2.61) was the highest of the four samples.

Concluding Remarks

In this chapter, we have described how job insecurity has been operationalized in previous research and emphasized that fear or worry of job loss is a central characteristic in these measures. Based on this, we also described the job insecurity measure used in the present project and evaluated its measurement properties. In general, the results show that the job insecurity scale represents a single dimension and that it offers satisfactory reliability in each country. Although we did not find support for the proposition that all factor analysis parameters are identical across countries, we are convinced that the job insecurity measure under investigation may be used reliably and with validity to assess job insecurity in different settings. Also, the similarity of the results across the four countries indicates that the measure functions comparably in all countries. Despite construct validity being a continual process and something that can never be proven (Cronbach & Meehl, 1955), our results suggest that the job insecurity measure in this study may be used to capture job insecurity and to assess how this stressor is related to predictors and outcomes. Given the results presented in this chapter, we increase the possibility of being able to compare results between different countries more appropriately in the subsequent chapters.

CHAPTER 5

Predicting the Experience
of Job Insecurity

In Chapter 3 we described job insecurity as a subjective experience, where individuals perceive a threat to their employment or current working situation. This perception of threat may arise during turbulent times, when there are clear signals from the organization of upcoming changes. However, as we saw in Chapter 3, individual employees may perceive their situation as threatened – that is, experience job insecurity – even if there is no apparent objective threat. This raises the question of why some individuals are more prone to worry about job loss, and many researchers have put forward hypotheses on the antecedents of job insecurity. Considering the factors presumed to give rise to this experience, it is possible to differentiate between those factors that relate mainly to the environment and those relating to the individual (cf. Kinnunen & Nätti, 1994; Sverke & Hellgren, 2002). The environmental factors are comprised of organizational and social characteristics, such as the organization's way of dealing with changes and cutbacks, social support from actors within and outside of work, and the support obtained through union membership. Examples of individual factors are personal background, position in the organization and professional role, as well as attitudes and personality (see, e.g., Greenhalgh & Rosenblatt, 1984; Van Vuuren, Klandermans, Jacobson & Hartley, 1991a; Kinnunen, Mauno, Nätti & Happonen, 2000; Näswall & De Witte, 2003; Roskies & Louis-Guerin, 1990).

A subjective perception, such as the experience of job insecurity, is likely to be interpreted in different ways by different people. That is, employees in the same objective work situation will experience different levels of job insecurity, depending on their interpretation of the situation (Jacobson, 1991b). This description echoes the ISR model (Katz & Kahn, 1978) described in Chapter 3, and the interactionist theories (e.g., Ekehammar, 1974; Endler & Magnusson, 1976), in that it highlights how the interaction between the objective environment and the way that individuals interpret it shapes the reactions to certain situations. People differ in their perceptions of how serious a threat is, that is, how much they worry about losing their job. When the threat is considered to be serious, the level of job insecurity is likely to be higher. Another factor influencing the level of threat experienced concerns how severe a threat would be if realized. Employees who feel that losing their job would be very serious will probably experience higher levels of job insecurity than employees who consider themselves able to handle job loss (Jacobson, 1991b).

Perceptions of vulnerability may help explain this connection (Lazarus & Folkman, 1984). It appears that the intensity of the job insecurity experience can be explained by the degree of vulnerability felt by individuals. The degree of vulnerability may in turn vary with different attributes and individual differences. The experience of vulnerability also depends on the extent to which individuals feel that they have the resources necessary to handle threats and challenges. The extent to which individuals feel they possess these necessary resources for handling the consequences of a realized threat differs from one person to the next. Various groups may not necessarily have the same perceptions of what resources are available to them (Frese, 1985), which would result in different levels of job insecurity. In previous research, there have been great variations in the reported levels of job insecurity, both between samples and within samples (*e.g.*, Sverke *et al.*, 2002). One meta-analysis showed that the strength of the relation between job insecurity and its outcomes differs, in varying degrees, between demographic groups (Näswall, Sverke & Hellgren, 2001).

In this chapter, we take a closer look at a few common demographic variables and personality characteristics that may give rise to different levels of vulnerability and, thus, job insecurity. We emphasize the subjective interpretation and experience of the phenomenon, and our investigations focus on factors which may predispose individuals to the perception of job insecurity. We discuss the influence of individual factors (for example, personal background and demographic characteristics) as well as environmental factors (such as union membership) on the subjective interpretation of threat. In our empirical investigations we return to the samples from the four European countries (please note that for the analyses in the present chapter, the data for Sweden come from the alternative data set; for a more detailed description of the samples, see Chapter 2).

Individual Characteristics

Age and gender are two frequently studied variables that are often included as control variables in many analyses. This implies that we consider men and women, and the younger and older, to differ from each other in the outcome variables we investigate. They have also been

72

reported as correlates of job insecurity in previous research. For example, Mohr (2000) found a strong positive correlation between age and job insecurity, which is taken as evidence for older employees experiencing more job insecurity than younger employees. Other studies, such as the one by Van Vuuren *et al.* (1991a), also reported a positive relationship between age and job insecurity, suggesting that older employees experience more job insecurity than younger. Age may influence an employee to appraise the alternatives in the labor market differently. Younger persons usually have more alternatives, and companies value youth and competence, whereas older employees may feel that they have fewer alternatives. With fewer alternatives, potential job loss becomes more serious, and the perceived threat is stronger.

As far as gender is concerned, previous research studies have identified some differences. One study (Näswall *et al.*, 2001) showed that men exhibited a stronger relation between the experience of job insecurity and its negative outcomes than women. This may be an indication that men experience more job insecurity than women. This has been supported by earlier research, for example, Kinnunnen and her colleagues (1999) as well as Rosenblatt, Talmud, and Ruvio (1999). We therefore expect men to report higher levels of job insecurity than women.

However, it has been suggested that the influence of age is related to gender in the sense that men and women in the same age group have different expectations placed on them (De Witte, 1999). Men are probably more vulnerable to the experience of job insecurity during midlife (30 to 50 years of age). This is attributable to their traditional role as the breadwinner who has the main responsibility of providing for the family. Even if women are gradually sharing more of this responsibility, the traditional role of the man as provider may make the prospect of job loss more severe for men (Westman, 2000). Women, on the other hand, may be more likely to experience job insecurity as they get older, since their prospects for obtaining new employment after a layoff usually decline with age. Thus, we expect men in the middle age category, and women in the older category, to report the highest levels of job insecurity. In order to test this, we followed what was suggested in previous research (De Witte, 1999), and divided our sample into three age categories before comparing the levels of job insecurity in these age groups, (<30; 30–50; >50) among men and women respectively.

The results of the analyses of variance (ANOVA) are reported in Table 5.1. There was a significant main effect of age in two of our samples, Belgium and Sweden. Post-hoc tests (Bonferroni) revealed that in both these samples, those in the younger age category (those younger than 30) reported the highest levels of job insecurity. This result is contrary to previous research, where older workers reported more job insecurity (*e.g.*, Mohr, 2000; Van Vuuren *et al.*, 1991a).

Table 5.1. Impact of age and gender on job insecurity

	Belgium	Italy	The Netherlands	Sweden[a]
Age				
Young	2.21	2.60	1.91	2.09
Middle	2.30	2.62	1.86	1.79
Older	2.57	2.69	1.81	1.74
Df	2,1088	2,448	2,605	2,1401
F	5.00**	.14	.52	4.34*
Gender				
Men	2.15	2.57	1.87	1.90
Women	2.58	2.71	1.85	1.85
Df	1,1088	1,448	1,605	1,1401
F	29.92***	1.25	.07	.24

*$p<.05$, **$p<.01$, ***$p<.001$.
[a] For these analyses, the alternative Swedish data set was used.

Perhaps this may be explained by differences in country policies. In Sweden, for example, workforce reductions are largely based on seniority; the last person to be hired would have to be the first one to leave. Younger persons often have shorter tenure than older workers, which may put them more at objective risk, and predispose them to interpreting the situation as threatening, resulting in higher levels of job insecurity.

There was a main effect of gender in one of our samples. In the Belgian sample, the women consistently reported higher levels of job insecurity than the men, regardless of age. This may indicate that they perceive themselves less securely employed, and that they feel less attractive on the labor market. This result was contrary to our initial expectation and previous research, which suggests that men would report higher levels of job insecurity. One possible explanation may be found in earlier research studies, where women are reported to experience a higher level of job insecurity when they are responsible for supporting a family (De Witte, 1999).

In the Belgian and Italian samples, we detected an interaction effect between age and gender. These effects did not, however, point in the same direction. The interaction effect in Belgium ($F_{[2,448]}=5.82$, $p<.01$), as illustrated in Figure 5.1, reflects that women consistently reported higher levels of job insecurity than men. It is also evident that the level of job insecurity was higher among women in the oldest age group (those above 50 years of age). This may be attributable to difficulties for those over 50 years of age to obtain new employment in the event of job loss. For women, this seems to be a greater concern than for men. However, as Figure 5.1 also shows, the interaction effect in the Italian sample ($F_{[2,1088]}=4.23$, $p<.05$) indicates that the experience of job insecurity was stronger among older men than among younger, and that younger women experienced more job insecurity than older women and men.

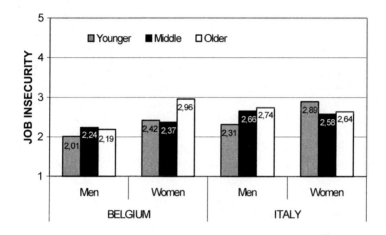

Figure 5.1. Interaction of age and gender in Belgium and Italy

Family Situation

Recent research (Näswall *et al.*, 2001) has suggested that men experience higher levels of job insecurity than women. As mentioned above, this may be due to the traditional role of the man as family provider and as the worker in the family (Barnett & Brennan, 1997). The threat of losing one's job would be regarded as a threat to the fulfillment of this role (Warr, 1987) since it requires that one is employed. However, our results in the previous section are not particularly supportive of this notion, and previous studies have suggested that women, too, experience a higher level of job insecurity when they are the sole breadwinner of the family (De Witte, 1999). Having children living at home is one indication that a person is providing for a family.

In this section, we report the results of tests that were performed in order to try and determine whether those women and men who have family responsibilities experience higher levels of job insecurity, where family responsibility is operationalized as children living at home. The potential difficulties (*i.e.*, economic strain and feelings of responsibility) associated with having children to support may be alleviated by the presence of a partner, since this may result in a generally better economic situation. Individuals with a partner may be expected to be less dependent on their income since their partners may be able to provide for them in the event of job loss. It has been suggested that cohabitating also provides a benefit in the form of the social support that a family or partner provides, which has been found to have a buffering effect against the experience of job insecurity (Lim, 1996). The family situation may thus influence the level of job insecurity experienced by the employee. With this in mind, this section presents the results of our investigation of how gender and family situation influence the level of job insecurity experienced. We expect that men and women in similar life situations will experience similar levels of job insecurity. Individuals with a partner at home should experience less job insecurity, as they would benefit from the positive support a partner can provide as well as the potential extra income. Also, we expect single parents with children living at home to report the highest levels of job insecurity, regardless of gender.

The results of the analyses are presented in Table 5.2. In the Belgian data set, there was no information included pertaining to family situation (partner or children), and consequently, we could not report any results for Belgium in this section. Main effects of gender, partner, or children living at home were not detected in any of the three samples that we were able to test our hypotheses on (Italian, Dutch, and Swedish data sets). Nor did we find any interaction effects between any of the three variables in our samples (in the Dutch data, the three-way interaction could not be tested due to there being too few cases in some combinations).

Table 5.2. Impact of family situation on job insecurity

	Italy	The Netherlands	Sweden[a]
Gender			
Men	2.50	1.73	1.70
Women	2.62	1.76	1.86
Df	1,450	1,332	1,1394
F	.38	.43	1.22
Partner			
No	2.52	1.62	1.78
Yes	2.61	1.85	1.78
Df	1,450	1,332	1,1394
F	.25	.84	.00
Children			
No	2.64	1.81	1.83
Yes	2.49	1.67	1.73
Df	1,450	1,332	1,1394
F	.67	1.10	.42

[a] For these analyses, the alternative Swedish data set was used.

Thus, contrary to our expectations, family situation did not have any effect on the level of job insecurity in any of the countries where this could be investigated. This suggests that the factors constituting family situation are not that important to the perception of job insecurity among employees. A possible explanation is that these variables do not concern attributes of the individual person, but rather, of his or her life situation. Factors such as age and gender are directly related to the person and may therefore be considered more salient on the labor market than factors concerning life outside of work. It has previously been suggested that the feeling of job insecurity reflects a feeling of vulnerability (Van Vuuren *et al.*, 1991a), and that this feeling of vulnerability to some extent arises from a person's evaluation of his/her own attributes. If employees feel that some of their attributes (*e.g.*, gender, age, or family situation) put them at a disadvantage, they may feel more insecure. Perhaps factors such as having a partner or children at home do not seem important in deciding whether one is more or less attractive to the labor market, and therefore do not affect the feeling of job insecurity. Also, one potential drawback of our data is that we have not specifically measured whether or not the respondents are actually the chief income bringers. Perhaps the use of "children at home" as an indicator of this is too rough a measure. In this context, future research would benefit from ascertaining whether employees feel that they alone are responsible for their family's subsistence.

Social Status

Work status (*i.e.*, blue- or white-collar employees and professionals/managers) and level of education are two related variables. In this section, we describe tests of the different levels of job insecurity among blue-collar workers, white-collar employees, and professionals/managers with different levels of education. Previous research has suggested that blue-collar workers, since they are generally more income-dependent than both white-collar workers and managers, will experience a threat of layoff more acutely than other groups who are less dependent (Frese, 1985; Gallie *et al.*, 1998; Kinnunen *et al.*, 1999). In addition, data from Great Britain show that blue-collar workers consistently reported higher levels of job insecurity than white-collar workers during a period of 20 years (starting in 1966) (Burchell, 2002). Based on this, it is reasonable to assume that blue-collar workers experience higher levels of job insecurity than employees in the other categories.

However, the opposite has also been suggested, that is, that white-collar and professional employees are becoming increasingly more prone to job insecurity. During the 1990s, reports of job insecurity began coming out of the professional and financial sectors, which had previously enjoyed less unpredictable employment (Burchell, 2002). This may be explained, in part, by the fact that downsizing was becoming a much more common measure for nearly all types of organizations that were trying to cope with turbulent times, and not just for the larger industrial factories that, traditionally, had been the ones most apt to utilize such measures (Burke & Nelson, 1998). The increased turbulence now found in traditional white-collar sectors has exposed both employees and managers to uncertainty. In relation to the increased flexibility of working life, it has been suggested that non-manual workers (*i.e.*, white-collar and professional employees) face growing threats of unemployment (Rifkin, 1995). The concept of "status inconsistency" has been brought up in this context (Schaufeli, 1992). This concept suggests that those in higher occupational positions, such as managers, who experience job insecurity, perceive this to be inconsistent with their status in that the position of manager or professional should not entail (the risk of) unemployment. Thus, the experience of job insecurity may become more severe for those who feel that it is something they should not have to worry about (see also Brockner, Tyler & Cooper-Schneider, 1992).

Another factor related to work status is the amount of education a person has acquired. The level of education completed influences the number of choices that workers have on the labor market. It seems reasonable to expect that people with only the lower levels of education completed (*i.e.*, compulsory school), in many cases, would lack the skills and knowledge needed in order to provide themselves with many alternative choices. In the event of job loss, they would probably have more difficulties securing new employment than those who have a more extensive education. These workers would consequently be more vulnerable to the experience of job insecurity and, in turn, report higher levels. This hypothesis builds on work by Van Vuuren *et al.* (1991a), who concluded that people with higher levels of education tend to experience less job insecurity.

In the present section, we compare the levels of job insecurity of groups with different levels of education and social status. In addition to this, we investigate whether these two variables interact. It has been suggested that since white-collar workers and professionals usually have a higher educational level, they will be less vulnerable to job loss than employees with lower levels of education (Schaufeli, 1992). Our hypothesis is that blue-collar workers and employees with less education will experience more job insecurity than white-collar workers and people with higher education. We expect that blue-collar workers with the lowest levels of education will report the highest level of job insecurity.

In our data we detected a main effect of work status in one of the four European countries (see Table 5.3). In the Swedish sample, those in blue-collar jobs reported the highest levels of job insecurity. It is believed that in the past, blue-collar workers were subjected to reorganizations and layoffs more often than other types of employees. Although the Swedish results follow the traditional suggestion that blue-collar workers are more exposed to uncertainty (Frese, 1985), work status had no significant influence on the level of job insecurity reported in three of our samples. Lately, however, layoffs and other types of organizational restructurings have influenced the workplaces of white-collar workers as well. This is a potential explanation of the fairly similar levels of job insecurity among employees with different work status in Belgium, Italy, and the Netherlands. Our results thus suggest, that work status is less important as a predictor of job insecurity than previously thought, and may reflect that the various occupational groups are more equally exposed to uncertainty in these samples.

Table 5.3. Impact of social status on job insecurity

	Belgium	Italy	The Netherlands	Sweden[a]
Work status				
Blue-collar	2.29	2.80	1.91	2.01
White-collar	2.40	2.19	1.84	1.63
Professional/Manager	2.24	2.62	1.77	1.66
Df	2,1041	2,390	2,300	2,1217
F	1.21	1.66	.44	19.30***
Education				
Compulsory	2.59	2.33	1.92	–
High-school	2.22	2.70	1.80	–
University	2.13	2.59	1.78	–
Df	2,1041	2,390	2,300	–
F	6.69**	.84	.51	–

$*p<.05, **p<.01, ***p<.001.$
– Data not available.
[a] For these analyses, the alternative Swedish data set was used.

Our data showed a significant main effect of level of education in only one sample – the Belgian. The highest levels of job insecurity were reported by those with compulsory school as their highest level of education completed. This finding concurs with the literature which suggests that people with less education would experience more insecurity (Van Vuuren *et al.*, 1991a). The lower level of education may in turn yield fewer options in the labor market, which is attributable to the lower skill level associated with less education. Fewer options in the labor market, *i.e.*, low employability (Rajan, 1997), may be associated with higher levels of job insecurity. The lack of impact of education in the other three samples may reflect, just as in the case of work status, an increased exposure to the threat of job loss, even among the highly educated, during the last decade (Burke & Nelson, 1998; Cascio, 1995).

In one of the samples we detected an interaction effect (note that the interaction effect could not be tested in Sweden due to lack of data on level of education). This interaction effect, which was found in the Belgian sample ($F_{[2,1041]}=2.60$, $p<.05$), and is illustrated in Figure 5.2, indicates that work status and education interact to make certain groups more vulnerable to the experience of job insecurity. Here, those in professional or managerial positions who also reported their highest level of education completed as compulsory school (*i.e.*, the lowest category of education) experienced the highest levels of job insecurity. This may potentially be explained by the feeling among these employees that their opportunities in the labor market are limited, and that their possibilities of finding new employment after being laid-off are slim.

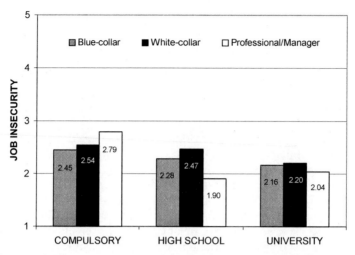

Figure 5.2. Interaction of work status and education in Belgium

Employment Contract

Given the different types of situations that employees under different contracts may encounter, we shall now look at how the type of employment contract may relate to the level of job insecurity experienced. As mentioned in Chapter 3, temporary employment has mainly been studied as one of the aspects of "flexibility" (*e.g.*, Reilly, 1998). By hiring employees on a temporary basis, and thus putting a time limit on their contracts, organizations achieve more flexibility, motivated by more competitive economic conditions. Fluctuations in demand make it difficult to anticipate how many employees will be needed at a given time. By temporarily hiring the extra staff needed, organizations are able to meet the demands without long-term commitments to new employees (De Witte & Näswall, 2003; Goslinga & Sverke, 2003; McLean Parks *et al.*, 1998).

Previous research studies have found that workers with temporary employment contracts report more job insecurity than those who have contracts without a time limit (Näswall & De Witte, 2003; Sverke *et al.*, 2000). Temporary work has also been described as an objective type of job insecurity (Pearce, 1998), in that it makes it difficult for the employee to envision his or her future employment. This may in turn give rise to uncertainty. Even if we subscribe to the subjective definition of job insecurity, we can still believe that the time limit put on the temporary contracts is likely to make these employees find their future to be less predictable, and thus report higher levels of job insecurity. This expectation is in agreement with previous research and theory.

Another important aspect of the employment contract is whether it is a part-time or full-time contract. Part-time workers may not feel they are part of the "core" staff in the same sense as those working full-time. Part-time contracts may, like in the case of temporary contracts, be turned to when there is a need to hire someone to put in only a little bit of work on a project, or a demand for someone who can work with a certain task, where hiring a full-time employee would be uncalled for (Barling & Gallagher, 1996; Sverke *et al.*, 2000). Part-time workers may, just as temporary employees, consequently feel that they will not be prioritized in the event of a downsizing, believing that the employer will choose to retain those workers who are considered to be part of the organization's "core staff". Previous research has moreover identified part-time workers as being less satisfied with their employment security than full-time employees (Levanoni & Sales, 1990; Still, 1983).

In order to take both kinds of employment contracts into account, in this section we investigate the interactive effect of the two aspects of employment contract (permanent *vs.* temporary and full-time *vs.* part-time contracts) on the levels of job insecurity in our four samples. The results of the analysis of variance (see Table 5.4) showed no main effect of part-time work in any of the samples. This indicates that part-time workers did not experience more job insecurity than those working full-time. We did, however, detect a main effect of temporary employment contract. In Belgium, the Netherlands, and Sweden, temporary workers reported higher levels of job insecurity than those permanently employed.

Table 5.4. Employment contract and job insecurity

	Belgium	Italy	The Netherlands	Sweden[a]
Contract type				
Permanent	2.26	2.84	1.79	1.63
Temporary	2.59	2.90	2.31	2.56
Df	1,1089	1,383	1,607	1,1368
F	4.44*	.08	27.92***	177.74***
Work hours				
Part-time	2.46	2.68	2.10	2.03
Full-time	2.39	3.07	1.99	2.17
Df	1,1089	1,383	1,607	1,1368
F	.23	3.69	1.22	3.80

*$p<.05$, ***$p<.001$.
[a] For these analyses, the alternative Swedish data set was used.

The results also revealed a significant interaction effect of the two contract types in the Swedish sample ($F_{[1,1368]}=4.07$, $p<.05$). Figure 5.3 illustrates this interaction effect by plotting the levels of job insecurity for the different categories in the Swedish sample. Here we see that those holding temporary contracts while also working part-time reported the highest levels of job insecurity. However, there was no significant interaction effect in Belgium, Italy, or the Netherlands.

The results partially confirm our initial suggestion that those without permanent contracts report higher levels of job insecurity. In contrast part-time work in itself does not seem to contribute to the experience of job insecurity. The notion that these workers are less attached to the organization and therefore perceive themselves more at risk did not receive support in our data. It is important to note, however, that our data do not take into account whether workers hold a certain employment contract voluntarily or not. For instance, it may be that those who are forced to work part-time against their wishes feel less attached to the organization. Those choosing to work part-time, on the other hand, may be pleased with their level of attachment to the organization. Since we have no record of this factor, we can only suggest that this may explain the lack of differences between contracts.

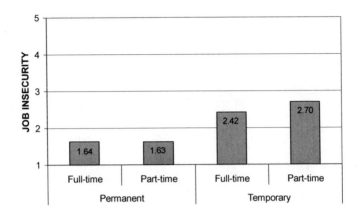

Figure 5.3. Interaction between contract types in Sweden

However, it is also possible that part-time work in itself does not result in more job insecurity. Those working part-time may not be more prone to perceptions of job insecurity than those working full-time. In our data, the only exception to this is the Swedish sample, where those working part-time *and* under temporary contracts reported higher levels of job insecurity than the other groups. This implies that part-time workers to some extent experience more job insecurity than other workers, if they are working under temporary contracts. Temporary employees, on the other hand, reported more job insecurity in two of our samples. This is in accordance with previous research and theory, and is a partial confirmation of the assumption that those not permanently attached to the organization are more uncertain about the future of their employment.

Union Membership

Social support is suggested as a factor that may decrease the level of job insecurity experienced and diminish its influence on health and work related attitudes (Armstrong-Stassen, 1993; Lim, 1996). The union may be one important source of social support (Armstrong-Stassen, 1993; Dekker & Schaufeli, 1995; Hellgren & Sverke, 2001). Union membership can lessen the perception of powerlessness in that the union has the function of speaking for the employees (Barling *et al.*, 1992; Hellgren & Chirumbolo, 2003; Sverke & Hellgren, 2001). One of the tasks of the union is to make sure that the needs of the members, that is, the employees, are met. A perception of a strong union should decrease the experience of job insecurity since the union negotiations with employers are supposed to be a benefit to employees (Johnson *et al.*, 1992). Further-more, unions are not necessarily without influence or involvement in processes of organizational change, and it has an interest in, as well as influence on, ensuring that the employees are treated fairly (Mellor, 1992; Sverke & Hellgren, 2001). Insofar as the employees feel protected by the union, they may not feel powerless in trying to avoid negative situations at work.

In this section, we examine the plausibility of the idea that union members should report less job insecurity than non-members. This test was carried out using a univariate analysis of variance, where we compared the levels of job insecurity reported by union members to the levels reported by non-members. This hypothesis could not be tested in the Netherlands since the entire sample was comprised of union members.

The results reveal a significant difference between union members and non-members in the level of job insecurity experienced. This was found in two samples, Belgium ($F_{[1,1058]}$=33.37, $p<.001$) and Sweden ($F_{[1,1374]}$=5.09, $p<.05$). Figure 5.4 displays the results of this comparison. In the Belgian sample, union members reported significantly higher levels of job insecurity than non-members. However, as the figure also shows, the results pointed to the opposite in the Swedish sample, where union members, as we initially expected, reported less job insecurity than non-members. There was no significant difference between members and non-members in Italy.

The results in the Belgian sample were contrary to our expectation that union membership would be associated with lower levels of job insecurity. This could be explained by the reasoning that union members might be more aware of the risk of job loss, since this is something the union is trying to prevent. The fact that the employees are aware that the union is working towards preventing job insecurity may make the members more vigilant, and lead them to interpret ambiguous messages as a prelude to uncertain employment and threats of job loss. An alternative explanation to the higher levels of job insecurity among union members (in Belgium) is that individuals who work in areas where their employment is less secure are more likely to join a trade union (*cf.* Bender & Sloane, 1999; Brett, 1980; Klandermans, 1986). Previous research also suggests that unionized workers tend to rate job security as one of the most important issues for the union to work towards (Allvin & Sverke, 2000; Lind, 1996). The results in Sweden are consistent with our hypothesis, indicating that employees without union protection report higher levels of job insecurity.

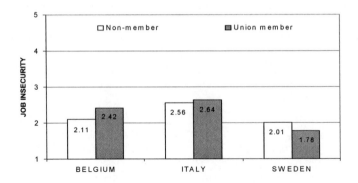

Figure 5.4. Union membership and job insecurity

Personality

Job insecurity is determined by how individuals evaluate and inter-pret their work situation. This interpretation is influenced, as we have seen, by several background factors. One important factor that contrib-utes to individuals' outlooks on both the present and the future concerns their general dispositions. Fortunately, in one of our European data sets (the alternative data for Sweden), personality was included, allowing us to investigate the question of how personality affects the experience of job insecurity.

According to the previous theoretical discussions, personality char-acteristics are important for coping processes and the appraisal of a situation as positive or negative, as well as for self-reports on well-being (Hart & Cooper, 2001; Lazarus & Folkman, 1984). Hart and Cooper (2001), for example, present results indicating that a high degree of extraversion would make the individual more likely to use problem-focused coping strategies. These strategies are considered more effective than those focusing on the emotion elicited by the stressor, since they are directed at solving the problem and changing the situation (Callan, 1993).

In the present section, three aspects of personality are discussed, namely locus of control, self-efficacy, and affectivity, and their relations to job insecurity are investigated. We shall, first of all, discuss the rele-vant theories along with our hypotheses for all three personality charac-teristics, and then proceed to report on our results.

The central tenet of theories of attribution rests on the idea that peo-ple are interested in understanding their environment. Individuals are also concerned with trying to understand what specific events lie behind various occurrences. Those who can understand and interpret these events are in a better position to influence and affect future occurrences (Augostinos & Walker, 1996). At the heart of attribution theories is the assumption that the individual judges events to have either internal or external causes. More specifically, events are attributed causes that originate either from the individual (internal) or from the environment (external). Rotter (1966) has developed this line of reasoning to account for perceptions of internal and external locus of control in reference to occurrences that the individual experiences. He argues that events not exclusively attributed as caused by the individual him- or herself are, in our culture, referred to as luck, fortune, destiny, or being under the control of somebody else. This means that individuals who attribute the cause of events in life to themselves have an internal locus of control, while those who attribute the cause of events to factors beyond their control have an external locus of control.

Spector (1982) suggests that locus of control is one of the most important variables in explaining human behavior in organizations. Anderson, Hellriegel, and Slocum (1977) found that individuals making internal attributions reported lower levels of perceived threat and stress compared to those who made external attributions. Van Vuuren *et al.* (1991a) postulated that individuals making internal attributions should experience lower levels of stress and less job insecurity. The appraisal individuals make of their locus of control will also affect their choice of coping strategies, as well as how they feel about their ability to cope with the situation at all (Judge, Locke, Durham & Kluger, 1998). A feeling of personal control is usually related to lower levels of perceived stress and increases the use of problem-focused strategies (Parkes, 1994).

Self-efficacy has been shown to influence the way in which an individual copes with a stressful situation (Judge, Thoresen, Pucik & Welbourne, 1999). Higher levels of self-efficacy facilitate a positive evaluation of the situation and function as a coping resource, which increases the individual's perception of being able to handle the situation. Self-efficacy also increases the likelihood of the utilization of problem-focused strategies (Lazarus & Folkman, 1984).

Bandura defines self-efficacy as the "beliefs in one's capability to organize and execute the courses of action required to produce given attainments" (1997, p. 3). Self-efficacy thus refers to the individual's belief in his or her ability to attain a desired outcome in any given situation. Bandura (1997) argues that self-efficacy is one of the strongest determinants of the individual's behavior, and this includes situations involving stress. He considers the degree of self-efficacy to be related to an individual's coping strategies and ability to handle stress. Several studies have found that self-efficacy is associated with coping strategies for career changes, unemployment, and resistance to change (see Judge *et al.*, 1999, for a review). The literature thus proposes that high self-efficacy is a necessary condition for positive evaluations of critical events at work.

Positive and negative affectivity are distinct emotional dimensions that are presumed to roughly reflect the personality attributes neuroticism and extraversion (Watson & Clark, 1997). More specifically, research on affectivity indicates that it represents parts or subscales of neuroticism (negative affectivity) and extraversion (positive affectivity). Individuals characterized by a high level of negative affectivity are presumed to be more negative towards themselves, others, and the world in general, compared to individuals with less pronounced negative emotions. Positive affectivity, on the other hand, is presumed to be associated with such characteristics as well-being, sociability, enthusiasm, and a generally positive outlook on life (Judge *et al.*, 1999).

Bowman and Stern (1995) found a positive correlation between positive affectivity and problem-focused coping in stressful organizational circumstances. Cohen and Wills (1985) argue that positive affectivity can function as a moderator between experiences of organizational change and stress. Roskies, Louis-Guerin, and Fournier (1993) suggest that positive affectivity should have an equally strong but reverse relation to stress and health as negative affectivity. It has been argued that perceptions of stress at work (*e.g.*, job insecurity) and reduced well-being are expressions of neurotic personality traits, which are tantamount to negative emotions (*e.g.*, Brief, Burke, George, Robinson & Webster 1988; Schaubroeck, Ganster & Fox, 1992).

We suggest that the personality factors described above have an impact on the interpretation that individuals make of their environment, and thus on the level of job insecurity experienced. Individuals with an internal locus of control are expected to report lower levels of job insecurity. We also anticipate that people high in self-efficacy will exhibit the same pattern. Positive affectivity is expected to be associated with lower levels of job insecurity, whereas negative affectivity is proposed to accompany higher levels of job insecurity.

Table 5.5. Effects of personality traits on job insecurity (standardized multiple regression coefficients): Sweden[a]

Predictor	Job insecurity
Age	.07*
Gender (women)	.03
Employment contract (temporary)	.18***
Locus of control (internal)	-.30***
Self-efficacy	.03
Positive affectivity	.01
Negative affectivity	.10**
R^2 adjusted	.14***

*$p<.05$, **$p<.01$, ***$p<.001$.
[a] For these analyses, the alternative Swedish data set was used.

As mentioned above, only one of our data sets, the Swedish alternative one, contained information on dispositional characteristics. As Table 5.5 illustrates, job insecurity was predicted by individuals' perceptions of locus of control. This relation was negative, which means that individuals perceiving that the control over life events generally is external, that is, out of their own hands, tend to experience higher levels of job insecurity than individuals making internal attributions. Contrary to our hypothesis, the results did not show that individuals with higher levels of self-efficacy experienced lower levels of job insecurity. Self-efficacy does not, therefore, appear to have an impact on an individual's interpretation of the situation as being characterized by uncertainty, and this factor is perhaps a more important determinant of reactions to job insecurity. Also, there was no significant relationship found between positive affectivity and perceived job insecurity. A generally positive outlook does thus not seem to matter for the perception of job insecurity in our sample. However, the results indicate that individuals characterized by high negative affectivity experience higher levels of job insecurity than those with lower levels on this attribute.

Two of the personality dispositions we investigated may be considered predictors of job insecurity. Individuals who feel that life's events are out of their control were more prone to job insecurity. This corresponds to the description of job insecurity as a feeling of powerlessness to counteract a negative situation (Greenhalgh & Rosenblatt, 1984). This finding also replicates results obtained by Van Vuuren *et al.* (1991a). Our second predictor of job insecurity was negative affectivity. People who tended to describe events and the future in negative terms, and considered themselves in a negative light, tended to also report higher levels of job insecurity. This is also consistent with previous research by Van Vuuren *et al.* (1991a), who found that people who are more pessimistic typically feel more job insecurity. The personality attributes and the control variables explained a total of 14 percent of the variation in job insecurity.

Concluding Remarks

This chapter has shown that personality, age and gender, as well as social status, temporary employment contract, and union membership all seem to be of some significance in determining the level of job insecurity experienced. Contrary to our hypothesis, however, family status did not appear as an important factor. We would argue that attributes more central to the individuals, such as age, gender, and level of education, would make them feel that they are running a higher risk of job loss, than factors that are more related to the general life situation.

The results presented here are based on investigations in four different countries. However, we do not compare the results between the four countries; rather, our results show how generalizable the results are. Some background variables, such as temporary work, can generally be said to be predictive of job insecurity, for example. However, as we have seen, the investigated countries exhibit quite different patterns in some cases. At this point it is time to take the reactions to job insecurity into account.

CHAPTER 6

Consequences of Job Insecurity

Given the previous discussion of job insecurity as an experience that may evoke stress reactions and/or be interpreted as a breach of the psychological agreement existing between the individual and the organization, it is not difficult to imagine that job insecurity may have psychological effects. Concern over losing an important feature in life is something that affects most individuals in a negative way. In Chapter 3, we described how the very apprehension of a negative occurrence might be just as difficult to cope with as the actual event. Some researchers even suggest that a threat of job loss may be more detrimental to the individual than the realization of these threats (Dekker & Schaufeli, 1995; Latack & Dozier, 1986). Such a view concurs with the findings of stress research, where it has been shown that the anticipation of a stressful event may be an equal, if not greater, source of stress than the actual event itself (Lazarus & Folkman, 1984).

Since job insecurity reflects the perceived anxiety about losing one's job, this anxiety may be expected to have consequences for the individual. Work is a central part of life to many people – it fulfills both financial and social needs. Jobs provide individuals with income, social contacts, possibilities of personal development, as well as daily and weekly structure (Jahoda, 1982). If the individual is at risk of not being able to fulfill these needs, in that he or she perceives the employment to be threatened, he/she is liable to feel a sense of frustration. Losing one's job would entail the loss of financial as well as social resources, and result in the individual no longer feeling needed (De Witte, 1999; Levi, 1999).

According to the stress models we discussed in Chapter 3, a situation brings about stress when the individual feels that he/she cannot meet the demands perceived to be made on him/her (Katz & Kahn, 1978; Lazarus & Folkman, 1984; Siegrist, 1996). From a theoretical point of view the negative consequences of job insecurity can be explained by the uncertainty involved in the situation. The individual does not know if the threat of unemployment will be realized – or how to counteract it. Consequently, the individual has difficulties in assessing whether he or she can meet the demands posed on him or her since it is unclear what these demands entail.

We have also discussed that job insecurity can be described as a breach of the psychological contract (Robinson & Morrison, 2000). Individuals react strongly when they feel that the implied contract existing between them and the employer is breached, for example when job insecurity breaks an implicit agreement on long-term employment in the organization. In such an event, employer confidence is eroded, as the employer is no longer seen as a trustworthy partner.

Because of its potential function as a breach of psychological contracts and its nature as a work stressor, job insecurity is associated with a number of negative consequences (Barling & Kelloway, 1996; Chirumbolo & Hellgren, 2003; Davy *et al.*, 1997; Van Vuuren, Klandermans, Jacobson & Hartley, 1991b; Hellgren *et al.*, 1999; Sverke *et al.*, 2002). The anxiety experienced is expected to have negative consequences for the individual's health and well-being. But job insecurity also appears to affect attitudes towards work and the organization, especially when the individual holds the organization responsible for his or her stress experience. Job insecurity may also, in a similar way, result in a negative evaluation of the labor union and its performance, if the individual feels that the union does not protect his/her interests well enough.

In this chapter, we focus on the consequences of job insecurity and discuss the findings of previous research regarding its consequences for the individual, the organization, and the labor union. This discussion is accompanied by empirical analyses of data from the four countries. The use of four European countries allows us to fulfill a secondary purpose of this chapter, namely, to investigate whether the effect sizes may be generalized over samples. This does not imply a comparison between countries, but rather a testing of to what extent the respondents in the different samples react to job insecurity in similar ways.

In the empirical analysis, we investigate the effects of job insecurity on three potential areas of outcomes, namely, consequences for the individual, consequences for the organization and, finally, consequences for the union (see Figure 6.1). The analysis also includes demographic variables. It has been suggested in the literature that the relation between predictor variables and outcomes may be influenced by additional variables like demographic characteristics. This is also the case regarding the relation between job insecurity and its potential outcomes (Hellgren & Sverke, 2003), such as subjective well-being (Diener, Eunkook, Suh, Lucas & Smith, 1999; Näswall *et al.*, 2001) and work and organizational attitudes (Van Vuuren *et al.*, 1991b). Therefore, demographic variables – age, gender, and temporary work – are controlled for in the empirical investigations in order to better understand the association between job insecurity and its potential consequences.

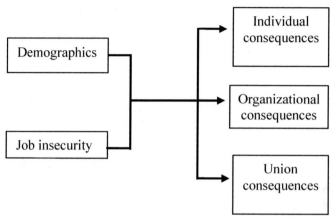

**Figure 6.1. Empirical model of the relation
between job insecurity and three different areas of outcomes**

This chapter first investigates the association between job insecurity experiences and individual consequences (health complaints). The analysis includes mental as well as physical health complaints. Secondly, the relationship between job insecurity and the organizational consequences (job satisfaction, organizational commitment, and turnover intention) is addressed. This is followed by an investigation of the relationship between job insecurity and union-related consequences (union satisfaction, union commitment, and union turnover intention). Finally, we discuss the results of the empirical tests, putting particular emphasis on both how job insecurity relates to the three different categories of outcomes and where job insecurity seems to have the most serious impact.

Consequences for the Individual

It is to be expected that job insecurity will result in some sort of strain, as do other stressors (Jex & Beehr, 1991; Lazarus & Folkman, 1984), and this strain has often been hypothesized to reduce well-being. Job insecurity may be taxing for the individual since it involves prolonged exposure to uncertainty (Jacobson, 1991a; Joelson & Wahlquist, 1987; Van Vuuren, 1990). Because of this uncertainty, it is more difficult for individuals to use effective coping strategies (Lazarus & Folkman, 1984), since they are unable to foresee what might happen.

When individuals are in a state of unsuredness over whether job loss will actually occur, they do not know which coping strategies are appropriate. In contrast, the event of actual job loss may trigger coping strategies that can be effectively employed, such as the act of mourning or the initiative to look for a new job. It is the actualization of the threat that relieves the confusion over whether the threat will be realized or not, which thus eases the stress of uncertainty (Lazarus & Folkman, 1984).

The stress of job insecurity may result in many different types of outcomes for individuals, but in the present chapter we focus on two major outcomes – mental health complaints and physical health complaints. Mental health complaints relate to how the individual feels. Mental health represents the operationalization of subjective well-being, indications of which include a good self-image, a general positive subjective evaluation of one's own well-being, and a lack of symptoms such as worry and despondency (*cf.* Goldberg, 1972). Physical health complaints, on the other hand, refer to the individual's reported symptoms like headaches, muscle tension, and tiredness (*cf.* Bishop, 1994; Diener *et al.*, 1999). There are several different ways to describe and assess an individual's health; it can be done through, for instance, medical examinations, measurements of biological markers, or through the study of records. However, among the different methods in use, self-reports are by far the most common (Bishop, 1994). Self-report measures, as indicators of health, are subjective in that no one other than the individual is involved in the assessment. This type of measurement reflects how individuals actually feel. It could, for example, reveal that a person feels tired or has headaches despite the fact that he or she may have a close to perfect health status from a medical perspective. This measurement method is of particular importance to us, in our analyses, since we are chiefly interested in investigating how the employees perceive and rate their own health.

The potential long-term consequences of job insecurity on the individual's health and well-being have also been documented. Because job insecurity is a stressor, it can be expected to have consequences on well-being and health just like other factors that trigger stress. A stressor arises from the individual's perception of lacking the resources necessary to counteract a threat. This results in tension, which gives rise to stress reactions that may include psychosomatic symptoms or lower psychological well-being. In accordance with this, it has been shown that perceived job insecurity can be linked to lower general well-being (Barling & Kelloway, 1996; De Witte, 1999; Van Vuuren *et al.*, 1991b; Hellgren *et al.*, 1999; Jick, 1985). Both physical and mental health problems, it has also been found, appear to increase with the degree of job insecurity (Ashford *et al.*, 1989; Isaksson, Hellgren & Pettersson, 2000; Lim, 1996). Meta-analyses show that job insecurity, in the population as a whole, has a relatively strong negative relation to psychological well-being and a somewhat weaker negative relation to physical health (Näswall *et al.*, 2001; Sverke *et al.*, 2002).

The strengths of the links vary somewhat between previous studies investigating the effects of job insecurity on psychological well-being. Some studies have found strong associations between job insecurity and health complaints, while others report a weaker connection. For example, Roskies and Louis-Guerin (1990) studied managers at different levels in three corporations. Two of the organizations were judged to be at a great risk of having to get rid of employees, while the third appeared to be on the verge of employing more people (which thus implied objective job security). The authors found a strong relation between perceived job insecurity and mental health complaints, regardless of organization. The objectively observed job insecurity was not related to health complaints or work attitudes. Roskies and Louis-Guerin went on to conclude that the subjective perception of job insecurity, in this case, added to an increase in psychological problems such as worry and anxiety.

Most studies in this area have investigated the relation between job insecurity and self-reported health. There are also studies investigating how job insecurity could be linked to objective measures of health, such as cardiovascular diseases and blood pressure (*e.g.*, Ferrie *et al.*, 1998; Mattiasson, Lindgärde, Nilsson & Theorell, 1990). These studies indicate that job insecurity has negative effects on physiological health indicators as well.

Turning now to our empirical data, the question remains how job insecurity relates to individual consequences in terms of mental and physical health complaints in the four countries. However, we first need to examine whether the samples differ in their levels of mental and physical health complaints. The Belgian data were omitted from the mean comparison since mental health complaints in Belgium were assessed with a yes/no response mode, and physical health complaints were not assessed at all. Table 6.1 shows mean levels for both health variables in the respective country together with tests for mean level differences between countries (ANOVA).

Table 6.1. Tests for mean differences in mental and physical health complaints between countries

Country	Mental health complaints	Physical health complaints
Belgium	#	–
Italy	2.07	2.04
The Netherlands	1.58	1.67
Sweden	1.99	2.13
Df	2,3156	2,2784
F	286.426***	81.820***

***$p<.001$.
Scale range: 1–4 (mental health complaints) and 1–5 (physical health complaints).
Not included in the means comparisons because of different response scale.
– Data not available.

The *F*-tests for mean differences between countries show that there were significant differences in both mental health complaints and physical health complaints between the three countries. The post-hoc tests (Bonferroni) revealed that all countries differed from each other regarding the mean levels of both outcome variables. The highest average level of mental health complaints was found in Italy and the lowest in the Netherlands. When it comes to physical health complaints, the Swedish sample reported the most frequent perceptions of somatic complaints and, again, the Netherlands the fewest. Thus, the Dutch sample reported fewer health complaints as compared with the other two countries. It can also be concluded that the Italian participants reported the highest level of mental health complaints and Sweden the highest level of physical health complaints.

The next question to be answered, however, concerns whether job insecurity perceptions are associated with mental and physical health complaints in the respective country. In order to answer this question, a series of multiple regression analyses were performed, using age, gender, and temporary work as control variables. The results of the multiple regression predicting mental health complaints are displayed in Table 6.2.

Job insecurity was positively associated with mental health complaints, in all participating countries, after controlling for age, gender, and temporary work. The results indicate that higher levels of job insecurity are related to more frequently reported mental health complaints. As can be seen from Table 6.2, the association between job insecurity and mental health complaints was strongest in Italy (which also was the country reporting the highest mean level of mental health complaints) and weakest in the Netherlands. It can also be concluded that age emerged as a significant predictor of mental health complaints in Belgium and Italy, suggesting that older people tend to report more mental health complaints as compared to the younger. However, no such relation was obtained for the Netherlands and Sweden. Gender was a significant predictor of mental health complaints in the Netherlands and Sweden, but not in the Belgian and Italian samples. The relationship in the Netherlands and Sweden was positive, suggesting that women tend to report higher levels of mental health complaints than men do. Finally, it was found that temporary work did predict mental health complaints in three of the participating countries (Belgium, the Netherlands, and Sweden); this relation was negative, indicating that temporary workers typically report fewer mental health complaints as compared to workers with permanent employment contracts.

Table 6.2. Results of multiple regression predicting mental health complaints (standardized regression coefficients)

Predictor	Belgium	Italy	The Netherlands	Sweden
Age	.09*	.12*	.06	.02
Gender (women)	.04	.05	.14**	.06*
Temporary work	-.11*	.03	-.10*	-.07*
Job insecurity	.23***	.31***	.16***	.23***
R^2 adjusted	.07***	.10***	.04***	.05***

$*p<.05, **p<.01, ***p<.001.$

In total, the regression model accounted for between four (the Netherlands) and ten percent (Italy) of the variance in mental health complaints. We can conclude that job insecurity was significantly associated with mental health complaints in all four countries. It can also be concluded that job insecurity emerged as a predictor of mental health complaints after controlling for individual demographics (age, gender) and temporary work. The results also indicate that being employed on a contingent basis is not associated with more frequent reports of mental health complaints but, rather, with a more positive subjective well-being.

Our next step is to look at the association between job insecurity and physical health complaints. Table 6.3 reveals that job insecurity was associated with physical health complaints in Italy and Sweden, but not in the Netherlands (physical health problems were not assessed in Belgium). The direction of the relation was positive in both Italy and Sweden, indicating that job insecurity perceptions are associated with more frequent reports of physical health complaints. The results also show that gender was positively associated with physical health complaints in Italy, suggesting that women tend to report more physical health complaints than men. In Sweden, all control variables were related to physical health complaints, such that younger individuals reported more frequent physical health complaints as compared to older individuals, and also in this case, that women reported more frequent physical health problems. In addition, the results also show that temporary workers reported fewer physical health complaints compared with permanent employees. None of the predictor variables, it should be added, reached significance in the sample from the Netherlands. In total, the control variables and job insecurity perceptions explained eight (Italy) and four (Sweden) percent of the variance in physical health complaints.

Table 6.3. Results of multiple regression predicting physical health complaints (standardized regression coefficients)

Predictor	Belgium[a]	Italy	The Netherlands	Sweden
Age	–	.08	.04	-.06*
Gender (women)	–	.15*	.02	.12***
Temporary work	–	-.03	-.05	-.06*
Job insecurity	–	.25***	-.02	.16***
R^2 adjusted	–	.08***	-.00	.04***

*$p<.05$, **$p<.01$, ***$p<.001$.
– Not applicable.
[a] Data on physical health complaints were not available in the Belgian sample.

To summarize, job insecurity predicted mental health complaints, as expected, in all four countries. Individuals experiencing high levels of job insecurity reported more mental health complaints than those characterized by lower levels of job insecurity. Job insecurity also predicted symptoms of physical ill-health in Italy and Sweden, as expected. However, in the Netherlands, job insecurity was not related to physical health complaints. Overall, this provides support for the idea that job insecurity is a significant work stressor in today's working life and reinforces results obtained in previous research (*e.g.*, Burchell, 1994; De Witte, 1999; Kinnunen *et al.*, 2000; Kuhnert, Sims & Lahey, 1989; Sverke *et al.*, 2002). These results also give support for the central assumption of most stress theories – the anticipation of a fundamental and involuntary event may lead to strain reactions (*e.g.*, Lazarus & Folkman, 1984). Further support is also found for the view that threats to a person's present employment situation may threaten critical social roles for the individual and thereby generate feelings of distress and ill-health (Siegrist, 1996, 2000). It has also been argued that the possibility of exerting control over the situation is a necessary condition for being able to handle the situation in a constructive way (Theorell, 2003), and that job insecurity, by definition, contains an element of uncontrollability and powerlessness (Greenhalgh & Rosenblatt, 1984; Sverke & Hellgren, 2002) – all of which renders this stressor one that may have serious consequences for the individual.

Consequences for the Organization

Job insecurity may obviously affect the well-being of individuals. In this sense, job insecurity is a significant stressor with consequences for the individual. However, the consequences are not limited to just the individual. The situation is, rather, often such that individuals experiencing job insecurity also tend to react to the dissatisfying circumstances in ways that affect the organization as well (Greenhalgh & Rosenblatt, 1984; Sverke *et al.*, 2002).

One of the most researched outcomes of job insecurity is job satisfaction. This concept has been defined as a positive attitude that is based on the perception of the job as something pleasant that provides the individual with what he or she needs. Job satisfaction represents an employee's degree of contentment with his or her job (Locke, 1976). Since job insecurity arises from the individual evaluating the security of the employment as being less than desirable, we would expect individuals experiencing job insecurity to be dissatisfied with their jobs. Several studies have also found a strong negative association between job insecurity and job satisfaction (*e.g.*, Ashford *et al.*, 1989; Lim, 1996; Rosenblatt & Ruvio, 1996), indicating that employees who perceive their employment as uncertain also feel more dissatisfied with their work tasks (for meta-analysis results, see Sverke *et al.*, 2002).

Organizational commitment is a central topic of interest in the area of organizational research (see, *e.g.*, Griffin & Bateman, 1986; Mathieu & Zajac, 1990; Meyer, 1997; Morrow, 1983). The idea that employees who are committed to the organization identify with and share the values and goals of the organization is fundamental in this regard, as the concept reflects a wish to be loyal to the organization (Allen & Meyer, 1990; Mowday, Steers & Porter, 1979). An organization needs its employees to be committed in order to properly achieve the desired goals. Previous research has related the experience of job insecurity to lower levels of commitment to the organization (*e.g.*, Armstrong-Stassen, 1993; Borg & Elizur, 1992; McFarlane, Shore & Tetrick, 1991), and meta-analysis results confirm this view (Sverke *et al.*, 2002). This can be put into the context of theories on the psychological contract (Davy *et al.*, 1997; Rousseau, 1989). The employee may perceive job insecurity as a breach of the psychological contract, especially if he/she entered the employment relationship under the implicit understanding that a job well-done would guarantee continued employment. Job insecurity would then be a signal that the organization is not keeping its end of the deal. As a consequence, the employee may then react by lowering his or her level of commitment, or also by getting the feeling that the employer can no longer be trusted. Lowered commitment would result in an organization's employees no longer feeling they want to exert themselves for the benefit of the organization. As a consequence, they may opt to leave the organization.

One of the most serious consequences associated with job insecurity is that of voluntary turnover. Previous research has shown that individuals who are able to, tend to leave the organization as the situation becomes more uncertain and less satisfactory (Ashford *et al.*, 1989; Cavanaugh & Noe, 1999; Hellgren *et al.*, 1999; Sverke *et al.*, 2002). It is not hard to imagine that if one has the opportunity to find more favorable employment in another organization, and is not content with the present situation, changing jobs is a natural reaction (Hirschman, 1970). Such a reaction affects the organization in that it is often the most competent employees who leave since they also are the most attractive for other companies to hire (Kozlowski *et al.*, 1993; Pfeffer, 1998). As a consequence, the organization is left with a staff of less competent employees (who also may have developed negative attitudes toward their work) with which to try and revitalize the organization and bring it back on its feet.

The reactions to job insecurity described above can all impact the organization in some way. In this section, we will investigate whether these organizational consequences also apply to our European samples by analyzing the impact of job insecurity on job satisfaction, organizational commitment, and the intention to leave the organization. First, however, we shall look at the mean levels of the organizational variables in each country.

Table 6.4 shows mean levels as well as tests for significant differences in job satisfaction, organizational commitment and turnover intention between countries (Belgium was omitted from the mean comparison involving turnover intention since in Belgium this variable was assessed with a yes/no response mode).

**Table 6.4. Tests for mean differences
in work-related attitudes between countries**

Country	Job satisfaction	Organizational commitment	Turnover Intention
Belgium	3.70	3.39	#
Italy	3.60	3.20	2.63
The Netherlands	3.79	3.52	2.85
Sweden	3.68	2.54	2.30
Df	3,4082	3,4033	2,2937
F	4.93**	318.70***	58.978***

**p<.01; ***p<.001.
Scale range: 1–5 (all outcome variables).
Not included in the means comparisons because of different response scale.

The results of the *F*-tests show that there were mean differences between countries in all three attitude variables. The follow-up post-hoc tests (Bonferroni) reveal that the average level of job satisfaction in the Netherlands differed from that in Italy and Sweden; in both cases, the level of job satisfaction was higher in the Netherlands. No other country differences were obtained regarding job satisfaction. In terms of organizational commitment, all four countries differed from one another, with the highest level of organizational commitment being found in the Netherlands and the lowest in Sweden. There were also country differences when it comes to turnover intention. The average level of turnover intention was highest in the Netherlands and lowest in the Swedish sample.

However, the main question is whether job insecurity is related to such organizational attitudes as job satisfaction, organizational commitment, and turnover intention. In order to test this, we used multiple regression analysis, where we again included age, gender, and temporary work as control variables in the four samples.

The results of the regression analyses (see Table 6.5) show that job insecurity was negatively related to job satisfaction in all participating countries, thus indicating that experiences of job insecurity are connected with lower levels of perceived job satisfaction. Among the control variables, age was positively related to job satisfaction in the Swedish sample, implying that older people report more job satisfaction compared to the younger. In Belgium, gender was identified as a predictor of job satisfaction, and the relation was negative which suggests that women report less job satisfaction compared with men. Temporary work showed an association with job satisfaction in three of the four countries (not in Belgium). The association was positive, indicating that people with temporary work arrangements are more satisfied with their jobs as compared with permanent workers. In total, the amount of explained variance in job satisfaction ranged from six (the Netherlands and Sweden) to ten percent (Italy).

Table 6.5. Results of multiple regression predicting job satisfaction (standardized regression coefficients)

Predictor	Belgium	Italy	The Netherlands	Sweden
Age	.05	-.08	.02	.23***
Gender (women)	-.09*	.07	.05	.02
Temporary work	.05	.16*	.10*	.07*
Job insecurity	-.28***	-.28***	-.25***	-.10***
R^2 adjusted	.09***	.10***	.06***	.06***

*p<.05, ***p<.001.

Organizational commitment was also significantly predicted by job insecurity, in all participating countries (see Table 6.6). Furthermore, also in this case, the direction of the relation was negative, indicating that job insecurity perceptions tend to reduce individuals' loyalty and attachment to the organization. With regard to the control variables, it was found that age predicted organizational commitment in three of the four countries (not in Italy). The association was positive, thus indicating that older workers typically report higher levels of organizational commitment than younger. Gender was negatively associated with organizational commitment in Italy and Sweden, implying that men tend to be more committed to their organization than women. There was no relation between temporary work and organizational commitment in the four samples. In all samples, the model variables explained a total of four percent of the variance in organizational commitment.

Table 6.6. Results of multiple regression predicting organizational commitment (standardized regression coefficients)

Predictor	Belgium	Italy	The Netherlands	Sweden
Age	.10*	.05	.10*	.19***
Gender (women)	-.07	-.14*	.07	-.06**
Temporary work	.03	.06	.04	.04
Job insecurity	-.16***	-.18**	-.18***	.05*
R^2 adjusted	.04***	.04***	.04***	.04***

*p<.05, **p<.01, ***p<.001.

As can be seen in Table 6.7, job insecurity was also related to turnover intention in all of the samples. The relationships were positive, suggesting that job insecurity perceptions are associated with an increasing desire to voluntarily withdraw from the organization. Among the control variables, only age reached significance in three of the countries (not in Italy); the relation between age and turnover intention was negative, which suggests that younger employees have a higher level of turnover intention than older employees. Together, the control variables and job insecurity accounted for between three (Belgium) and fourteen (Italy) percent of the variance in turnover intention.

From our empirical analyses it is clear that job insecurity had an impact on all organizational variables in all four participating countries, suggesting that job insecurity experiences may have severe consequences for employee attitudes and, thereby, also for their behavior in the organization (*e.g.*, Steel & Ovalle, 1984). These results are consistent with both previous theoretical arguments and empirical research. Our findings underscore the impact of job insecurity on attitudes toward work and the organization, and support arguments for the necessity of preventing this stressor. The deterioration of satisfaction and commitment is expected to have a negative impact on employee job performance, and also to augment the impact that job insecurity already has on turnover intention (Davy *et al.*, 1997).

**Table 6.7. Results of multiple regression predicting
turnover intention (standardized regression coefficients)**

Predictor	Belgium	Italy	The Netherlands	Sweden
Age	-.16****	-.08	-.25***	-.28***
Gender	.00	.00	-.00	-.02
Temporary work	.00	-.09	-.06	-.03
Job insecurity	.13**	.39***	.11**	.08**
R^2 adjusted	.03***	.14***	.06***	.08***

**p<.01, ***p<.001.

These results can be explained with the aid of psychological contract theory. Job insecurity, as a breach of the psychological contract, is assumed to have an impact on an employee's attitudes toward the job and the organization. This means that an individual's loyalty and willingness to stay with the organization decrease as the relationship with the organization becomes more characterized by fault-finding or tainted by feelings of dishonesty and betrayal (Rousseau, 1989; Rousseau & McLean Parks, 1993). Also, Davy *et al.* (1997) argue that the negative relation between job insecurity and organizational commitment will increase as the individual's sense of a breach of the psychological contract intensifies. There may thus be a direct connection between the psychological contract and the individual's loyalty to, or attitudes toward, the organization. All in all, job insecurity is perceived as one of the more important aspects of the psychological contract, and is the most vital to restore in order to maintain or rebuild the relationship between the individual and the organization (Allen *et al.*, 2001).

Consequences for the Union

As we have seen above, job insecurity has implications for the well-being of individuals, as well as for the organization since employees react to job insecurity with dissatisfaction and lowered commitment. Since many organizations have a strong union presence, we were also interested in investigating how experiences of job insecurity affect members' attitudes toward their union.

Previous research has established that the need for protection against the threat of unemployment is one of the main motives for joining as well as staying in a union (Bender & Sloane, 1999; Klandermans, 1986; Visser, 1995; Wheeler & McClendon, 1991). During uncertain times, members are known to seek out the help of their unions, perhaps by attaining information about changes at work or by inquiring about what the union can do to improve their situation or secure their jobs (Barling *et al.*, 1992; Greenhalgh & Rosenblatt, 1984; Johnson *et al.*, 1992).

However, positive reactions toward the union are only expected to occur if the union is perceived as independent of the negative changes in the organization. If the members hold the union responsible for the uncertainty, or do not believe that the union has done enough to prevent negative events, then more negative attitudes toward the union are to be expected (Mellor, 1992; Sverke & Goslinga, 2003). Also, the consequences of job insecurity for the union can be explained with the help of psychological contract theory (Rousseau, 1995). As we saw in Chapter 3, the psychological contract involves the expectations that individuals have on another party. In the present context, this concerns the expectations that the members have on their union.

Within this psychological contract, the idea of balance is central; the member needs to feel that what he/she brings into the relation is balanced by what is being offered by the union. We assume that job insecurity disturbs this balance, and that job insecurity in this sense constitutes a breach of the psychological contract (King, 2000). After all, union members who feel that the union has failed in securing their future employment might think that the psychological contract with the union has not been honored, while the very reason people become members stems from the wish to be protected against uncertain employment and work environment hazards. A perceived breach of the psychological contract has been shown to have effects on a variety of attitudes and behaviors (*e.g.*, Davy *et al.*, 1997; Robinson, 1996; Robinson *et al.*, 1994; Schalk, Freese & Van den Bosch, 1995). A violation of the psychological contract reduces organizational commitment and satisfaction, and increases the intention to leave the organization (turnover). Based on these general assumptions, we have developed similar hypotheses regarding how job insecurity may affect union commitment, union satisfaction, and union turnover intention.

Union satisfaction can be described as a result of how members perceive that their union has met their needs (Barling *et al.*, 1992). It involves the result of an evaluation done by the members of how content they are with union activities and the services provided (Kuruvilla, Gallagher & Wetzel, 1993). Within union research, satisfaction with the union is an important factor (for a review, see Barling *et al.*, 1992; Gallagher & Strauss, 1991). Union satisfaction is related to union commitment (Goslinga & Klandermans, 2001) and involvement in the union (Aryee & Debrah, 1997). The association between union satisfaction and job insecurity, however, has not been extensively investigated. Since job insecurity implies a violation of the psychological contract with the union, we expect that job insecurity will be related to lower levels of union satisfaction.

Union commitment relates to members' attachment to their union, based on the extent of their identification with the union's goals and values (Gordon, Philbot, Burt, Thompson & Spiller, 1980; Sverke & Kuruvilla, 1995). Affective commitment promotes union participation, such as holding a representative position and attending union meetings (Barling *et al.*, 1992; Gallagher & Strauss, 1991), and is negatively related to union turnover intentions (Klandermans, 1989; Sverke & Sjöberg, 1995). The concept of affective union commitment, developed by Goslinga (1996, 2001), is in part analogous to the conceptualization of affective organizational commitment (see Allen & Meyer, 1990). According to this view, there are three dimensions of commitment, namely, affective, normative, and continuance commitment. For our purposes, we have focused on the dimension of union commitment known as affective commitment, which closely resembles the ideological commitment discussed by Sverke and Kuruvilla (1995) and the union loyalty component advocated by Gordon *et al.* (1980). Based on our theoretical discussion of the psychological contract, we expect union commitment to be lower among members experiencing job insecurity.

The attitudes members have toward their union reflect their perceptions of the performance of the union and the benefits of union membership. The member evaluates how well his or her expectations have been met, that is, whether the psychological contract has been honored, and then decides whether to keep his/her end of the deal and remain a member. It thus follows that these attitudes will affect the intention of individual union members to remain members of the union or discontinue their union membership. This has been demonstrated in a number of studies. For instance, Goslinga and Sverke (2003) found union satisfaction and commitment to predict union turnover intention. We thus expect that the experience of job insecurity, as a breach of the psychological contract, will predict a higher union turnover intention. The disappointment felt over the union's failure to provide a secure work environment results in members wishing to resign their membership.

Again, we first have a look at the mean level differences between the four countries (see Table 6.8). The *F*-tests for mean differences between countries were significant for all three union-related variables, thus indicating that there were differences between countries in all outcomes. The subsequent post-hoc tests (Bonferroni) showed that all countries differed from one another in terms of union satisfaction (with the exception of a non-significant difference between Belgium and the

Netherlands); the highest level of union satisfaction was obtained in Belgium and the lowest in Italy. Regarding union commitment, all mean values were significantly different from each other, with the highest level found in Italy and the lowest in Belgium. Furthermore, the average levels of union turnover intention were found to differ between all samples (except between the Netherlands and Sweden), the Belgian sample showing the highest turnover intention, and the Netherlands and Sweden the lowest.

Table 6.8. Tests for mean differences in union related attitudes between countries

Country	Union satisfaction	Union commitment	Union turnover Intention
Belgium[a]	3.77	2.62	2.98
Italy	2.86	3.50	2.58
The Netherlands	3.70	2.89	2.34
Sweden	3.07	2.75	2.25
Df	3,3978	3,3946	3,3936
F	244.09***	94.09***	63.901***

***$p<.001$.
Scale range: 1–5 (all outcome variables).
[a] For these analyses the alternative Belgian data set was used.

The results of the multiple regression analyses, where union satisfaction was regressed on job insecurity and the control variables, are presented in Table 6.9. Job insecurity predicted union satisfaction in two of the four countries (Belgium and Italy). In both cases, the relationship was negative, suggesting that job insecurity experiences are related to less satisfaction with the union. Age was a predictor of union satisfaction in Italy and Sweden. The relation was negative in Italy, which suggests that younger employees are more satisfied with the union as compared with older. However, in the Swedish sample, the direction of the relation was the opposite, suggesting, in this case, that older workers are more satisfied with the union. Gender was also found to predict union satisfaction in two of the four countries (the Netherlands and Sweden), where, in both cases, the positive relation indicates that women are more satisfied with the union than men. Finally, in the Belgian sample, it was found that temporary work predicted union satisfaction and that this relation was positive, which implies that temporary workers are more satisfied with the union in comparison to their non-contingent counterparts. Although the predictive power of the regression model was limited, it could explain variance proportions ranging from one percent (Belgium and the Netherlands) to six percent (Italy).

Table 6.9. Results of multiple regression predicting union satisfaction (standardized regression coefficients)

Predictor	Belgium[a]	Italy	The Netherlands	Sweden
Age	.00	-.17**	-.02	.06*
Gender (women)	.05	.04	.11**	.15***
Temporary work	.10*	-.05	.02	.03
Job insecurity	-.10*	-.20**	.05	-.04
R^2 adjusted	.01***	.06***	.01***	.02***

*$p<.05$, **$p<.01$, ***$p<.001$.
[a] For these analyses the alternative Belgian data set was used.

Table 6.10 shows that union commitment was predicted by job insecurity in Italy and Sweden, whereas no significant relation between the variables was obtained for Belgium and the Netherlands. The direction of the relation was negative in the Italian sample and positive in the Swedish sample. This implies that job insecurity experiences were associated with lower levels of commitment to the union in Italy, while in Sweden job insecurity perceptions were associated with higher levels of union commitment. Among the control variables, age predicted union commitment in all samples and the relation was positive, suggesting that older people report more union commitment compared to the younger. In the Netherlands, gender was also significantly related to union commitment, and the association was negative, suggesting that men report more union commitment than women. Temporary work was unrelated to union commitment in all four samples. Again, the regression model explained a fairly small amount of variance in the dependent variable, with numbers ranging from one (Belgium) to five percent (the Netherlands) of explained variance.

Table 6.10. Results of multiple regression predicting union commitment (standardized regression coefficients)

Predictor	Belgium[a]	Italy	The Netherlands	Sweden
Age	.15**	.13*	.17***	.18***
Gender (women)	.01	-.01	-.14**	.04
Temporary work	.01	-.01	.06	.02
Job insecurity	.01	-.15*	.05	.05*
R^2 adjusted	.01***	.02***	.05***	.03***

*$p<.05$, **$p<.01$, ***$p<.001$.
[a] For these analyses the alternative Belgian data set was used.

Finally, Table 6.11 presents the results for union turnover intention. Job insecurity was positively related to union turnover intention in Belgium and Italy, which indicates that job insecurity tends to be related to an increased intention to voluntarily terminate the union membership. However, in the Netherlands and Sweden, no such pattern was found. Regarding the control variables, age and temporary work were recognized as significant predictors of membership turnover in the Netherlands, suggesting that younger employees are more inclined to voluntarily quit their union membership than older employees, and that temporary workers are less inclined to leave the union in comparison to permanently employed workers. In the Swedish sample, gender emerged as a predictor of union membership turnover intention, and the direction of the relation was negative, suggesting that men are more prone to hand in their union membership in comparison to women. Viewed altogether, the predictor variables were able to account for between one (Belgium and Sweden) and three percent (Italy) of the variance in union turnover intention.

To some extent, the results confirm our hypotheses. However, a few of the results do diverge from what we had expected. Union satisfaction was lower among individuals with higher levels of job insecurity, in both Belgium and Italy, as expected, but in the Netherlands and Sweden, no such relationship was found. On the contrary, union satisfaction appeared to be unrelated to job insecurity in these two countries. It may be that other factors are more important to union satisfaction. Perhaps job insecurity is not attributed to the union in these countries, and therefore would not affect satisfaction with the union.

Table 6.11. Results of multiple regression predicting union turnover intention (standardized regression coefficients)

Predictor	Belgium[a]	Italy	The Netherlands	Sweden
Age	-.08	.05	-.13**	-.02
Gender (women)	-.03	-.02	-.05	-.08**
Temporary work	-.01	-.01	-.11**	-.04
Job insecurity	.11*	.19**	.04	.04
R^2 adjusted	.01***	.03***	.02***	.01***

$*p<.05, **p<.01, ***p<.001.$
[a] For these analyses the alternative Belgian data set was used.

Union commitment was negatively related to job insecurity only in Italy, while in Belgium and the Netherlands union commitment was unrelated to job insecurity. In Sweden, however, job insecurity was positively related to union commitment. This could be explained by the reasons for membership discussed above. Individuals who experience uncertainty would look to the union for help (Bender & Sloane, 1999; Iverson, 1996), thereby possibly strengthening their commitment. In these cases, the union would most likely not be blamed for the perception of job insecurity (*cf.* Mellor, 1992); rather, the union would be seen as a solution to the problems concerning uncertainty.

This explanation may also apply to the lack of significant relationships found between job insecurity and union turnover intention in both the Netherlands and Sweden. While the results for Belgium and Italy followed predictions, in that job insecurity was associated with the intention to withdraw membership, in the Netherlands and Sweden the respondents' negative reactions to job insecurity were not directed at the union. It may be that the organization, instead, was blamed for the unsatisfactory level of employment security (*cf.* Sverke & Goslinga, 2003; Sverke & Hellgren, 2001). In these two countries, the union may be seen as an agent with the ability to help their members in times of uncertainty.

Concluding Remarks

From these results it can be concluded that, in general, job insecurity is associated with all three domains investigated in the study – individual consequences, organizational consequences, and union consequences. The results also indicate that job insecurity, on a general level, appears to be clearly associated with one of the individual consequences (*i.e.*, mental health complaints) since this relationship was significant and in the expected direction in all participating countries, but less consistently related to physical health complaints (significant associations were obtained in two of the three countries where this relation could be tested). These results are also in line with previously reported results, which suggest that job insecurity has a stronger association with mental health complaints as compared with physical complaints (Hellgren *et al.*, 1999; Mattiasson *et al.*, 1990; Mohr, 2000; Sverke *et al.*, 2002).

It can also be concluded that job insecurity seems to have the strongest association with organizational variables in terms of job and organizational attitudes. In this case, job insecurity was found to be significantly related to all three of the investigated outcomes (job satisfaction, organizational commitment, and turnover intention), in all four countries. These relationships followed an expected direction of association, which previous research has also found (*e.g.*, Ashford *et al.*, 1989; Davy *et al.*, 1997; Lim, 1996; Sverke *et al.*, 2002). Given this, it can be concluded that job insecurity perceptions seem to be associated with decreased job and organizational attitudes as well as with an increased propensity for the employee to voluntarily leave the organization. These results therefore indicate that not only the individual may be negatively affected by job insecurity experiences, but also the organization as a whole.

When it comes to the relation between job insecurity and union attitudes, the results are more inconsistent. It can be concluded, however, that job insecurity was associated with all union outcomes in Italy, whereas no associations between job insecurity and union attitudes were found in the Dutch sample. Despite this, it appears that job insecurity perceptions may have some effects also for the union, in that members may hold the union responsible for their job insecurity experience. When this is the case, they can respond with negative attitudes toward the union (Mellor, 1992) and an increased propensity to withdraw their union membership (Sverke & Goslinga, 2003).

CHAPTER 7

Reducing the Negative Consequences?

In Chapter 6 we learned that job insecurity, in accordance with previous theory and research, can have consequences not only for the individual but also for the organization and the union. Job insecurity was a predictor of health complaints and negative attitudes toward work and the organization, in all our samples. It also predicted negative attitudes toward the union, in some of our samples. With these results as a background, we will now shift focus to how these negative relations may be moderated, that is, how the negative consequences of job insecurity may be prevented or alleviated. We investigate this by introducing two variables that may affect how the employee reacts to job insecurity. These variables, both related to the union, are union membership and the level of perceived union support among members. Figure 7.1 provides an illustration of the model we test in this chapter. It can be seen from the model that we depict job insecurity as predicting the same outcomes as in the previous chapter, and that we control for the same demographic variables. For the purposes of the present chapter, we have added the potential moderating effects of union membership and perceived union support. We will be testing, using the same data as in the previous chapter, whether these union factors buffer the negative impact of the job insecurity experience. Before we turn to the empirical tests, however, it is important to discuss why we expect that these factors may alleviate the consequences of job insecurity.

Social Support

The support obtained from family, friends, managers, and colleagues is considered an important factor in predicting how employees react to and cope with stress (Callan, 1993; Dekker & Schaufeli, 1995; House, 1981; Lim, 1996). Through contact with other people, individuals have the opportunity to stay informed of recent happenings and can receive help in handling different situations. Access to social support is presumed to strengthen one's self-confidence (Heaney, Price & Rafferty, 1995). Talking to others, and getting their point of view of the situation, can provide valuable information on how to improve the situation, or just be an outlet for upset feelings. To reflect the different ways of how the individual may benefit from social support, the concept has been divided into instrumental and emotional support, and it has been described as having an informative function as well (House, 1981). According to the literature, social support may help individuals to vent their frustrations as well as facilitate their learning of methods for dealing with undesirable situations.

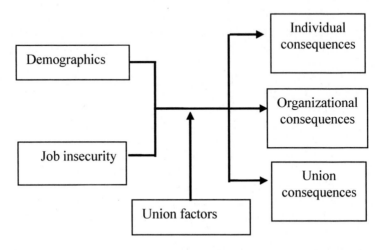

Figure 7.1. Empirical model of the relation between job insecurity and three different areas of outcomes, as well as the moderating effect of union membership and support

In order to cope effectively with a stressful situation, individuals make appraisals of what resources are needed in order to do so (Lazarus & Folkman, 1984). Social support is a type of external resource, as opposed to internal, personal resources (Callan, 1993). In constituting such an external resource, social support from others may increase the likelihood of the individual reacting in a problem-focused manner (Callan, 1993; Scheck, Kinicki & Davy, 1997). This is considered to be more constructive and useful in the long run than acting in an emotion-focused manner and trying to repress the feelings evoked by a situation (Callan, 1993). Problem-focused coping is usually characterized by actions that are directed at removing or dealing with the source of the problem, rather than any attempt to alleviate the negative emotional reactions (Lazarus & Folkman, 1984). Social support also affects the individual's interpretation of the situation in a positive way, in that the reaction to a stressor is mitigated by the positive feelings brought on by the support (LaRocco, House & French, 1980; Scheck *et al.*, 1997). In addition, a social network can function as a source of information in uncertain circumstances, and using social support can be a way of working through one's feelings. Moreover, to receive support can represent instrumental help, for example in the search for a new job.

Social support has been suggested as a key variable in reducing the perception of stress (Viswesvaran, Sanchez & Fisher, 1999), and has been empirically identified as a moderator of the relationship between stress and health problems (Frese, 1999; Jackson, 1992). Those reporting that they feel strong social support appear to be better equipped to cope with stressful situations (Quick, Quick, Nelson & Hurrell, 1997). Several studies have investigated how various coping resources influence the way individuals handle stress, and how these different ways of dealing with stress affect its consequences. It appears that some coping strategies are slightly more effective than others. For instance, individuals who try to share their uncertainty by talking to others tend to experience less stress reactions than those who do not talk to others about their feelings (Ashford, 1988; Frese, 1999; Jackson, 1992).

We consider social support to be important in the context of job insecurity. As any stressor, perceived job insecurity affects individuals negatively, as we saw in Chapter 6. The negative feelings that job insecurity evokes may prompt employees to seek out the support of each other, to express their frustration or fears, but also to seek alternatives and strategies for coping with the negative situation (Callan, 1993). The importance of social support in alleviating the negative effects of job insecurity has been investigated empirically as well. Armstrong-Stassen (1993) found that support from supervisors during restructuring worked as a moderator of the effect of job insecurity on organizational attitudes. She suggests that it is vital for the organization to proactively provide support in order to prevent employees' attitudes toward the organization from deteriorating. Another study investigated how support at work and from sources outside of work influenced the reactions to job insecurity (Lim, 1996). Employees who received more social support at work were described as being more willing to remain with the organization, in spite of turbulence. According to Lim (1996), support outside of work influenced the relation between job insecurity and life satisfaction. Individuals experiencing more support were more satisfied with life, despite job insecurity, than those reporting less support. The individuals receiving support from their spouse or family may also feel that they have access to economical support, which in turn can decrease the worry about job loss that is attributable to economical problems (see also Chapter 5).

Employees who learn the value and usefulness of their social network strengthen their sense of possessing the resources necessary for coping with stress-provoking situations (Heaney *et al.*, 1995). Our interpretation of this is that people who feel that they have strong social support, and also know how to make effective use of it, experience the negative consequences of job insecurity to a lesser extent than people who receive less social support. Employees can learn how these networks should be utilized through workshops initiated by the organization (Heaney *et al.*, 1995).

Social support can roughly be divided according to whether they originate mainly from work or non-work sources (Jackson, 1992). Naturally, important sources of support outside of work are family and friends, and any other social network one may have that is not related to, or dependent on, one's employment. At work the employees may benefit from talking to colleagues, supervisors, or perhaps counsellors at the workplace. There is also the support that the union can provide (Armstrong-Stassen, 1993). Theoretical arguments in previous literature have suggested that perceived union support will operate in a manner similar to social support (Shore, Tetrick, Sinclair & Newton, 1994), since it is based on a social exchange between the union and its members. Union representatives at a workplace may thus be significant providers of support, and there is some evidence in the literature indicating a moderating or buffering effect of perceived union support on the relation between stressor and strain (*e.g.*, Bluen & Edelstein, 1993; Fried & Tiegs, 1993).

To provide an overview of the potential buffering variables examined in this chapter – union membership and perceived union support – we present descriptive statistics in Table 7.1. In order to gain a general idea of the levels of the union variables in relation to those of the outcomes, the means values of the outcome variables, also presented in Chapter 6, are reiterated in the table.

Table 7.1. Mean levels of job insecurity,
the buffer variables and the outcomes

	Belgium	Italy	The Netherlands	Sweden
Job insecurity	1.83	2.61	1.85	2.09
Union factors				
Union support	3.81	3.24	3.70	3.19
Union members (%)	58	63	100	92[b]
Individual consequences				
Mental health complaints	#	1.58	2.07	1.99
Physical health complaints	–	1.67	2.04	2.13
Organizational consequences				
Job satisfaction	3.70	3.79	3.60	3.68
Organizational commitment	3.39	3.52	3.20	2.54
Turnover intention	#	2.85	2.63	2.30
Union consequences				
Union satisfaction[a]	3.77	3.70	2.86	3.07
Union commitment[a]	2.62	2.89	3.50	2.75
Union turnover intention[a]	2.98	2.34	2.58	2.25
N	1,482	451	799	1,904

[a] Data for Belgium were derived from the alternative Belgian data set, which includes union-related variables.
[b] All analyses concerning union membership are based on the alternative Swedish data set, which contains both members and non-members.
Scale range: 1–5 for all variables except mental health complaints (1–4) and union membership (no/yes).
Mental health complaints and turnover intention in Belgium were omitted from the table since they were assessed with a yes/no response mode.
– Data not available.

Univariate tests of the difference in mean values between countries showed that there were significant differences between all our four samples in the levels of perceived union support ($F_{[3,3955]}=172.89$, $p<.001$) as well as the levels of job insecurity ($F_{[3,4460]}=84.32$, $p<.001$). These mean values suggest how union support may be related to job insecurity. In the two samples with the lowest levels of job insecurity (Belgium and the Netherlands), union support was perceived as higher than in the countries with higher levels of job insecurity.

Union Membership

Even though the experience of job insecurity is an increasingly important factor at workplaces with, as well as without, union representation, only a limited amount of international research has delved into the importance of union membership for the experience of job insecurity and its consequences (Bender & Sloane, 1999; Mellor, 1992; Sverke & Hellgren, 2002). Without access to the collective support union membership may provide, an individual, we can assume, would have more difficulties in coping with insecurity (Dekker & Schaufeli, 1995). On the other hand, it may be that individuals who choose to remain outside of unions have a greater confidence in their own ability to deal with feelings of insecurity.

Shaw, Fields, Thacker, and Fisher (1993) included union membership as a possible source of external social support. They found a positive correlation between union membership and expressions of loyalty to the organization (*i.e.*, the company) as well as positive attitudes toward changes in the organization, but no interaction effects when it came to insecurity and membership on these reactions. Another study (Sverke & Hellgren, 2001) showed that union members were less prone to manage their feelings of uncertainty by leaving the organization they worked for, or by individual protests against downsizing; instead, they displayed more loyalty to the organization than non-members. Dekker and Schaufeli (1995), on the other hand, found that the social support given by union membership, colleagues, and other employees could not mitigate the negative consequences of job insecurity on employee well-being.

However, there is research to suggest that, on a general level, the importance an individual attributes job security represents a central determinant of union membership (Crockett & Hall, 1987). It appears, for example, that both members and officers of labor organizations rank job security as perhaps the most important bargaining issue (Dworkin, Feldman, Brown & Hobson, 1988; Lind, 1996). Furthermore, union members appear to give job security a higher priority than non-members (Johnson *et al.*, 1992). While this suggests that unionized workers differ from their non-unionized counterparts in terms of the priority placed on job security, as well as the appraisal of the degree of insecurity in the surrounding work situation, there is likely to be substantial variation also among the union members – even if they are employed at the same workplace.

By belonging to a union, the member has access to a number of different supportive functions. The collective support that a union provides may prevent the members from feeling that they are without a protective network in the event of a reorganization or restructuring in their organization. Since unions often are in a negotiating relationship with the organization, and may be able to influence the organization's treatment of the employees, union membership may serve to decrease the perceived probability of job loss (Johnson *et al.*, 1992). The union may also provide a social context for the members, where they can get in touch with people in similar situations, or staff members who are available to discuss employment rights issues. The collective bargaining conducted by unions may help individual employees feel that their interests are being looked after, which constitutes one source of support. Members of a union may feel that the collectivity of the union can protect them from, for instance, organizational interventions that may be of detriment to employees (Heller, Pusic, Strauss & Wilpert, 1999).

Greenhalgh and Rosenblatt (1984) suggested that unions may alleviate feelings of job insecurity by decreasing the sense of powerlessness associated with job insecurity. By being part of a group which works collectively for the attainment of common goals, the member/employee can gain a sense of control and influence over events, which may lessen the feeling of powerlessness. Labor unions may also work to reduce job insecurity by providing assistance for employees who are trying to cope with such an experience; they could, for example, aid in the job search, or provide information and tools that would help employees find an education that would prepare them for another career. In so doing, unions may facilitate the use of problem-focused coping strategies, which has been associated with a decrease in the negative consequences and negative reactions to job insecurity (*cf.* Callan, 1993; Lazarus & Folkman, 1984; Sverke & Hellgren, 2001).

The effects of job insecurity on the outcome variables have already been presented in Chapter 6 and will not be discussed in detail here. In this section, we investigate how union members differ from non-members in their reactions to job insecurity. We also examine the main effect of union membership, that is, how the members and non-members differ in the outcome variables. In regard to our procedure, in the present section we focus on the effects of job insecurity and union membership on individual (well-being) and organizational (work attitudes) outcomes. (For obvious reasons, our data cannot be used to compare members' and non-members' attitudes and behavioral orientations toward unions.) Again, the data originate from the same samples as in Chapter 6; however, since the respondents in the Dutch sample were all union members, the Netherlands was not included in this section's analyses.

In Figure 7.2, we present a typology of job insecurity and union membership that is designed to help clarify the relations we are testing in this section. The combining of high and low levels of job insecurity (after median split) with affiliation/non-affiliation created four different groups. The category labeled "Insecure members" comprises those workers who belong to a trade union and perceive a relatively high subjective probability of job loss. The "Insecure non-members" have similar experiences of job insecurity but are not affiliated with a union. The high level of job insecurity shared by individuals in these groups is likely to result in similar reactions, but it is possible that unionized and non-unionized employees, because of union membership, differ in terms of individual and organizational consequences of job insecurity (Rosenblatt & Ruvio, 1996; Sverke & Hellgren, 2001). "Secure members" and "Secure non-members" share similar perceptions of low job uncertainty, which suggests that their reactions to job insecurity will be less negative as compared with the insecure employees. Secure members and non-members do differ, however, when it comes to their formal relationships with labor organizations, which is something that potentially may be observable as different ways to deal with a relatively secure employment situation.

In order to test how union members and non-members differ in their reactions to job insecurity, that is, in their well-being and attitudes toward the organization, we used multivariate analysis of variance (MANCOVA) controlling for age, sex, and type of employment con-tract. For these analyses the job insecurity was dichotomized into high and low using median split. The results revealed significant main (mul-tivariate) effects of job insecurity in all three samples containing both members and non-members (Belgium: $F_{[4,1026]}=21.59$; $p<.001$; Italy: $F_{[5,376]}=8.95$; $p<.001$; Sweden: $F_{[5,1324]}=2.84$; $p<.05$). There were also multivariate effects of union membership in Belgium ($F_{[4,1026]}=3.77$; $p<.001$) and Italy ($F_{[5,376]}=3.62$; $p<.01$), but not in Sweden ($F_{[5,1324]}=1.99$; $p>.05$). No effects of the interaction between job insecu-rity and union membership status were obtained in Belgium ($F_{[4,1026]}=1.17$; $p>.05$), Italy ($F_{[5,376]}=1.59$; $p>.05$), or Sweden ($F_{[5,1324]}=1.90$; $p>.05$), indicating that there was no buffering effect of union membership on the consequences of job insecurity.

Union member

		Yes	No
High	Job insecurity	**Insecure members** Belgium 26% Italy 27% Sweden 49%	**Insecure non-members** Belgium 18% Italy 14% Sweden 4%
Low		**Secure members** Belgium 25% Italy 27% Sweden 43%	**Secure non-members** Belgium 31% Italy 32% Sweden 4%

Figure 7.2. Categorization of union membership and job insecurity including the proportion of employees in each category in the respective countries

The effects of job insecurity have already been discussed in Chapter 6. However, to further investigate the significant main effect of union membership discovered in the multivariate test, individual follow-up tests of the differences between members and non-members on each outcome were conducted, retaining the same covariates (ANCOVA). The results of these tests are displayed in Table 7.2.

There were no differences between members and non-members in health complaints, neither mental nor physical, in any of the samples. In contrast, union membership was significantly associated with job satisfaction in the Belgian sample, members reporting less job satisfaction, but no differences between members and non-members were found in Italy or Sweden. In the case of organizational commitment, non-members reported higher levels of commitment to their organization than union members, in the Italian and Belgian samples. In Sweden the opposite was found, in that union members reported more organizational commitment than non-members. However, the multivariate test of significance for union membership effects failed to reach significance in the Swedish sample, indicating that this result should be taken as preliminary and interpreted with great care.

The main effects of union membership generally show that union members were less satisfied with their job, and expressed lower commitment to the organization they are employed by. The higher levels of negative attitudes employees expressed toward the organization may support the notion that employees become union members as an attempt to cope with their negative experiences of the organization. By joining a union, the employees may hope to get assistance with issues that are disquieting to them in their organization (*e.g.*, Barling *et al.*, 1992; Brett, 1980; Klandermans, 1986; Premack & Hunter, 1988; Waddington & Whitston, 1997; Wheeler & McClendon, 1991). Previous research appears to confirm this, in suggesting that the experience of job insecurity is one of the often-quoted reasons for joining a labor union (Bender & Sloane, 1999; Lewis & Murphy, 1991).

On the other hand, the results also revealed that no multivariate or univariate effects were obtained for the postulated moderating effect of union membership. This implies that union membership may not alleviate the negative effects of job insecurity, that is, protect the members against the adverse consequences of employment uncertainty. These results are also in accordance with previous studies that have investigated the potential buffering effects of union membership in the relationship between job insecurity and various outcome variables (*e.g.*, Dekker & Schaufeli, 1995; Shaw *et al.*, 1993; Sverke & Hellgren, 2001).

The lack of buffering effects of union membership can potentially be explained by the fact that membership status *per se* does not tell us anything about how much support the members actually perceive they get from their union. Union activities may have a beneficial impact on the relation between job insecurity and its outcomes – but presumably only if the members feel that their membership status actually helps them in difficult situations.

122

Table 7.2. Mean values of health and attitude variables and test for direct and interaction effects of job insecurity and union membership

	Insecure Member	Secure member	Insecure non-member	Secure non-member	Effects (F)[c] Insecurity	Union	I x U
Belgium[a]							
Mental health complaints	1.32	1.20	1.29	1.23	27.86***	.05	3.36
Physical health complaints	–	–	–	–	–	–	–
Job satisfaction	3.39	3.85	3.56	3.92	70.42***	5.92*	1.19
Organizational commitment	3.14	3.41	3.38	3.57	18.84***	13.77***	0.64
Turnover intention	1.34	1.26	1.32	1.25	11.61***	.25	0.00
Italy							
Mental health complaints	2.17	1.97	2.16	2.04	16.10***	.64	1.07
Physical health complaints	2.25	1.94	2.05	1.93	10.25**	2.54	2.20
Job satisfaction	3.31	3.71	3.48	3.89	18.68***	3.05	.01
Organizational commitment	2.87	3.17	3.31	3.39	3.46	9.52**	1.05
Turnover intention	3.10	2.36	2.78	2.42	29.68***	1.50	3.52
Sweden[b]							
Mental health complaints	1.80	1.65	1.77	1.77	3.58	1.25	3.58
Physical health complaints	2.20	2.03	2.16	2.01	5.46*	.12	.01
Job satisfaction	3.65	4.04	3.62	3.71	6.01*	3.08	2.33
Organizational commitment	2.71	2.77	2.46	2.51	.43	7.97**	.00
Turnover intention	2.45	2.09	2.72	2.26	10.84**	2.93	.15

*p<.05, **p<.01, ***p<.001.
[a] Data for Belgium were derived from the alternative Belgian data set, which includes union-related variables.
[b] Data for Sweden were derived from the alternative Swedish data set, which comprises both members and non-members.
[c] Degrees of freedom for univariate F tests: Belgium 1,1029; Italy 1,380; Sweden 1,1328.
Scale range: 1–5 for all variables except mental health complaints (1–4). However in Belgium mental health and turnover intention was measured with a yes/no response range; – Data not available

Union Support

Following the notion that members' perceptions of how their unions actually perform are of significance (Shore *et al.*, 1994), our next step is to investigate how perceived union support, that is, the members' opinions on how well the union supports them, affects the reactions to job insecurity. These analyses include only those who belong to a union.

Even if management usually initiates organizational restructuring and downsizing, unions are not necessarily without influence over the process. On the contrary, the local union of an organization initiating restructuring could be an integral part of the process and may try to influence the development of the restructuring in order to protect its members. Employees often rely on the union as a source of power with the potential to influence events and decrease the uncertainty that restructurings bring about. The extent to which this results in positive outcomes depends on the union's collectivity and ability to defend the interests of their members (Van Vuuren *et al.*, 1991b).

Naturally, what the members expect to get out of their union membership is important. These expectations may concern what membership should guarantee and, hence, shape the attitudes that the members hold toward their union (Brett, 1980; Goslinga & Klandermans, 2001; Gallagher & Strauss, 1991; Hellgren & Chirumbolo, 2003). This may be compared to what is found in the psychological contract theories mentioned in Chapter 3 (*e.g.*, Rousseau, 1989). Another similar theoretical framework used to understand work-related attitudes and behaviors is social exchange theory. This framework suggests that it is people's self-interest that determines their social interactions (Sinclair & Tetrick, 1995).

Social exchange theory has been expanded, by Eisenberger and his colleagues (Eisenberger, Huntington, Hutchinson & Sowa, 1986), to include relationships between employees and their organization and the support the employees feel they receive from the organization. According to this theoretical framework, the employees personify the organization and perceive that they have a social exchange relationship with this personified organization (Eisenberger *et al.*, 1986; Sinclair & Tetrick, 1995). Different aspects of the interaction between employee and organization (as perceived by the employee) affect the employee's opinion of the organization. The degree to which the employee feels that the organization supports and appreciates him or her, and is committed to him/her in terms of ensuring need fulfillment, growth, and well-being, form the employee's attitudes toward the organization (Aryee & Chay, 2001; Eisenberger *et al.*, 1986; Lim, 1996). Union support is suggested to influence members in a similar manner (Hellgren & Chirumbolo, 2003; Goslinga & Sverke, 2003; Shore *et al.*, 1994), as it is based on an exchange between the union (or the organization) and its members (or the employees).

Union support can be considered one type of social support (Armstrong-Stassen, 1993; Johnson & Johnson, 1992; Shore *et al.*, 1994). The union may provide the employee with a social context to discuss events at the workplace. A supportive presence at the workplace may make the employee feel less threatened in a turbulent environment. Union support is a form of instrumental support in that it functions as a safeguard for the interests of the employees, provides them with protection in the event of downsizing, and ensures that the organization does not mistreat the employees (Heller *et al.*, 1998). The union may also provide the informational type of support, when it acts as a link between management and the workforce, relaying information about company decisions, *etc.* Of course, the union may relay information and complaints from the workforce to management as well, and here act as a liaison for the employees. Union representatives can serve to help clarify the motives and rationales for restructuring, which may decrease the uncertainty and rumors circulating in an organization (Hellgren & Sverke, 2001). If these union tasks actually work, and the members perceive that they work, the members are expected to experience union support. Van Vuuren *et al.* (1991b) found that employees who feel that they can depend on a strong union to defend their interests also perceive their jobs as less insecure.

At this point, we return to our data in order to test the potential buffering effect that perceptions of union support among union members may have on the relation between job insecurity and our outcome variables of health complaints, work attitudes, and union attitudes. In order to investigate this, multiple regressions analyses were performed. In addition to the main effect of job insecurity, which has been reported in Chapter 6, we also investigate the main effect of union support as well as the interaction effect of job insecurity and union support on the same outcome variables (the interaction term was created using the procedure recommended by Aiken and West, 1991). This allows us to investigate both whether union support alone has any impact on employee well-being and attitudes, and whether perceived union support can alleviate the negative consequences of job insecurity. As in previous analyses, age, gender, and type of employment contract were used as covariates.

Consequences for the Individual

We first begin with an investigation of mental and physical health complaints as outcome variables. The results of the regression analyses are displayed in Table 7.3. Because the standard Belgian data set did not include perceived union support, and the alternative data set for this country, which comprised support, did not incorporate mental and physical health complaints, Belgium is not included in these analyses.

The regression results reveal that mental health complaints were predicted by job insecurity, as stated already in Chapter 6, in Italy, the Netherlands, and Sweden. In all samples, the relation between job insecurity and mental health complaints was positive, indicating that individuals perceiving higher levels of job insecurity also reported mental health complaints more frequently than individuals experiencing lower levels of job insecurity.

Union support predicted mental health complaints only in the Swedish sample. The negative relationship between union support and mental health complaints that we obtained in Sweden suggests that individuals perceiving low levels of union support would be more inclined to report mental health complaints than individuals experiencing high levels of union support. This suggests that perceptions of union support may reduce union members' experiences of mental health complaints. However, the interaction effect of job insecurity and union support on mental health complaints was not found to be significant in any of the samples. Thus, we did not identify any buffering effect of union support, but what we did notice was that perceived union support itself could be beneficial to the members' mental health. An explanation for this may be found in previous research on social support in general, which has stated that there is a direct negative relationship between support and strain (*e.g.*, Vieswesvaran *et al.*, 1999). This negative relationship implies that the presence of social support (of which union support is one type) reduces strain, independent of the type of stressor (Vieswesvaran *et al.*, 1999). In total, the regression model explained a small proportion of variance in mental health complaints, ranging from five to eleven percent.

Table 7.3. Results of multiple regression predicting mental and physical health complaints with direct and interactive effects of job insecurity and union support

Predictor	Mental health complaints	Physical health complaints
Italy		
Job insecurity	.31***	.24***
Union support	-.07	-.10
Insecurity x Support	-.01	-.04
R^2 adjusted	.11***	.08***
The Netherlands		
Job insecurity	.16***	-.01
Union support	-.07	.04
Insecurity x Support	-.03	.01
R^2 adjusted	.05***	.00
Sweden		
Job insecurity	.22***	.16***
Union support	-.13***	-.07**
Insecurity x Support	-.03	-.06*
R^2 adjusted	.07***	.04***

*$p<.05$, **$p<.01$, ***$p<.001$.
Note: the effects of the covariates (age, gender, and temporary work) are omitted from the table (for information of these effects, see Chapter 6).
Data for these analyses were not available for Belgium.

In our second set of regression analyses, we tested how union support may interact with job insecurity to decrease members' reports of physical health complaints. The regression model accounted for up to eight percent of the variance in the level of physical health complaints in the three samples. The results in Table 7.3 reveal that job insecurity was positively related to this outcome in Italy and Sweden, indicating, as reported in Chapter 6, that those experiencing higher levels of job insecurity also tend to report more physical health complaints. In the Netherlands, job insecurity did not explain the variation in physical health complaints. It was only in the Swedish sample that we detected any main effect of union support. This effect was negative, indicating that the more support members feel from their union, the less physical health complaints they report. In this sample we could also identify an interaction effect between job insecurity and union support on physical health complaints. Mean values and an illustration of the interaction effect in Sweden are displayed in Figure 7.3.

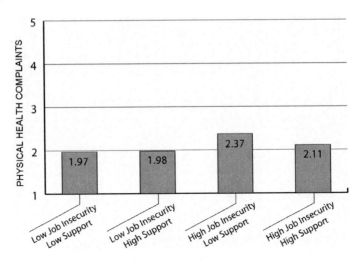

**Figure 7.3. Interaction effect of job insecurity and union support
on physical health complaints in the Swedish sample**

The direction of this interaction effect followed our theoretical dis-cussion above. In Figure 7.3, we see that individuals experiencing high levels of job insecurity in combination with low levels of union support reported more physical health complaints than the other combinations. The group experiencing high levels of job insecurity in combination with high levels of union support reported lower levels of physical health complaints. However, in both groups with lower levels of job insecurity, even fewer physical health complaints were reported, regard-less of the extent of union support felt. This implies that union support may buffer against physical health complaints when a high level of job insecurity is experienced, but has no effect when the level of job insecu-rity is lower.

Although our hypothesis concerning the moderating effect of union support was only confirmed in one of the three samples, this result is encouraging since it is in line with previous theoretical discussions. The literature suggests that members who perceive that their union is able to provide them with the support they expect and need, will react less negatively to job insecurity. Our results in the Swedish sample point to the feasibility of this hypothesis.

Consequences for the Organization

In this section we return to the work attitudes of job satisfaction, organizational commitment, and turnover intention. Our focus is on how job insecurity and perceptions of union support relate to these organizational outcomes, specifically whether union support buffers the negative effects of job insecurity. Table 7.4 displays the results of the regression analyses predicting job and organizational attitudes. Again, as in the case of health complaints, there was lack of data for the testing of the effects of union support on the outcome variables in Belgium.

Let us first look at the results concerning job satisfaction. As described in Chapter 6, this work-related attitude was predicted by job insecurity in Italy, the Netherlands, and Sweden. In all cases the relation was negative, indicating that higher levels of job insecurity are associated with lower levels of job satisfaction.

Union support predicted job satisfaction in both the Netherlands and Sweden, but failed to reach significance in Italy. The relation between union support and job satisfaction was positive in both of these samples, implying that perceived union support is associated with higher levels of job satisfaction. However, there was no significant interaction effect of job insecurity and union support on job satisfaction in any of the three countries. Although work-based social support appears to moderate the negative effects of job insecurity on employee satisfaction (Büssing, 1999; Lim, 1996), our findings could be taken to suggest that support from the union does not necessarily buffer the negative effects of job insecurity, but rather works directly on job satisfaction (Hellgren & Sverke, 2001). Those who felt that they received support from their union were also more content at their workplace, which may be because their unions have a strong presence and are involved in issues regarding the work environment. However, union efforts to protect the membership from the consequences of employment uncertainty appear to have mattered little, since perceptions of union support failed to alleviate the negative effects of job insecurity on job satisfaction. In total, the regression model accounted for between seven and eleven percent of the variation in job satisfaction.

Table 7.4. Results of multiple regression predicting job satisfaction, organizational commitment and turnover intention with direct and interactive effects of job insecurity and union support

Predictor	Job satisfaction	Organizational commitment	Turnover Intention
Italy			
Job insecurity	-.25***	-.16**	.40***
Union support	.11	.01	.02
Insecurity x Support	-.07	-.15*	.02
R^2 adjusted	.11***	.06***	.17***
The Netherlands			
Job insecurity	-.23***	-.17***	.10*
Union support	.13**	.13**	-.08*
Insecurity x Support	.07	.01	-.01
R^2 adjusted	.07***	.05***	.07***
Sweden			
Job insecurity	-.10***	.06**	.07**
Union support	.17***	.29***	-.14***
Insecurity x Support	.04	.05*	-.02
R^2 adjusted	.09***	.12***	.09***

*$p<.05$, **$p<.01$, ***$p<.001$.
Note: the effects of the covariates (age, gender and temporary work) are omitted from the table (for information of these effects, see Chapter 6).
Data for these analyses were not available for Belgium.

When it comes to organizational commitment, the results in Table 7.4 reveal that job insecurity was a significant predictor in all our samples. In total, the regression model (including control variables, job insecurity, union support, and the interaction term) explained between five and twelve percent of the variation in organizational commitment. As discussed in Chapter 6, the relation between job insecurity and organizational commitment was of the expected negative direction in Italy and the Netherlands, suggesting that perceptions of job insecurity are connected with lower levels of identification and commitment to the organization (*cf.* Armstrong-Stassen, 1993; Sverke *et al.*, 2002). In contrast, the relation was positive in Sweden, which indicates that perceptions of job insecurity were associated with higher levels of organizational commitment in the Swedish sample.

Union support was a significant predictor of organizational commitment in the Netherlands and in Sweden. Support from the union was positively related to organizational commitment, such that positive evaluations of the support gained from the union were associated with higher levels of organizational commitment. This may be discussed in light of the results obtained for job satisfaction. A strong and potent union presence may provide some guarantee for the members that their employment situation will be positive, in that the union will work to secure their interests in the workplace. This may prompt the members to be positively inclined toward their organization and report higher levels of commitment to the organization (Hellgren & Sverke, 2001; Sverke & Hellgren, 2001).

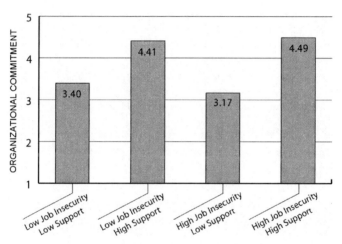

Figure 7.4. Interaction effect of job insecurity and union support on organizational commitment in the Italian sample

Moreover, the interaction effect of job insecurity and union support was significant in the Italian and Swedish samples. In Italy, as Figure 7.4 shows, the lowest levels of organizational commitment were obtained in the group experiencing high levels of job insecurity in combination with low levels of union support. The group reporting the strongest commitment to the organization was characterized by high job insecurity in combination with high union support. In line with the interaction found in Italy, the results for Sweden (Figure 7.5) show that the two groups characterized by high levels of union support, irrespective of the degree of job insecurity, also reported higher levels of organizational commitment. Also in Sweden, the individuals reporting less organizational commitment were found among those experiencing high or low levels of job insecurity in combination with low union support. It can be concluded that individuals experiencing low levels of job insecurity and high levels of union support also reported high levels of organizational commitment. In accordance with predictions, then, perceived union support related to high levels of organizational commitment in two of the three countries, regardless of the perceptions (*i.e.*, high or low) of job insecurity.

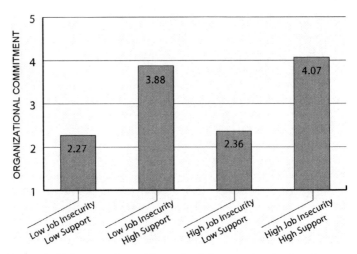

Figure 7.5. Interaction effect of job insecurity and union support on organizational commitment in the Swedish sample

Table 7.4 also shows how turnover intention may be affected by job insecurity and union support. The regression model explained between seven and seventeen percent of the variance in turnover intention in the three samples. Job insecurity predicted turnover intention in all samples. The relations were all in the same, positive, direction, indicating that job insecurity is associated with stronger organizational turnover intention. In addition, union support predicted turnover intention in the Netherlands and Sweden. In both countries, the relation was negative, such that individuals experiencing higher levels of union support expressed a weaker intention to leave the organization voluntarily. This may indicate that those who do not perceive their union as supportive may be of the opinion that the union is not capable of alleviating the negative conditions at the workplace. These members may wish to leave the organization, which is then reflected in turnover intention (*cf.* Goslinga & Sverke, 2003; Sverke & Goslinga, 2003). Those members who believe their union to be supportive and able to make sure their interests are looked after, are not as willing to leave the organization, as is also reflected in the higher levels of organizational commitment observed above. However, in neither of the samples did the interaction between job insecurity and union support reach significance, which suggests that union support does not buffer the effect of job insecurity on turnover intention.

Consequences for the Union

We have seen that job insecurity and union support have significant effects on both well-being and work-related attitudes. However, it is conceivable that these factors also affect attitudes related to the union (Armstrong-Stassen, 1993; Goslinga & Sverke, 2003; *cf.* Johnson & Johnson, 1992; Shore *et al.*, 1994). In this section we investigate whether job insecurity and union support predict union satisfaction, union commitment, and union turnover intention, as well as if union support may buffer the effect of job insecurity on these factors. In contrast to the previous sections, the analyses pertaining to union-related variables make use of data from all four countries, since the alternative Belgian data set contained data on the relevant variables. The results of the regression analyses are presented in Table 7.5. The main effects of job insecurity were discussed in Chapter 6, but will be mentioned briefly here as well.

In our first set of regression analyses relating to the objective of this section, we tested how union satisfaction could be predicted by job insecurity and union support, respectively. Job insecurity predicted union satisfaction only in the Dutch sample, after control variables and union support were also taken into account. The relationship between job insecurity and union satisfaction was weak, yet significant and positive, which indicates that members with higher levels of job insecurity also tend to report higher levels of union satisfaction. In the remaining three countries, however, job insecurity was unrelated to union satisfaction.

Union support, on the other hand, was a significant and strong predictor of union satisfaction in all four samples. The relation between union support and union satisfaction was positive, indicating, as expected, that those perceiving strong union support also are more satisfied with their union. This is not surprising given that feelings of support from one's organization would make the member embrace more positive attitudes toward that organization (Armstrong-Stassen, 1993; Shore *et al.*, 1994). However, there was no interaction effect of job insecurity and union support in any of the samples; on the other hand, there was not much effect to buffer against since job insecurity was unrelated to union satisfaction in three of the countries (and, in fact, evidenced a positive relation with union satisfaction in the fourth – the Netherlands). The model also explained a larger portion of the variance in the dependent variable than we saw in the previous analyses, ranging from 24 up to as much as 48 percent.

Table 7.5. Results of multiple regression predicting union satisfaction, union commitment and union turnover intention with direct and interactive effects of job insecurity and union support

Predictor	Union satisfaction	Union commitment	Union turnover intention
Belgium			
Job insecurity	-.03	.06	.06
Union support	.49***	.39***	-.35***
Insecurity x Support	.07	-.06	.02
R^2 adjusted	.25***	.16***	.12***
Italy			
Job insecurity	-.10	-.08	.13*
Union support	.45***	.37***	-.44***
Insecurity x Support	-.05	-.05	-.07
R^2 adjusted	.24***	.15***	.21***
The Netherlands			
Job insecurity	.08*	.07	.03
Union support	.52***	.42***	-.40***
Insecurity x Support	.00	.01	.03
R^2 adjusted	.28***	.22***	.18***
Sweden			
Job insecurity	-.02	.08***	.02
Union support	.68***	.69***	-.46***
Insecurity x Support	.03	.03	.01
R^2 adjusted	.48***	.50***	.22***

*$p<.05$, ***$p<.001$.
Note: the effects of the covariates (age, gender and temporary work) are omitted from the table (for information of these effects, see Chapter 6).

In the case of union commitment, we found a similar pattern of results. Job insecurity was a significant predictor of union commitment only in the Swedish sample, and, as in the case of union satisfaction in the Netherlands, the relation was positive. This indicates that those experiencing job insecurity actually reported stronger union commitment than those with lower levels of job insecurity. This was observed in Chapter 6 as well, and explained by the conjecture that those experiencing job insecurity are likely to turn to the union for help and, in doing so, their commitment may actually be strengthened (Bender & Sloane, 1999; Iverson, 1996).

Union support was a strong and positive predictor of union commitment in all our samples. The direction of the relation was positive in all cases, such that perceptions of union support were associated with higher levels of union commitment. Again, this was an expected and not very surprising result. It appears that those who feel that they benefit from union support tend to remain loyal to their union, which also is in accordance with previous research on job insecurity (Armstrong-Stassen, 1993; Goslinga & Sverke, 2003; Johnson & Johnson, 1992) as well as the theories of the psychological contract (*cf.* Rousseau, 1989) and social exchange (Eisenberger *et al.*, 1986). The tie between the union and its members is strengthened as the members feel that the union is holding up its end of the bargain. In total, the regression model explained 16 percent of the variance in union commitment in Belgium, 15 percent in Italy, 22 percent in the Netherlands, and 50 percent in Sweden.

With respect to union turnover intention, the results (shown in Table 7.5) show that job insecurity was unrelated to this outcome in all samples but one – Italy. In this case, the data indicated that a higher level of job insecurity was related to a higher intention to give up the union membership. This may be explained by the conjecture that the union can be blamed for the causes of the uncertainty (Mellor, 1992), which leads to the members wishing to resign their membership from a union that apparently cannot prevent job insecurity.

Union support was negatively related to union turnover intention, in all participating countries. The negative relation suggests that experiences of union support are associated with lower levels of the intention to terminate the union membership (Goslinga & Klandermans, 2001; Goslinga & Sverke, 2003). The results also revealed that no interaction effects of job insecurity and union support were obtained in any of the participating countries. This may be attributable to the low impact of job insecurity on turnover intention in three of the samples. Job insecurity was not found to be associated with the intention to leave the union (except in the Italian sample), and hence there was no negative effect of job insecurity to be moderated by union support. Also, where the impact of perceived union support was strong, the impact of job insecurity was non-significant. This indicates that despite the interaction effect not reaching significance, union support may help the individual to deal with job insecurity. In total, the predictor variables explained 12 percent of the variance in Belgium, 21 percent in Italy, 18 percent in the Netherlands, and 16 percent in Sweden.

Concluding Remarks

The results presented in this chapter lead to some important conclusions concerning the role of the union in the understanding of the effects of job insecurity. For one, union members were found to differ from non-members in their reactions to job insecurity in a few important variables, namely, job satisfaction, and organizational commitment. However, the way in which members differed from non-members varied between the countries in our study. This suggests that the members' perceptions of their union and the benefits associated with membership are important. Because of this, we investigated the effects of perceived union support on individual, organizational, and union-related consequences of job insecurity. The results corroborated the notion that perceived union support is an important factor in shaping members' attitudes toward the organization and the union.

However, union support was only occasionally found to buffer against the negative effects of job insecurity. On the one hand, these findings could be taken to suggest that perceptions of union performance, on a general level, tend not to decrease the negative impact of job insecurity on its individual and organizational consequences (in terms of union-related outcomes, there was not much to buffer against since job insecurity, with a few exceptions, was unrelated to union attitudes). On the other hand, the results also indicate that receiving support from the union may make the member better equipped to cope with the consequences of job insecurity. For instance, union support moderated the negative effects of job insecurity on physical health complaints (in the Swedish sample) and organizational commitment (Italy and Sweden). Perceived union support also appears to be important in that it had positive main effects on well-being and attitudes – those who felt that their union is supportive reported less health complaints and were more positively disposed toward both the organization and the union.

CHAPTER 8
Conclusions

In recent decades, a vast number of companies and organizations have carried out organizational changes and restructurings, resulting in many employees receiving notice, being laid off, or just feeling uneasy or worried about their future in the organization. This has created, in many segments of the labor market, a climate characterized by uncertainty, which has caused many employees to experience job insecurity. Job insecurity has become an increasingly more important and urgent problem in the work environment, developing in the wake of economic globalization, increased internal and external competition, technological changes, and organizational unpredictability. The experiencing of job insecurity has been described as a significant stressor and is believed to have a number of consequences, including negative health symptoms, a desire to leave the organization, and decreased satisfaction and loyalty.

Given these circumstances, the general objective of this book has been to increase the understanding of the phenomenon of job insecurity and its consequences. Survey data have been utilized to empirically address three important areas of theoretical as well as practical interest. One of these areas concerns personal demographics and other characteristics that may make individuals more inclined to experience job insecurity, which has prompted us to examine whether certain groups of individuals may be more vulnerable to job insecurity. A second area, concerning the consequences of perceived employment uncertainty, has been focused on testing how job insecurity relates to individual factors such as health complaints, organizational factors like job and organizational attitudes, and union factors, including attitudes towards the union. The third and final area has to do with the prevention of these detrimental effects, and we have investigated if factors associated with union membership can reduce the negative effects of job insecurity for the individual, the organization, and the union.

By using data obtained from workers in four European countries – Belgium, Italy, the Netherlands, and Sweden – our ambition has primarily been to evaluate the extent to which the results can be generalized or, in other words, to explore whether the experience of job insecurity, its consequences, and the role of the union appear to be akin in a broader, international context.

The Nature and Measurement of Job Insecurity

Before discussing our results, it is appropriate to return briefly to the theoretical foundations that have guided the research presented in this book. Our empirical examinations have emanated from a definition of job insecurity based on stress theory and theories of psychological contracts between employees and their employers. These theories were discussed in depth in Chapter 3 where we also provided an overview of how job insecurity has been conceptualized in previous research.

In this book, job insecurity is regarded as a perceptual phenomenon and defined as the individual's subjective experience of an involuntary event. This implies that the job insecurity experience is personal and unwanted, and may differ among individuals exposed to the same objective environment. This "subjective" definition differs from more "objective" definitions that describe job insecurity as a characteristic of the situation (*e.g.*, organizational change, temporary work, high unemployment rate) without reference to the individual's experience and interpretation of the situation. To be able to detect an individual's subjective experiencing of job insecurity, we have to use some kind of measure. In this book, we have relied on a five-item scale developed within the project. This measure has proven to have sound psychometric properties in all four participating countries (see Chapter 4).

Theoretically, job insecurity is defined as a type of stressor, involving an uncertainty and unpredictability about the future that is often experienced over an extended period of time. In order to understand the process involved in the job insecurity phenomenon, and how it may evolve and result in various consequences, we have presented and discussed different theoretical stress frameworks and related the job insecurity phenomenon to these theories. In general, it can be concluded that the lack of control and sense of powerlessness accompanying the experience of job insecurity is intimately connected with the individual's experience of stress and discomfort. We have also related job insecurity to psychological contract theories that postulate that employees who experience job insecurity may regard it as a breach, or even a violation, of the psychological agreement existing between the organization and the individual. This perception, that promises have been broken, is more apt to arise when the individual has entered an organization under the impression that he or she would be provided with an employment that is permanent and secure for the future.

Who Feels Job Insecurity?

One of the aims of this book is to attempt to contribute to a better understanding of those factors that could be seen as being at the root of the job insecurity experience. Previous research has shown that the levels of job insecurity can vary considerably from study to study, which suggests that there are factors in the work environment that can make individuals more or less prone to experiencing job insecurity. Previous research, however, has also shown that the levels of job insecurity can vary considerably among individuals within the same organization despite the fact that they share the same actual working conditions, which implies that individual factors also have an influence on the degree of job insecurity perceived. As we described in Chapter 3, it is the combination of environmental and individual factors that is central to those theories which suggest that a stressor, such as job insecurity, is a subjective experience. Chapter 5 was dedicated to a systematic analysis of how a subjective experience results as a consequence of an individual interpreting a given situation, based on his or her own individual qualities and previous experiences. With the use of the survey data from the four countries, this chapter investigated to what extent the experiencing of job insecurity can be said to stem from individual factors (personal background, family situation, social status, and personality dispositions) and environmental factors (employment contract and union membership).

The investigations reported in Chapter 5 showed some mixed results, making it difficult to come to any general conclusions about which characteristics make individuals prone to experiencing job insecurity. Although there do seem to be some influences of age, gender, social status, and employment contract on the job insecurity experience, the results, however, point in different directions in the different countries. It can also be concluded that family situation, like cohabiting or having children living at home, was not associated with job insecurity experiences in any of the participating countries. The results, however, support the notion that individual factors have an effect on the experiencing of job insecurity, which is in line with the stress model presented by Katz and Kahn (1978; see Figure 3.1), suggesting that both individual and environmental factors interact and shape the individual's appraisal of a given situation.

It is not possible to draw any firm conclusions regarding the effects of age and gender since, for Sweden, the results suggest that younger individuals experience more job insecurity, while, in Belgium, it was the older who reported higher levels of insecurity. In the Belgian sample women reported more job insecurity as compared to men, and the tests for interaction effects of age and gender revealed that older women experienced more job insecurity. In contrast to this, in Italy it was the older men who reported stronger experiences of job insecurity. Given these results, it can be concluded that demographics, such as age and gender, may have some impact on the job insecurity experience, despite us not being able to draw any general conclusions about these relationships. This means that no support was found in our study for those previous results which have indicated that women experience less job insecurity compared with men (*e.g.*, Ferrie, Shipely, Marmot, Stansfeld & Smith, 1995), and that those in the middle age category (30 to 50 years) should be the most likely to experience job insecurity (De Witte, 1999). Consequently, it is still unclear how age and gender relate to job insecurity.

With regard to social status, the results for the Swedish sample showed that blue-collar workers experienced more job insecurity than white-collar workers, while the results for Belgium showed that those individuals who had only finished compulsory school reported more job insecurity compared to individuals with higher levels of education. There was also an interaction effect in the Belgian sample, suggesting that professional/management level workers experience more job insecurity if they have only completed a compulsory school education, compared to those professionals/managers with high school or university educations. These results suggest that individuals who have both blue-collar jobs and less education may be more prone to experiencing job insecurity, and, moreover, that a lower level of education may also leave professionals and managers more prone to experiencing job insecurity. These results are also in accordance with previous arguments that have suggested that blue-collar workers may be more income-dependent and thereby more inclined to experience job insecurity (Gallie *et al.*, 1998; Kinnunen *et al.*, 1999). It has also been suggested that individuals with higher levels of education should typically be more attractive to the labor market and have a higher degree of employability, thereby making them less vulnerable to job insecurity. Results obtained by Van Vuuren *et al.* (1991a) have also indicated that individuals with higher levels of completed education experience less job insecurity (see also Näswall & De Witte, 2003). All of this indicates that more highly educated white-collar and professional workers are less inclined to experience job insecurity, at the same time as blue-collar workers and individuals with lower educational levels are more likely to experience job insecurity.

Type of employment contract also appears to be related to job insecurity perceptions. In the Netherlands and Sweden, individuals with temporary employment contracts reported more experiences of job insecurity than full-time or part-time employees. In Sweden, the results also indicate that the combination of having a temporary position and working part-time is related to perceived job insecurity. This result follows previous research suggesting that working under a temporary contract may intensify an individual's experiencing of job insecurity. Other researchers have also reported temporary work to be associated with perceptions of job insecurity (*e.g.*, De Witte & Näswall, 2003; Näswall & De Witte, 2003; Sverke *et al.*, 2000). Again, the results suggest that type of employment contract is related to the level of job insecurity experienced, and that individuals working under temporary contracts are more inclined to experience job insecurity, and, moreover, that those who are both temporarily employed and hold part-time positions are more vulnerable to job insecurity than those with just temporary or part-time contracts.

Regarding union membership and job insecurity, we postulated that union members would be less inclined to experience job insecurity than non-members. The reasoning behind this was based on the idea that unions function as a form of collective social support (Dekker & Schaufeli, 1995; Lim, 1996). Our analysis showed mixed results for the association between union membership status and job insecurity experiences, and in the Belgian sample union members even reported more job insecurity compared to non-members. The opposite was found in the Swedish sample, where non-members reported more job insecurity than union members did, and, in the Italian sample we did not discover any differences between union members and non-members regarding job insecurity experiences. Such results make it difficult to reach any firm conclusions over the impact of union membership on job insecurity perceptions; however, it may be concluded that union membership status seems to have some association with the level of job insecurity experienced, but to what extent and in which direction is unclear. It may, for example, be that some workers turn to unions when they are experiencing job insecurity, while others work in unionized settings characterized by uncertain employment relations.

Chapter 5 also investigated the association between perceptions of job insecurity and personality characteristics such as positive and negative affectivity, self-efficacy, and attributional style (locus of control). Since an individual's interpretation of the environment, according to interactionist theories (*e.g.*, Ekehammar, 1974; Endler & Magnusson, 1976), is based on a combination of the objective environment and the individual's subjective interpretation of this environment, it is likely that dispositions may impact this process and thereby influence the individual's experiencing of a stressor such as job insecurity (see the Katz &

141

Kahn, 1978, model in Figure 3.1). The results of the empirical analysis revealed that locus of control and negative affectivity both were related to job insecurity. In the case of locus of control, the results suggest that individuals with an external attribution style were more likely to experience job insecurity compared with individuals with more internal attributions. These results support those presented by Van Vuuren *et al.* (1991a) who also reported that those with an external locus of control tend to experience more job insecurity than those with an internal locus of control. The fact that negative affectivity also predicted job insecurity experiences indicates that individuals who are disposed to negative emotions also tend to report job insecurity. However, neither positive affectivity nor self-efficacy showed any relation to job insecurity experiences. Similar results were also reported by Roskies *et al.* (1993). All in all, this indicates that dispositions may have an impact on the degree of job insecurity a person experiences. It should also be mentioned that dispositions, in the present study, were only assessed in the Swedish sample, so the results should therefore be interpreted somewhat carefully.

In conclusion, we can say that the bulk of the research addressing the issue of who feels job insecurity is rather limited and the results thus far contradictory, which makes it difficult to draw any sound conclusions on how demographics and personal characteristics influence job insecurity perceptions. It is possible that factors like education and social status have more clear associations with the perceptions of job insecurity if this is investigated in regions that are severely affected by unemployment and economic decline. Naturally, it is likely that there are regional fluctuations, but when aggregated to the national level such differences may not be detected. However, the results presented here show, at least, that these factors do influence job insecurity to some extent. More research is obviously needed in order to better understand what may trigger job insecurity and what it is that makes individuals more or less susceptible to this work stressor (see also Näswall & De Witte, 2003, for a discussion).

Consequences of Job Insecurity

Another important area of consideration for building a better understanding of the uncertain employment relations that characterize the modern working life has to do with the consequences of job insecurity. A review of previous research that has examined the relationships between job insecurity and its consequences can be found in Chapter 6. This chapter was also dedicated to empirically addressing this book's secondary aim – to investigate the extent to which job insecurity brings about similar consequences in different contexts – by examining whether the effect sizes may be generalized over the samples drawn from the four European countries. Our purposes are grounded in the premise that job insecurity can have significant consequences for the various actors involved, namely the individual, the organization he or she works for, and the union.

Consequences for the Individual

The theories used to define and explain job insecurity all point out the negative consequences that the experience of employment uncertainty is likely to have on the individual. Our investigations have confirmed these suggestions to a large degree. In all four European countries, job insecurity was associated with higher frequencies of mental health complaints. The present results thus provide convincing support for the notion that those who experience job insecurity also tend to experience more mental health complaints. We also found that physical health complaints were to some extent predicted by job insecurity. This was not confirmed in all countries, however. In one of the three samples where data on this variable were available (the Netherlands), job insecurity was found to not be related to physical health complaints. It should be noted, however, that in this sample the level of physical health complaints was also lower than in Italy and Sweden.

These results point out that the job insecurity experience is severe for the individual employee. This is not surprising, given the definition of job insecurity as a stressor. Stress arises when individuals encounter a situation that they evaluate as threatening, and where they feel they cannot effectively counteract the threat (Lazarus & Folkman, 1984). The feeling that the threat to one's job cannot be neutralized brings a sense of lack of control into the situation. The degree to which the outcome of the threat is seen as undesirable will also affect the severity of the threat – the anticipation of very negative outcomes makes the threat appear stronger. Job insecurity entails the features just described. It is the perception of a threat against the current employment situation, a threat with outcomes that the person experiencing the threat would rather not face. Job insecurity also entails a sense of powerlessness (Greenhalgh & Rosenblatt, 1984), which comes along with the individual not being able to neutralize the threat. These experiences give rise to strain in the individual, which is manifested in health complaints and decreased well-being (Hellgren & Sverke, 2003). Our data show no general exception to this.

These negative consequences for the individual may also be explained by the theory of effort–reward imbalance (*cf.* Siegrist, 2000).

This theory postulates that the employee exerts a certain effort, and aims to receive rewards that are equivalent to this effort. When there is an imbalance in that the effort exceeds the perceived rewards, the individual experiences emotional distress, which is associated with mental and physical strain. Job insecurity represents one aspect of this imbalance. When the employees cannot control their work status, which is the implication of job insecurity, even if they have put a lot of effort into their job, the perception of an imbalance will occur (Siegrist, 1996). This imbalance results in emotional distress, as mentioned above. Job insecurity is thus a stressor in the sense that it represents a lack of sufficient rewards given to the employee.

Consequences for the Organization

The employee is not the only party that is affected by job insecurity. As Chapter 6 showed, employees' reactions to job insecurity affect the organization as well. This is rather intuitive. Employees who are suffering from stress, and who are experiencing stress symptoms such as lowered well-being and mental health complaints, are probably not functioning to their full potential at the workplace. Also, employees whose well-being is suffering will probably have some sort of reaction against the source of the stress, and in the event of job stress, this source is often the organization or representatives of the organization, such as the supervisors. In Chapter 6, we saw evidence of this. Job insecurity was associated with lower levels of job satisfaction, a pattern that appeared in all four samples. These results are consistent with much of previous research (*e.g.* Ashford *et al.*, 1989; Heaney *et al.*, 1994; Hellgren *et al.*, 1999), and these four samples, exhibiting the same pattern, add to the weight of such evidence.

Loyalty towards the organization also suffers when job insecurity is prevalent. As expected, organizational commitment was lower in the samples where job insecurity levels were higher. There was, however, one exception. In the Swedish sample, organizational commitment and job insecurity were positively related, indicating that higher levels of job insecurity may also be associated with stronger organizational commitment. The result obtained in the Swedish sample contradicts previous research (*e.g.*, Armstrong-Stassen, 1993; McFarlane Shore & Tetrick, 1991; Sverke *et al.*, 2002) and theoretical arguments (Allen & Meyer, 1990; Morrow, 1993). One explanation may be that insecure employees actually try to secure their jobs by expressing more commitment to their organization during turbulent times, working harder to show that they should be allowed to stay in the event of downsizing (*cf.* the loyalty hypothesis advocated by Hirschman, 1970). There is some evidence of this in previous research (Bergman & Wigblad, 1999). However, the effect of job insecurity on organizational commitment was not very strong in the Swedish sample, and the level of commitment may thus not increase radically when job insecurity is present. In the three samples where higher job insecurity predicted lower organizational commitment, the effect sizes were somewhat larger, suggesting that this negative relation is stronger than the positive relation found in Sweden.

Another sign of employee loyalty is the willingness to remain with the organization as is expressed by low turnover intention. In all four samples, job insecurity was associated with stronger turnover intentions. As employees come to feel more uncertain about their future employment, they gradually prepare themselves mentally for a possible change of workplace, which is reflected in turnover intention. Even if we do not have an objective measure of actual turnover rates, a previous meta-analysis has shown a substantial degree of concurrence between the intention to quit and the actual behavior (Steel & Ovalle, 1984). Our results also correspond with previous empirical findings (*e.g.*, Davy *et al.*, 1997; Sverke *et al.*, 2002). Those who report job insecurity also report a corresponding wish to seek out alternative employment.

These attitudinal outcomes of job insecurity reflect the consequences of a breach of the psychological contract and reactions to an imbalance between effort and reward. These two theoretical frameworks may be simultaneously applied in order to explain these reactions to job insecurity. The psychological contract existing between employees and their organization contains expectations regarding the obligations and rewards that are to follow the completion of one's responsibilities (Rousseau, 1989; Robinson *et al.*, 1994). If the employee feels that the organization has failed to fulfill its obligations to him or her, or has failed to reward the employee when he or she has accomplished his or her duties, the psychological contract is perceived to be breached (Robinson & Morrison, 2000). The employees may react strongly to this perceived breach, experiencing violation of the contract, where violation entails the strong negative emotional reaction to the breach (Morrison & Robinson, 1997). In Chapter 3 we described job insecurity as one type of breach of the psychological contract. This theoretical background facilitates the understanding of why the job insecurity experience elicits such negative attitudinal reactions. When employees fulfill their end of both the explicit and the implicit contracts, and in return receive indications that their jobs are in danger, it is understandable that they react with dissatisfaction and less loyalty. This has been observed in previous research as well, where the experience of job insecurity predicted dissatisfaction and decreased commitment, which in turn

145

predicted turnover intentions among the employees (Chirumbolo & Hellgren, 2003; Davy *et al.*, 1997).

Our results are thus in line with previous research and theoretical reasoning and point out how important it is for companies to make sure that the psychological contract is fulfilled. A workforce characterized by negative attitudes toward the employer will not put in the extra effort needed to bring a company in decline back on its feet (Noer, 1993). In addition, the augmented turnover intention associated with job insecurity, that we observed in all four samples, may result in that those who are able to find employment elsewhere leave the organization. Often these are the key persons that the employers need in order to revitalize the organization (Pfeffer, 1998).

The damage of trust in the employer that follows a breach of the psychological contract makes it difficult for the remaining employees to believe that their jobs will be safe in the future, regardless of what the organization assures them. One possible way of trying to prevent breach of the psychological contract is to try and mold the contract in such a way that secure employment is not necessarily what employees expect. It has been suggested that the content of the psychological contract is developing along such lines, which involves the organization providing the employees with resources for becoming more employable, *i.e.*, to increase the employees' alternatives on the labor market (Martin *et al.*, 1998). By not being as dependent on one particular job, the threat of job loss would become less severe, and job insecurity would not be as negative an experience.

Other theorists suggest that the most important task for an organization that has undergone restructuring or conducted cutbacks is to make significant efforts to restore the employees' sense of security (Kinnunen *et al.*, 2000). Such strategies may entail that management works actively to motivate employees and prevent them from feeling that their jobs are at risk (Kinnunen *et al.*, 2000). Another tactic involves the use of early and honest information and communication, which serves to prevent rumors and decreases the general sense of uncertainty during organizational change (Greenhalgh, 1991). The way in which the organization treats those who are forced to leave has a great impact on how secure the remaining staff feels (Isaksson, Pettersson & Hellgren, 1998). In addition, the fairness of layoffs and other types of change are likely to affect employees' trust in the organization (Brockner *et al.*, 1990). In general, the organization should be aware of the severe consequences of job insecurity and work to prevent those consequences as much as possible. Perhaps downsizings are difficult to avoid during periods of economic difficulties, but the way in which they are conducted is under the control of the employers. It is to their benefit, as well as the employees', to make sure that the employees are treated fairly and that they are able to accept the changes as much as possible.

Consequences for the Union

Since many of the organizations conducting cutbacks and reorganizations have a union presence (Mellor, 1992), the experiences of job insecurity among the employees may also affect the union. One possible manifestation of this is when the negative attitudes toward the organization, discussed in previous sections, spill over to the union. On the other hand, it is also plausible that the members could turn to their union for help, which would be reflected in them having positive attitudes towards the union. In Chapter 6 we investigated how job insecurity also predicted attitudes toward the union. In the cases where we found even the slightest indication of job insecurity having an impact, we also tended to find negative attitudes toward the union. From our investigations, it can be concluded that job insecurity predicts lower union satisfaction (in two samples), along with weaker union commitment (in one country) and increased turnover intention (in two samples).

These results contradict previous research to some degree. Even though very few studies have related job insecurity to factors associated with union membership, of those investigating this relation, most found that job insecurity tends to be positively related to union membership (Bender & Sloane, 1999; Iverson, 1996). Hence, employees who worry about losing their jobs may turn to the union for protection against uncertain employment relations. Our results, on the other hand, indicate that unionized employees do not necessarily see their union as being a great source of help during uncertain times. Rather, the negative attitudes toward the organization among employees experiencing job insecurity are accompanied by negative attitudes, albeit weaker, toward the union as well. In one sample (Sweden), however, we found the opposite, that job insecurity was associated with higher levels of union commitment. It might be that in a country with a strong union presence, members are more committed to their union organization than to the organization in which they are employed (Gruen, 1954; Guest & Dewe, 1991). As noted in the previous section, however, job insecurity was also positively associated with organizational commitment in Sweden, which rules out the explanation maintaining that employees, in such a situation, would turn away from their employer and increase their loyalty to the union.

The lack of consistent results in our samples can be explained in part by the differences in the levels of job insecurity reported. The results for the Italian sample showed consistently negative attitudes and intentions toward the union, and in this sample the level of job insecurity was the highest (2.61 on the five-point scale). It is possible that attitudes towards the union are only affected when both job insecurity levels become higher and job insecurity is a major concern among the members. The results from Chapter 5 corroborate this, as we found that the Italian union members reported the highest levels of job insecurity. The higher levels of job insecurity among union members may thus have influenced their negative attitudes toward their union.

Although the results concerning consequences for the union were less uniform than the results concerning consequences for the individual and the organization, our study incidicates, however, that job insecurity can bring about negative attitudes toward the union. This may imply that the members have not entirely separated the union from the employing organization and react negatively toward all parties that may have anything to do with the experience of job insecurity. If the union is seen as being partly responsible for the negative situation at the workplace, the members will be less satisfied with, and express less commitment to, the union. To the extent that members feel that their union has not done enough to prevent negative circumstances at work, such as protecting job security, they will react negatively toward their union (Mellor, 1992). Again, the concept of the psychological contract is a useful explanatory framework. The union is supposed to protect the members' interests, and if this is not done to the members' satisfaction, the contract may be regarded as breached. As we discussed in the previous section, such perceptions of contract breach may have detrimental consequences for the members' attitudes. The unions therefore need to demonstrate that they are working with their members' interests as their primary focus and do all that they possibly can to prevent negative events from occurring.

The Importance of Union Membership and Support

We have already briefly discussed how important it is for organizations to prevent job insecurity, or at least try to mitigate its consequences. Most importantly, however, the presence of labor unions in organizations undergoing change may also affect the members' reactions to job insecurity. In Chapter 7 we investigated the moderating effect of union membership and union support on the relation between job insecurity and its outcomes. The rationale behind this was based on previous research describing the benefits of social support (*cf.* Armstrong-Stassen, 1993; Lim, 1996) and union membership (Bender & Sloane, 1999).

Our testing of how union members differed from non-members showed that members were generally less satisfied with their jobs and less committed to their employers. In two of the three samples that included unionized and non-unionized employees (Belgium and Italy), union members reported lower levels of organizational commitment than non-members. Job satisfaction was also lower among union members in one of the samples (Belgium). These findings contradict the observations made by Sverke and Hellgren (2001), who found that union members expressed more loyalty to their organization in comparison with non-members. There was no moderating or buffering effect detected of union membership, suggesting that union membership does not mitigate the negative effects of job insecurity that were discussed in the previous section. Our results indicate, rather, that employees become members in order to deal with their negative attitudes toward the organization, *i.e.,* their dissatisfaction with their employer.

We have discussed the possibility that the positive effects of union membership were being obscured by the fact that we had not taken into account to what extent the members regard their union organization as being able to protect them from uncertainty and negative events. Merely making a distinction between members and non-members does not address what those who are members actually think of their union. However, by taking the levels of perceived union support into account, we were able to more closely test whether the perception of having a supportive union may buffer against the negative consequences of job insecurity. This procedure allowed us to then test if the union's performance, as measured by the members' perceptions of union support, affects members' well-being, organizational attitudes, and feelings about their union.

Our results showed that it was only in the Swedish sample where union support had any main effect on well-being, which indicates that those perceiving more support from their union also tend to report fewer symptoms of ill-health and negative well-being. The main effect of union support on work related attitudes was not significant in all of the samples, but some general trends were revealed. Despite there being exceptions to the general trends, union support was, in most cases, associated with higher levels of job satisfaction and organizational commitment, as well as with a weaker intention to leave the organization. Perhaps not surprisingly, in all four countries union support was strongly related to the three union outcomes investigated, with positive relations to union satisfaction and union commitment, and a negative relation to the intention to resign union membership. Thus, union support seems to be quite strongly related to all outcome variables, except well-being.

However, the buffering effect of perceived union support was only evident in a small number of the cases. Union support had a moderating effect on the relation between job insecurity and physical health complaints in the Swedish sample. Those who experienced union support, to a greater extent, reported fewer health complaints, even when they experienced higher levels of job insecurity. In addition to this, we also detected a buffering effect of union support on the relation between job insecurity and organizational commitment. This moderating effect showed up in two of the four samples (Italy and Sweden) and indicated that higher levels of union support predicted high organizational commitment, regardless of the level of job insecurity experienced. However, in neither of the cases did union support moderate the relation between job insecurity and union attitudes.

These results point to the importance of social support and indicate that union support may be an effective source of support. This corresponds with previous research, which shows social support to have positive main effects on well-being and work related attitudes (Armstrong-Stassen, 1993; Vieswesvaran *et al.*, 1999). However, the hypothesized buffering effect of union support remains largely unconfirmed. Perhaps this is not surprising, given comments in previous publications on the lack of conclusive results on the buffering function of social support between stressor and outcome (Beehr, Farmer, Glazer, Gudanowski & Nair, 2003). Explanations for this lack of buffering effects have been offered. The first and most obvious one is that union or social support does not alleviate the negative consequences of job insecurity. This, however, cannot be a general conclusion since previous research has found that social support does indeed diminish the negative impact of job stress in general (*e.g.,* Billings & Moos, 1982; Frese, 1999; see Vieswesvaran *et al.*, 1999, for meta-analysis results) and job insecurity in particular (*e.g.,* Lim, 1996).

Another explanation that has been offered concerns the type of social support. It has been suggested that support only mitigates the negative effects of a stressor when the type of support matches the stressor or the type of reaction the individual has to the stressor (Jackson, 1992; LaRocco *et al.*, 1980). This would imply that certain sources of support are less effective as buffers in certain cases, as they either have nothing to do with the stressor, or are part of the problem (Jackson, 1992). For example, stress attributed to the supervisor (*e.g.,* role ambiguity) may not easily be alleviated by supervisor support, since the supervisor is the source of the problem (Beehr *et al.*, 2003). In the case of support from the union, this type of support may not alleviate dissatisfaction with the union that is related to job insecurity since the union could be held partly responsible for the source of the dissatisfaction (Hellgren & Chirumbolo, 2003; cf. Mellor, 1992). The buffering effect of union support on the negative relation between job insecurity and organizational commitment (in Italy and Sweden) may be partially explained by this reasoning. Perceived union support may help employees feel that they are able to remain with the organization in spite of uncertainty. The support received from the union may make the employees feel they can more easily deal with the perceived uncertainty, and the negative impact of job insecurity on organizational commitment is thereby not as great for these employees.

In conclusion, the results indicate that support from the union can be of considerable importance for the various actors, despite the buffering effects of union membership and union support only occurring sporadically in our analyses. The fact that union support, in a few cases, appeared to be connected with minor mental and physical health complaints suggests that union protection can be beneficial to the individual employee. Our results also suggest that employees who feel that they are supported by a union that provides them protection may be more positively disposed toward the employing organization. This indicates that the organization itself also has a great deal to gain from employees being members of a supportive union (regardless of the levels of perceived job insecurity), which is indicated by the main effects of union support on work-related attitudes. Not surprisingly, our data unequivocally show that perceptions of support from the union may typically result in members feeling more satisfied with the union, expressing more commitment to it, and wanting to retain membership. Thus, our results seem to be in accordance with previous research in which the evidence of a buffering effect of support is rare, but where a main effect of social support has been observed very often (Cohen & Wills, 1985; Scheck et al., 1997). This points to how important the presence of social support is – from the union, colleagues, supervisors, or other sources of work-based social support.

Methodological Issues

Naturally, there are a number of limitations and methodological aspects that may have affected the results presented in this book, and which therefore deserve commenting on. Firstly, all of the empirical work is based on self-reported survey data, which increases the risk of mono-method bias (Campbell & Fiske, 1959). This means that there may be systematic methodological errors built into the data source, and that these errors may have affected the results in a specific direction. One way of avoiding this is to use a multi-trait–multi-method design, which is recommended by Campbell and Fiske (1959). This design is, however, not very common in work and organizational research since it is often both difficult and costly to collect data from large samples and different sources at the same time (Bagozzi & Philips, 1982).

When it comes to research on job insecurity, it is also difficult to get organizations to agree to contribute data from personnel directories, supervisor ratings of staff, and other so-called "objective" sources of data, especially if the organization is engaged in reorganizations that involve personnel layoffs. To partly avoid these methodological problems, some authors in the field of employment uncertainty research rely on official statistics for rating job insecurity whereas measures of its outcomes are subjectively reported (*e.g.*, Burchell *et al.*, 1999; Gallie *et al.*, 1998; Heery & Salmon, 2000). However, one of the purposes of this book has been to assess the individual and subjective experience of job insecurity. We follow a more psychological definition that brings into question the validity of relying on official statistics or factual characteristics of employment status when investigating job insecurity, since such data sources do not address how individuals actually perceive their situation.

The health outcomes examined in the book are also based on self-reported symptoms, which naturally may have had an effect on the results. It would certainly have strengthened the study if the health outcomes could have been captured by biological or physical markers of health as well, which would have increased the validity and thereby the generalizability of the studies. However, studies investigating how job insecurity relates to biological, as opposed to self-reported, health indicators have obtained results which indicate that job insecurity is associated with ill-health regardless of how the outcomes are being assessed (*e.g.*, Lindström, Leino, Seitsamo & Torstila, 1997; Mattiasson *et al.*, 1990; Siegrist, Peter, Junge, Cremer & Siegel, 1990). Nevertheless, there are currently still relatively few studies that have investigated the relation between job insecurity and biological health indicators. This is probably a reflection of the fact that most research on individuals' health relies on self-reported data (Bishop, 1994), and studies relying on a variety of data sources are undoubtedly warranted.

It can also be said that the majority of the studies to investigate the effects of job insecurity have been cross-sectional (Sverke *et al.*, 2002), thus making it difficult to draw conclusions regarding the long-term consequences of this stressor. The empirical analyses in this book, as well, have been based on cross-sectional data, which limits the possibilities of drawing any firm conclusions about the development of the relations over time. There is, however, some support for the notion that job insecurity perceptions may lead to health complaints, rather than the other way around. For instance, Hellgren and Sverke (2003) conducted cross-lagged panel analyses of the relation between job insecurity and mental as well as physical health complaints over the course of one year. The results indicate that job insecurity may give rise to mental (but not physical) health complaints rather than the reverse scenario – that health complaints would generate perceptions of job insecurity. It can be concluded, then, that there is some support for the hypothesis that job insecurity causes mental health complaints, at least within the span of one year. The aspect of time is always a critical factor in stress research, and research has been conducted that identifies effects of job insecurity during periods of up to five years (Garst, Frese & Molenaar, 2000). It has also been argued that some stress reactions take longer to develop, while others are more immediate (Zapf, Dormann & Frese, 1996). This naturally has implications for the effects of job insecurity over time, since the detection of effects may be dependent on the time interval used in the study (for a more detailed discussion, see Hellgren & Sverke, 2003; Zapf *et al.*, 1996).

The measure used to assess job insecurity in this book was based on a five-item scale designed to capture the fear or worry employees may have over losing a present job in the foreseeable future. It thus reflects the core of job insecurity as the phenomenon was described in Chapter 3, and bears similarities to other global measures of job insecurity (*e.g.*, Johnson *et al.*, 1984; Mauno *et al.*, 2001). Moreover, as apparent from Chapter 4, the measure has proven to be both valid and reliable for all four countries and can therefore be seen as a good indicator of the experience of job insecurity in the different samples. However, this measure of job insecurity only reflects the fear or worry over losing the job as a whole. As noted in Chapter 3 and Chapter 4, several researchers have argued for the dividing of the construct into at least two different dimensions (*e.g.*, Ashford *et al.*, 1989; Greenhalgh & Rosenblatt, 1984; Hellgren *et al.*, 1999; Sverke & Hellgren, 2002). In such two-dimensional models, the first dimension typically reflects the fear of losing the job as a whole, while the second dimension focuses on the fear of losing valuable job features, such as challenging work tasks, career opportunities, salary increases, and improved working conditions. Since we in this book have relied on secondary data already collected within each country, we have been limited to this available measure of job insecurity, assessing only the fear of losing the job. It might be that our conclusions regarding the effects of job insecurity and the role of unions could have been slightly different had also other dimensions of job insecurity been assessed.

It should also be mentioned that the secondary data used in this book are based on different sampling procedures. The data cover a variety of occupations, industrial branches, and types of labor unions, but no attempts have been made at obtaining identical sample characteristics across countries. In two instances we also have had to rely on alternative data for countries where important information had not been collected in our standard data sets (*i.e.*, Belgium and Sweden; see Chapter 2 for a description of the samples used in the study). Because the samples are not taken from the total population within each country, our data are therefore not to be regarded as representative of each country. It is not possible, for instance, to reach any general conclusions about country differences since we do not know if the empirical findings reflect actual country differences or result from different sampling procedures in each country. In addition, the data for the different countries were collected using different methods, *i.e.*, mail questionnaires and standardized telephone interviews. Although questionnaires are considered efficient and appropriate for the assessment of attitudes (Nelson, 1985), telephone surveys are also less sensitive to social desirability effects in comparison with personal interviews (de Vaus, 1991). Despite these methodological issues, we do discuss and reflect over differences between the samples drawn from different countries. However, rather than attempting to uncover country differences, one of our objectives in this book has been to investigate the robustness of the results. By investigating job insecurity, its predictors and consequences, and the role of union membership using heterogeneous samples from four different countries, we have been able to investigate to what extent the psychological mechanisms underlying the experience of job insecurity, well-being, job and organizational attitudes, and union attitudes can be generalized.

Concluding Remarks

In the beginning of this book we presented four quotations. The first one declared that "job insecurity is a perceptual phenomenon" (Jacobson, 1991a, p. 31), and this subjective definition of job insecurity has guided our work throughout this book. The theoretical arguments and empirical analyses reported here have demonstrated that job insecurity can be described as a rather universal phenomenon, occurring in different countries with different labor market characteristics. In view of this, it becomes evident that job insecurity cannot simply be attributed to factors such as the general level of unemployment in a country or the proportion of the labor force holding "atypical" employment contracts.

Nor can the experience of job insecurity only be attributed to the objective situation or type of employment an individual has. Rather, we have shown that the experience of job insecurity depends upon how the individual interprets the objective situation. Some of the factors that can affect this interpretation have been identified in our study; they include age, gender, and personality dispositions.

As indicated by the second quotation in the opening of the book, job insecurity is a stressor that has negative consequences, which not only affects individuals, as "their reactions have consequences for organizational effectiveness" (Greenhalgh & Rosenblatt, 1984, p. 438) as well. Our results strengthens this assumption, and indicates, along with previous research (*cf.* the meta-analysis by Sverke *et al.*, 2002), that job insecurity is becoming an increasingly more significant problem in the work environment as well as an increasingly important issue for management.

Furthermore, the European results presented in this book also provide two important extensions of previous research. Firstly, we have shown that job insecurity also can have negative consequences for unions, in that members' attitudes towards the union may deteriorate and the intention to retain membership may decrease. Secondly, our data indicate that the consequences of job insecurity may be generalized over countries that differ in labor market characteristics and industrial relations climates. The association between job insecurity and the outcomes was evident in countries with different levels of unemployment, dissimilar composition of the labor force, varying rates of unionization, and differences in union–management climates. Our empirical data do show some differences in the consequences of job insecurity among the four samples; however, the fact that the results point to there being so many similarities between the countries is still a striking finding. Even if the strength of the associations varied between the countries, and sometimes there were divergences from the general trend, the pattern remains rather consistent. Our results indicate that experiences of job insecurity are related to mental as well as physical health complaints, more negative attitudes toward work and the organization, and, to some extent, more negative attitudes toward the union.

Job insecurity is thus a phenomenon worth taking seriously. Since it is related to stress and health complaints as well as a more negative experience of work, job insecurity is an important issue for the unions. For labor unions in Europe, the issue of stress prevention has gained increased prioritization (Koukolaki, 2002). In some countries, such as Sweden, stress prevention is regulated by collective agreements between employers and unions, while in other countries, such as the Netherlands, the labor legislation goes so far as to stipulate the obligations on the employers' side. Given this, it is, as stated in the third quote of the book's opening, remarkable that "the relationship between trade unions and job insecurity has been strangely neglected" (Bender & Sloane, 1999, p. 123). In an attempt to help in the remedying of such neglect, we have investigated if and how union membership can serve as a source of protection for the individual.

Our results show that union membership in itself does not seem to have such a great influence on how individuals react to job insecurity. Rather, there are indications that union members in general were less committed to the organization they work for as compared to non-members. An exception to this was found in the country where the rate of unionization was the highest, namely Sweden, which might indicate that unionization can have beneficial consequences for employers, when there is a strong union tradition and stable union–management relations (*cf.* Freeman & Medoff, 1984). Our results indicate, however, some significance of union support. Those who perceived strong support from their union generally expressed more positive work related attitudes and had a more positive opinion of the union. Even if social support from the union does not change the degree of job insecurity experienced, and just, so to say, eases the symptoms without curing the illness, it can still have a positive effect on individuals by preventing the most negative of reactions from occurring. It should be noted, however, that union support was shown to moderate the negative consequences of job insecurity in only a few cases, which is also in agreement with previous research results (*e.g.*, Dekker & Schaufeli, 1995).

However, providing members with collective support in times of flexibility and uncertainty is not necessarily an uncomplicated task for labor unions. Historically, the role of the union has been to look after and safeguard the collective interests of its members, but the increasing flexibility of working life today could potentially undermine the traditional forms of collective interest representation. With this change in the labor market climate comes a new and difficult situation for the labor unions. They have to represent increasingly diverse interest groups, each with their own special interests. In this environment, the increasing individualization becomes a challenge for the union since some groups may consider themselves better suited than the unions to take charge of their individual and professional interests at work (Allvin & Sverke, 2000; Dawson, 2003; Kjellberg, 2001; Sverke, 1997; Van Ruysseveldt *et al.*, 1995).

Should one then draw the conclusion that the role of the unions is to be a limited one when it comes to protecting the workforce from job insecurity and its consequences? This seems hasty from our point of view. We still subscribe to the optimistic view expressed by the fourth quotation in the opening of the book, that "unions may reduce both job insecurity and the stress associated with job insecurity" (Barling *et al.*, 1992, p. 187). To take the argument further, it could be said that unions *must* work to decrease job insecurity and its negative consequences – for the simple reason that if unions do not, they could face a backlash. Earlier research has shown that members may hold their union responsible for negative changes in their work environment, staff cuts, and job insecurity (*e.g.*, Hartley, 1991; Johnson *et al.*, 1992; Mellor, 1992), and our results concur, indicating that job insecurity can lead to more negative attitudes towards the union and an increased intention to resign membership.

The main issue before us concerns how unions are to protect employees against job insecurity and its consequences. Literature on the subject suggests that unions employ a variety of strategies and take on different roles in order to best look after the employees' interests (see, for instance, Beaumont, 1995; Boxall & Haynes, 1997; Hyman, 1996). Changing industrial and employment relations place demands on a labor movement that is strong both centrally and locally.

It is clear that strength and stability at the central level is important for a union to be able to effectively see to their members' interests. It is often said that union administered unemployment funds – the so-called Ghent system – not only have the potential of producing a high rate of union membership (as in, for example, Sweden and Finland), but can also help reduce national unemployment and create better conditions for the organization of temporary workers (e.g., Boeri *et al.*, 2001). A strong national union entails a stronger voice in central level bargaining and a better opportunity to oversee that collective agreements are followed, which is, not least of all, furthered by having the possibility of mobilizing members in industrial action (Freeman & Medoff, 1984; Korpi, 1978). Strength at the central level can also allow unions to offer greater legal protection and provide services that can be of help to a broad membership base.

However, having strong local union organizations at the workplace is also becoming increasingly important since the decentralization of working life has gradually resulted in the shift of collective bargaining from the central level to the workplaces. The local union has an important function to fulfill when it comes to the dissemination of information, especially in connection with reorganizations. In circumstances where there is a threat of staff reductions, or when it has actually been carried out, a strong local union can also counteract specific threats –

perhaps not so much through the negotiating of contract provisions as such, but by making sure that the contract and its stipulations are followed (Johnson *et al.*, 1992). We have already pointed out that perceptions of justice are important for how employees react in situations characterized by turbulence and uncertainty (Brockner, 1988), and unions can work towards the fair treatment of its members. In those situations where cutbacks are to be faced, union organizations at the workplace play an important role in the creation of support organizations, which can help employees to cope with their feelings of anxiety and uncertainty over the future and also provide assistance in finding new employment opportunities (Kieselbach, 2003). There are also advocates of the idea that unions can and should make efforts to minimize the experiencing of job insecurity by working for the provision of continuing education and competence training – measures that improve the employability of employees and their chances of obtaining alternative employment arrangements (*e.g.*, Dawson, 2003; Kieselbach, 2003; Van Ruysseveldt *et al.*, 1995).

In summary, individuals as well as organizations are harmed by the increased insecurity prevailing in the working life. Through elucidating and describing the factors resulting in job insecurity, and how this experience affects individuals, organizations, and unions, our ambition with this book has been to expand the body of knowledge surrounding job insecurity. Expanded knowledge leads to more attention being focused on this phenomenon of working life and an increased awareness of how prevention measures can be implemented in the future. One way in which to combat job insecurity's negative consequences is through the protection and support that a union can provide. Union organizations serve an important purpose when they organize stress prevention methods that can curtail the downsides of working life's increasing flexibility – and research on working life serves an important purpose by evaluating how successful these methods are.

References

Agho, A. O., Price, J. L. & Mueller, C. W. (1992). Discriminant validity of measures of job satisfaction, positive affectivity and negative affectivity. *Journal of Occupational and Organizational Psychology, 65*, 185–196.

Aiken, L. S. & West, S. G. (1991). *Multiple Regression: Testing and interpreting interactions.* Newbury Park, CA: Sage.

Akaike, H. (1987). Factor analysis and AIC. *Psychometrika, 52*, 317–332.

Allen, N. J. & Meyer, J. P. (1990). The measurement and antecedents of affective, continuance and normative commitment to the organization. *Journal of Occupational Psychology, 63*, 1–18.

Allen, T. D., Freeman, D. M., Russell, J. E., Reizenstein, R. C. & Rentz, J. O. (2001). Survivor reactions to organizational downsizing: Does time ease the pain? *Journal of Occupational and Organizational Psychology, 74*, 145–164.

Allvin, M. & Sverke, M. (2000). Do new generations imply the end of solidarity? Swedish unionism in the era of industrialization. *Economic and Industrial Democracy, 21*, 71–95.

Anderson, C. R., Hellriegel, D. & Slocum, J. (1977). Mangerial response to environmentally induced stress. *Academy of Management Journal, 20*, 260–272.

Andersson, K. (1986). *Utveckling och prövning av ett frågeformulärsystem rörande arbetsmiljö och hälsotillstånd* [Development and test of a questionnaire concerning work environment and health] (Rapport 2). Örebro: Yrkesmedicinska kliniken.

Angoff, W. H. (1988). Validity: An evolving concept. In H. Wainer & H. I. Braun (eds.), *Test Validity* (pp. 19–30). Hillsdale, NJ: Erlbaum.

APA. (1985). *Standards for Educational and Psychological Testing.* Washington, DC: American Psychological Association.

Armstrong-Stassen, M. (1993). Production workers reactions to a plant closing: The role of transfer, stress and support. *Anxiety, Stress and Coping: An International Journal, 6*, 201–214.

Aronsson, G. (1999). Contingent workers and health and safety. *Work, Employment, and Society, 13*, 439–459.

Aryee, S. & Debrah, Y. A. (1997). Members' participation in the union: An investigation of some determinants in Singapore. *Human Relations, 50*, 129–147.

Aryee, S. & Chay, Y. W. (2001). Workplace justice, citizenship behavior, and turnover intention in a union context: examining the mediating role of perceived union support and union instrumentality. *Journal of Applied Psychology, 86*, 154–160.

Ashford, S. J. (1988). Individual strategies for coping with stress during organizational transitions. *Journal of Applied Behavioral Science, 24*, 19–36.

Ashford, S. J., Lee, C. & Bobko, P. (1989). Content, cause, and consequences of job insecurity: A theory-based measure and substantive test. *Academy of Management Journal, 32*(4), 803–829.

Augoustinos, M. & Walker, I. (1995). *Social Cognition: An integrated introduction*. London: Sage.

Bagozzi, R. P. (1978). The construct validity of the affective, behavioral, and cognitive components of attitude by analysis of covariance structures. *Multivariate Behavioral Research, 13*, 9–31.

Bagozzi, R. P. & Phillips, L. W. (1982). Representing and testing organizational theories: A holistic construal. *Administrative Science Quarterly, 27*, 459–489.

Bagozzi, R. P., Yi, Y. & Phillips, L. W. (1991). Assessing construct validity in organizational research. *Administrative Science Quarterly, 36*, 421–458.

Bandura, A. (1982). Self-efficacy mechanism in human agency. *American Psychologist, 37*, 122–147.

Bandura, A. (1997). *Self-efficacy: The exercise of control*. New York: Freeman.

Barling, J., Fullagar, C. & Kelloway, E. K. (1992). *The Union and Its Members: A psychological approach*. New York: Wiley.

Barling, J. & Gallagher, D. G. (1996). Part-time employment. In C. L. Cooper & I. T. Robertson (eds.), *International Review of Industrial and Organizational Psychology* (pp. 243–277). New York: Wiley.

Barling, J. & Kelloway, E. K. (1996). Job insecurity and health: The moderating role of workplace control. *Stress Medicine, 12*, 253–259.

Barnett, R. C. & Brennan, R. T. (1997). Change in job conditions, change in psychological distress, and gender: A longitudinal study of dual-earner couples. *Journal of Organizational Behavior, 18*(3), 253–274.

Beard, K. M. & Edwards, J. R. (1995). Employees at risk: Contingent work and the psychological experience of contingent workers. In C. L. Cooper & D. M. Rousseau (eds.), *Trends in Organizational Behavior* (Vol. 2, pp. 109–126). Chichester, UK: John Wiley & Sons.

Beaumont, P. B. (1995). *The Future of Employment Relations*. London: Sage.

Beehr, T. A., Farmer, S. J., Glazer, S., Gudanowski, D. M. & Nadig Nair, V. (2003). The enigma of social support and occupational stress: Source congruence and gender role effects. *Journal of Occupational Health Psychology, 8*, 220–231.

Bender, K. A. & Sloane, P. J. (1999). Trade union membership, tenure and the level of job insecurity. *Applied Economics, 31*, 123–135.

Bergman, P. & Wigblad, R. (1999). Workers' last performance: Why some factories show their best results during countdown. *Economic and Industrial Democracy, 20*, 343–368.

Billings, A. G. & Moos, R. H. (1982). Work stress and the stress-buffering roles of work and family resources. *Journal of Occupational Behavior, 3*, 215–232.

Bishop, G. D. (1994). *Health Psychology: Integrating mind and body*. Boston: Allyn and Bacon.

Bluen, S. D. & Edelstein, I. (1993). Trade union support following an underground explosion. *Journal of Organizational Behavior, 14*, 473–480.

Boeri, T., Brugiavini, A. & Calmfors, L. (eds.). (2001). *The Role of Unions in the Twenty-First Century: A study for the Fondazione Rudolfo Debenedetti*. Oxford: Oxford University Press.

Bollen, K. A. (1989). *Structural Equations with Latent Variables*. New York: Wiley.

Borg, I. & Elizur, D. (1992). Job insecurity: Correlates, moderators and measurement. *International Journal of Manpower, 13*, 13–26.

Bowman, G. D. & Stern, M. (1995). Adjustment to occupational stress: The relationship of perceived control to effectiveness of coping strategies. *Journal of Counseling Psychology, 42*, 294–303.

Boxall, P. & Haynes, P. (1997). Strategy and trade union effectiveness in a neo-liberal environment. *British Journal of Industrial Relations, 35*, 567–591.

Brayfield, A. H. & Rothe, H. F. (1951). An index of job satisfaction. *Journal of Applied Psychology, 35*, 307–311.

Brett, J. M. (1980). Behavioral research on unions and union management systems. In B. M. Staw & L. L. Cummings (eds.), *Research in Organizational Behavior* (Vol. 2, pp. 177–213). Greenwich, CT: JAI Press.

Brief, A. P., Burke, M. J., George, J. M., Robinson, B. S. & Webster, J. (1988). Should negative affectivity remain an unmeasured variable in the study of job stress? *Journal of Applied Psychology, 73*(2), 193–198.

Brockner, J., Grover, S., Reed, T., DeWitt, R. & O'Malley, M. (1987). Survivors' reactions to layoffs: We get by with a little help for our friends. *Administrative Science Quarterly, 32*, 526–541.

Brockner, J. (1988). The effect of work layoffs on survivors: Research, theory, and practice. In B. M. Staw & L. L. Cummings (eds.), *Research in Organizational Behavior* (Vol. 10, pp. 213–255). Greenwich, CT: JAI Press.

Brockner, J., Grover, S. L. & Blonder, M. D. (1988). Predictors of survivors' job involvement following layoffs: A field study. *Journal of Applied Psychology, 73*, 436–442.

Brockner, J. (1990). Scope of justice in the workplace: How survivors react to co-worker layoffs. *Journal of Social Issues, 46*, 95–106.

Brockner, J., DeWitt, R. L., Grover, S. L. & Reed, T. F. (1990). When it is especially important to explain why: Factors affecting the relationship between managers' explanations of a layoff and survivors' reactions to a layoff. *Journal of Experimental Social Psychology, 26*, 389–407.

Brockner, J. & Greenberg, J. (1990). The impact of layoffs on survivors: An organizational justice perspective. In J. S. Carroll (ed.), *Applied Social Psychology and Organizational Settings* (pp. 45–75). Hillsdale, NJ: Lawrence Erlbaum Associates.

Brockner, J., Grover, S., Reed, T. F. & DeWitt, R. L. (1992). Layoffs, job insecurity, and survivors' work effort: Evidence of an inverted-U relationship. *Academy of Management Journal, 35*, 413–425.

Brockner, J., Tyler, T. R. & Cooper-Schneider, R. (1992). The influence of prior commitment to an institution on reactions to perceived unfair-ness: The higher they are, the harder the fall. *Administrative Science Quartely, 37*, 241–261.

Browne, M. W. & Cudeck, R. (1993). Alternative ways of assessing model fit. In K. A. Bollen & J. S. Long (eds.), *Testing Structural Equation Models* (pp. 136–162). Newbury Park, CA.: Sage.

Burchell, B. (1994). The effects of labour market position, job insecurity and unemployment on psychological health. In C. Marsh, C. Vogler & D. Gallie (eds.), *Social Change and the Experience of Unemployment* (pp. 188–212). Oxford: Oxford University Press.

Burchell, B. J., Day, D., Hudson, M., Ladipo, D., Mankelow, R., Nolan, J. P., Reed, H., Wichert, I. C. & Wilkinson, F. (1999). *Job Insecurity and Work Intensification*. York: Joseph Rowntree Foundation.

Burchell, B. (2002). The prevalence and redistribution of job insecurity and work intensification. In B. Burchell, D. Ladipo & F. Wilkinson (eds.), *Job Insecurity and Work Intensification* (pp. 61–76). London: Routledge.

Burke, R. J. & Nelson, D. (1998). Mergers and acquisitions, downsizing, and privatization: A North American perspective. In M. K. Gowing, J. D. Kraft & J. C. Quick (eds.), *The New Organizational Reality: Downsizing, restructuring, and revitalization* (pp. 21–54). Washington, DC: American Psychological Association.

Burke, R. J. & Cooper, C. L. (eds.). (2000). *The Organization in Crisis; Downsizing, restructuring, and privatization*. Oxford: Blackwell.

Büssing, A. (1999). Can control at work and social support moderate psychological consequences of job insecurity? Results from a quasi-experimental study in the steel industry. *European Journal of Work and Organizational Psychology, 8*, 219–242.

Callan, V. J. (1993). Individual and organizational strategies for coping with organizational change. *Work and Stress, 1*, 63–75.

Cameron, K., Freeman, S. J. & Mishra, A. K. (1991). Best practice in white-collar downsizing: Managing contradictions. *Academy of Management Executive, 5*, 57–73.

Camman, C., Fishman, M., Jenkins, D. & Klesh, J. (1979). The Michigan Organizational Assessment Questionnaire. University of Michigan, Ann Arbor, MI: Unpublished manuscript.

Campbell, D. T. & Fiske, D. W. (1959). Convergent and discriminant validation by the multitrait-multimethod matrix. *Psychological Bulletin, 56*, 81–105.

Caplan, R. D., Cobb, S., French, J. R. P., van Harrison, R. & Pinneau, S. R. (1975). *Job Demands and Worker Health*. Washington, D. C.: National Institute for Occupational Safety and Health.

Cappelli, P. (1999). *The New Deal at Work: Managing the market-driven workforce*. Boston: Harvard Business School Press.

Carmines, E. G. & Zeller, R. A. (1979). *Reliability and Validity Assessment* (Vol. 07–017). Beverly Hills and London: Sage.

Cascio, W. F. (1995). Whither industrial and organizational psychology in a changing world of work. *American Psychologist, 11*, 928–939.

Cascio, W. F. (1998). Learning from outcomes: Financial experiences of 311 firms that have downsized. In M. K. Gowing, J. D. Kraft & J. C. Quick (eds.), *The New Organizational Reality: Downsizing, restructuring, and revitalization* (pp. 55–70). Washington, DC: American Psychological Association.

Cavanaugh, M. A. & Noe, R. A. (1999). Antecedents and consequences of relational components of the new psychological contract. *Journal of Organizational Behavior, 20*, 323–340.

Chirumbolo, A. & Hellgren, J. (2003). Individual and organizational consequences of job insecurity: A European study. *Economic and Industrial Democracy, 24*, 217–240.

CIETT. (2000). *Orchestrating the Evolution of Private Employment Agencies towards a Stronger Society*. Paris: International Confederation of Private Employment Agencies.

Cohen, S. & Wills, T. A. (1985). Stress, social support, and the buffering hypothesis. *Psychological Bulletin, 98*, 310–357.

Conway, N. & Briner, R. B. (2002). A daily diary study of affective responses to psychological contract breach and exceeded promises. *Journal of Organizational Behavior, 23*, 287–302.

Cook, T. D. & Campbell, D. T. (1979). *Quasi-Experimentation: Design & Analysis Issues for Field Settings*. Boston. MA: Houghton Mifflin.

Crockett, G. & Hall, K. (1987). Salaried professionals and union membership: An Australian perspective. *The Journal of Industrial Relations, 29*, 49–65.

Cronbach, L. J. (1951). Coefficient alpha and the internal structure of tests. *Psychometrika, 16*, 297–334.

Cronbach, L. J. & Meehl, P. E. (1955). Construct validity in psychological tests. *Psychological Bulletin, 52*, 281–302.

Curtin, J. (1997). Engendering union democracy: Comparing Sweden and Australia. In M. Sverke (ed.), *The Future of Trade Unionism: International perspectives on emerging union structures* (pp. 195–210). Aldershot: Ashgate.

Davy, J. A., Kinicki, A. J. & Scheck, C. L. (1997). A test of job security's direct and mediated effects on withdrawal cognitions. *Journal of Organizational Behavior, 18*, 323–349.

Dawson, P. (2003). *Understanding Organizational Change: The contemporary experience of people at work*. London: Sage.

de Vaus, D. A. (1991). *Surveys in Social Research* (3rd ed.). London: UCL Press Limited.

De Witte, H. (1999). Job insecurity and psychological well-being: Review of the literature and exploration of some unresolved issues. *European Journal of Work and Organizational Psychology, 8*, 155–177.

De Witte, H. (2000). Arbeidsethos en jobonzekerheid: Meting en gevolgen voor welszijn, tevredenheid en inzet op het werk [Work ethic and job insecurity: Assessment and consequences for well-being, satisfaction and performance at work]. In R. Bowen, K. De Witte, H. De Witte & T. Taillieu (eds.), *Van groep naar gemeenschap* [From group to community]. *Liber Amicorum Prof. Dr. Leo Lagrou* (pp. 325–350). Leuven: Garant.

De Witte, H. & Näswall, K. (2003). "Objective" vs. "Subjective" job insecurity: Consequences of temporary work for job satisfaction and organizational commitment in four European countries. *Economic and Industrial Democracy, 24*, 209–312.

Dekker, S. W. A. & Schaufeli, W. B. (1995). The effects of job insecurity on psychological health and withdrawal: A longitudinal study. *Australian Psychologist, 30*, 57–63.

Delsen, L. (1995). *Atypical Employment: An international perspective. Causes, consequences, and policy*. Groningen: Wolters-Noordhof.

Diener, E., Eunkook, M., Suh, M., Lucas, R. E. & Smith, L. H. (1999). Subjective well-being: Three decades of progress. *Psychological Bulletin, 125*, 276–302.

Domenighetti, G., D'Avanso, B. & Bisig, B. (2000). Health effects of job insecurity among employees in the Swiss general population. *International Journal of Health Services, 3*, 477–490.

Dworkin, J. B., Feldman, S. P., Brown, J. M. & Hobson, C. J. (1988). Workers preference in concession bargaining. *Industrial Relations, 27*, 7–20.

Ebbinghaus, B. & Visser, J. (2000). *Trade Unions in Western Europe since 1945*. London: MacMillan.

Eisenberger, R., Huntington, R., Hutchinson, S. & Sowa, D. (1986). Perceived organizational support. *Journal of Applied Psychology, 71*, 500–507.

Ekehammar, B. (1974). Interactionism in personality from a historical perspective. *Psychological Bulletin, 81*, 1026–1048.

Elliott, L. & Atkinson, D. (1998). *The Age of Insecurity*. London: Verso.

Elsass, P. M. & Veiga, J. F. (1997). Job control and strain: A test of three models. *Journal of Occupational Health Psychology, 2*, 195–211.

Endler, N. & Magnusson, D. (1976). Toward and interactional psychology of personality. *Psychological Bulletin, 83*, 956–974.

Erikson, E. H. (1959). Identity and the life cycle. *Psychological Issues, 1*, 50–100.

European Commission. (2001). *Employment in Europe: Recent trends and prospects*. Luxembourg: Office for Official Publications of the European Communities.

European Foundation. (2001). *Third European Survey on Working Conditions 2000*. Dublin: European Foundation for the Improvement of Living and Working Conditions.

Fagan, C. & Burchell, B. (2002). *Gender, Jobs and Working Conditions in the European Union*. Dublin: European Foundation for the Improvement of Living and Working Conditions.

Ferner, A. & Hyman, R. (1998). Introduction: Towards European industrial relations. In A. Ferner & R. Hyman (eds.), *Changing Industrial Relations in Europe* (pp. xi–xxvi). Oxford: Blackwell.

Ferrie, J. E., Shipley, M. J., Marmot, M. G., Stansfeld, S. & Smith, G. D. (1995). Health effects of anticipation of job change and non-employment: Longitudinal data from the Whitehall 2 study. *British Medical Journal, 311*, 1264–1269.

Ferrie, J. E., Shipley, M. J., Marmot, M. G., Stansfeld, S. A. & Smith, G. D. (1998). An uncertain future: The health effects of threats to employment security in white-collar men and women. *American Journal of Public Health, 88*, 1030–1036.

Frankenhaeuser, M. & Johansson, G. (1986). Stress at work: Psycholbiological and psychosocial aspects. *International Review of Applied Psychology, 35*, 287–299.

Freeman, R. B. & Medoff, J. L. (1984). *What Do Unions Do?* New York: Basic Books.

Frese, M. (1985). Stress at work and psychosomatic complaints: A causal interpretation. *Journal of Applied Psychology, 70*, 314–328.

Frese, M. (1999). Social support as a moderator of the relationship between work stressors and psychological dysfunctioning: A longitudinal study with objective measures. *Journal of Occupational Health Psychology, 4*, 179–192.

Fried, Y. & Tiegs, R. B. (1993). The main effect model versus buffering model of shop steward social support: A study of rank-and-file auto workers in the USA. *Journal of Organizational Behavior, 14*, 481–493.

Furda, J. & Meijman, T. (1992). Druk en dreiging, sturing of stress [Pressure and threat, control and stress]. In J. Winnubst & M. Schabracq (eds.), *Handboek arbeid en gezondheid psychologie. Hoofdthema's* [Handbook on Work and Health Psychology. Core topics] (pp. 127–144). Utrecht: Uitgeverij Lemma.

Gallagher, D. G. & Strauss, G. (1991). Union membership attitudes and participation. In G. Strauss, D. G. Gallagher & J. Fiorito (eds.), *The State of the Unions* (pp. 139–174). Madison, WI: Industrial Relations Research Association.

Gallagher, D. G. & Sverke, M. (2000). *Contingent Employment Contracts: Are existing theories still relevant?* Paper presented at the The 12th World Congress on Industrial Relations Research Association, Tokyo, Japan.

Gallie, D., White, M., Cheng, Y. & Tomlinson, M. (1998). *Restructuring the Employment Relationship*. Oxford: Clarendon Press.

Ganster, D. C. & Fusilier, M. R. (1989). Control in the workplace. In C. L. Cooper & I. Robertson (eds.), *International Review of Industrial and Organizational Psychology* (pp. 235–280). London: Wiley.

Garst, H., Frese, M. & Molenaar, P. C. M. (2000). The temporal factor of change in stressor-strain relationships: A growth curve model on a longitudinal study in east germany. *Journal of Applied Psychology, 85*, 417–438.

Gold, M. & Weiss, M. (eds.). (1998). *Employment and Industrial Relations in Europe* (Vol. 1). Luxembourg: Office for Official Publications of the European Communities.

Goldberg, D. (1972). *The Detection of Psychiatric Illness by Questionnaire*. London: Oxford University Press.

Goldberg, D. (1979). *Manual of the General Health Questionnaire*. London: NFER Nelson.

Gordon, M. E., Philbot, J. W., Burt, R. E., Thompson, C. A. & Spiller, W. E. (1980). Commitment to the union: Development of a measure and an examination of its correlates. *Journal of Applied Psychology, 65*, 479–499.

Gorsuch, R. L. (1997). Explanatory factor analysis: Its role in item analysis. *Journal of Personality Assessment, 68*, 532–560.

Goslinga, S. (1996). *Voor wat hoort wat: Een ruiltheoretische benadering van vakbondsbinding* [Tit for tat: a social exchange perspective on union commitment]. Paper presented at the WESWA congress, Utrecht.

Goslinga, S. (1997). Relative groepsgrootte, binding en ingroep-favoritisme: Een onderzoek onder vakbondsleden [Relative group size, commitment and ingroup-favoritism: a study among union members]. In D. Daamen, A. Pruyn, W. Otten & R. Meertens (eds.), *Sociale psychologie en haar toepassingen* [Social psychology and its applications] (Vol. 11, pp. 41–54). Delft: Eburon.

Goslinga, S. (2001). Betrokkenheid bij een belangenorganisatie: De ontwikkeling van een meetinstrument op basis van het 3-componenten model van organisatiebetrokkenheid [Commitment to an interest group: the development of a measure based on the 3-component model of organizational commitment]. *Gedrag en Organisatie, 14*, 191–200.

Goslinga, S. & Klandermans, B. (2001). Union participation in the Netherlands: Differences between traditional and "new" employees. In G. Van Gyes, H. De Witte & P. Pasture (eds.), *Can Class Still Unite? The differentiated workforce, class solidarity and trade unions* (pp. 171–189). Aldershot: Ashgate.

Goslinga, S. & Sverke, M. (2003). Atypical work and trade union membership: Union attitudes and union turnover among traditional vs. atypically employed union members. *Economic and Industrial Democracy, 24*, 209–312.

Goudswaard, A. & de Nanteuil, M. (2000). *Flexibility and Working Conditions: The impact of flexibility strategies on "Conditions of work" and "Conditions of employment": A qualitative and comparative study in seven EU member states.* Dublin: European Foundation for the Improvement of Living and Working Conditions.

Greenhalgh, L. & Rosenblatt, Z. (1984). Job Insecurity: Toward conceptual clarity. *Academy of Management Review, 9*, 438–448.

Greenhalgh, L. (1991). Organizational coping strategies. In J. Hartley, D. Jacobson, B. Klandermans & T. Van Vuuren (eds.), *Job Insecurity* (pp. 172–198). London: Sage.

Greenhalgh, L. & Sutton, R. (1991). Organizational effectiveness and job insecurity. In J. Hartley, D. Jacobson, B. Klandermans & T. Van Vuuren (eds.), *Job insecurity* (pp. 151–171). London: Sage.

Griffin, R. & Bateman, T. (1986). Job satisfaction and organizational commitment. In C. L. Cooper & I. Robertson (eds.), *International Review of Industrial and Organizational Psychology* (pp. 157–188). New York: Wiley.

Gruen, W. (1954). A theoretical examination of the concept of dual allegiance. *Personnel Psychology, 7*, 72–80.

Guest, D. E. & Dewe, P. (1991). Company or trade union: Which wins workers allegiance? A study of commitment in UK Electronic Industry. *British Journal of Industrial Relations, 29*, 75–96.

Hackman, J. R. & Oldham, G. R. (1975). Development of the Job Diagnostic Survey. *Journal of Applied Psychology, 6*), 159–170.

Hart, P. M. & Cooper, C. L. (2001). Occupational stress: Toward a more integrated framework. In N. Anderson, D. S. Onez, H. K. Sinangil &

C. Viswesvaran (eds.), *Handbook of Industrial, Work, and Organizational Psychology* (Vol. 2, pp. 93–114). London: Sage.

Hartley, J. F. & Klandermans, P. G. (1986). Individual and collective responses to job insecurity. In G. Debus & H.-W. Schroiff (eds.), *The Psychology of Work and Organization* (pp. 129–136). Amsterdam: Elsevier Science Publishers.

Hartley, J. (1991). Industrial relations and job insecurity: A social psychological framework. In J. Hartley, D. Jacobsson, B. Klandermans & T. Van Vuuren (eds.), *Job Insecurity* (pp. 104–122). London: Sage.

Hartley, J., Jacobson, D., Klandermans, B. & Van Vuuren, T. (1991). *Job Insecurity*. London: Sage.

Hartley, J. F. (1995). Challenge and change in employment relations: Issues for psychology, trade unions, and managers. In L. E. Tetrick & J. Barling (eds.), *Changing Employment Relations: Behavioral and social perspectives* (pp. 3–30). Washington, DC: American Psychological Association.

Heaney, C. A., Israel, B. A. & House, J. S. (1994). Chronic job insecurity among automobile workers: Effects on job satisfaction and health. *Social Science and Medicine, 38*, 1431–1437.

Heaney, C. A., Price, R. H. & Rafferty, J. (1995). Increasing coping resources at work: A field experiment to increase social support, improve work team functioning, and enhance employee mental health. *Journal of Organizational Behavior, 16*, 335–352.

Heery, E. & Salmon, J. (eds.). (2000). *The Insecure Workforce*. London: Routledge.

Heller, F., Pusic, E., Strauss, G. & Wilpert, B. (1998). *Organizational Participation: Myth and reality*. Oxford: Oxford University Press.

Hellgren, J., Sjöberg, A. & Sverke, M. (1997). Intention to quit: Effects of job satisfaction and job perceptions. In F. Avallone, J. Arnold & K. De Witte (eds.), *Feelings Work in Europe* (pp. 415–423). Milano: Guerini.

Hellgren, J., Sverke, M. & Isaksson, K. (1999). A two-dimensional approach to job insecurity: Consequences for employee attidtudes and well-being. *European Journal of Work and Organizational Psychology, 8*, 179–195.

Hellgren, J. & Sverke, M. (2001). Unionized employees' perceptions of role stress and fairness during organizational downsizing: Consequences for job satisfaction, union satisfaction and well-being. *Economic and Industrial Democracy, 22*, 543–567.

Hellgren, J. & Chirumbolo, A. (2003). Can union support reduce the negative effects of job insecurity on well-being? *Economic and Industrial Democracy, 24*, 271–289.

Hellgren, J. & Sverke, M. (2003). Does job insecurity lead to impaired well-being or vice versa? Estimation of cross-lagged effects using latent variable modeling. *Journal of Organizational Behavior, 24*, 215–236.

Hirschman, A. O. (1970). *Exit, Voice, and Loyalty: Responses to decline in firms, organizations, and states.* Cambridge, MA: Harvard University Press.

House, J. S. (1981). *Work Stress and Social Support.* Reading, MA: Addison-Wesley.

Howard, A. (1995). *The Changing Nature of Work.* San Fransisco, CA: Jossey-Bass.

Hyman, R. (1996). Changing union identities in Europe. In P. Leisink, J. Van Leemput & J. Vilrokx (eds.), *The Challenges to Trade Unions in Europe: Innovation or adaptation.* Cheltenham: Edward Elgar.

ILO. (2000). *Yearbook of Labor Statistics.* Geneva: International Labour Office.

Isaksson, K. & Johansson, G. (1997). *Avtalspension med vinst och förlust: Konsekvenser för företag och medarbetare* [Early retirement agreement for better or worse: Consequences for companies and workers]. Stockholm: Folksam.

Isaksson, K., Pettersson, P. & Hellgren, J. (1998). Utvecklingscentrum: En verksamhet för uppsagda tjänstemän i KF [Development center: An activity for downsized salaried employees]. *Arbetsmarknad & Arbetsliv, 4,* 22–43.

Isaksson, K., Hellgren, J. & Petterson, P. (1999). Repeated downsizing: Attitudes and well-being for surviving personnel in a Swedish retail company. In K. Isaksson, C. Hogstedt, C. Eriksson & T. Theorell (eds.), *Health Effects of the New Labour Market* (pp. 85–101). New York: Kluwer Academic/Plenum Publishers.

Ivanchevich, J. M. (1974). Effects of the shorter workweek on selected satisfaction and performance measures. *Journal of Applied Psychology, 59,* 717–721.

Iverson, R. D. (1996). Employee acceptence of organizational change: The role of organizational commitment. *The International Journal of Human Resource Management, 7,* 122–149.

Jackson, P. B. (1992). Specifying the buffering hypothesis: Support, strain, and depression. *Social Psychology Quarterly, 55,* 363–378.

Jacobson, D. (1991a). The concepual approach to job insecurity. In J. Hartley, D. Jacobsson, B. Klandermans & T. Van Vuuren (eds.), *Job Insecurity* (pp. 23–39). London: Sage.

Jacobson, D. (1991b). Toward a theoretical distinction between the stress components of the job insecurity and job loss experiences. *Research in the Sociology of Organizations, 9,* 1–19.

Jacobson, D. & Hartley, J. (1991). Mapping the context. In J. Hartley, D. Jacobsson, B. Klandermans & T. Van Vuuren (eds.), *Job Insecurity* (pp. 2–22). London: Sage.

Jahoda, M. (1982). *Employment and Unemployment: A social-psychological analysis.* Cambridge, MA: Cambridge University Press.

Jenkins, A. (1998). Flexibility, "Individualization", and employment insecurity in France. *European Journal of Work and Organizational Psychology, 7*, 23–38.

Jex, S. M. & Beehr, T. A. (1991). Emerging theoretical and methodological issues in the study of work-related stress. In K. Rowland & G. Ferries (eds.), *Research in Personnel and Human Resources Management* (Vol. 9, pp. 311–365). Greenwich, CT: JAI Press.

Jick, T. D. (1985). As the axe falls: Budget cuts and the experience of stress in organizations. In T. A. Beehr & R. S. Bhagat (eds.), *Human Stress and Cognition in Organizations: An integrated perspective* (pp. 83–114). New York: Wiley.

Joelson, M. & Wahlquist, L. (1987). The psychological meaning of job insecurity and job loss: The results of a longitudinal study. *Social Science and Medicine, 25*, 179–182.

Johnson, C. D., Messe, L. A. & Crano, W. D. (1984). Predicting job performance of low income workers: The work opinion questionnaire. *Personnel Psychology, 37*, 291–299.

Johnson, N. B., Bobko, P. & Hartenian, L. S. (1992). Union influence and local union leaders' perceptions of job insecurity: An empirical test. *British Journal of Industrial Relations, 30*, 45–60.

Johnson, W. R. & Johnson, G. J. (1992). Union performance and union loyalty: The role of perceived steward support. *Journal of Applied Social Psychology, 22*, 677–690.

Judge, T. A., Locke, E. A., Durham, C. C. & Kluger, A. N. (1998). Dispositional effects on job and life satisfaction: The role of core evaluations. *Journal of Applied Psychology, 83*, 17–34.

Judge, T. A., Thoresen, C. J., Pucik, V. & Welbourne, T. M. (1999). Managerial coping with organizational change: A dispositional perspective. *Journal of Applied Psychology, 84*, 107–122.

Jöreskog, K.-G. & Sörbom, D. (1996). *Lisrel 8: Users Reference Guide.* Chicago, IL: Scientific Software.

Karasek, R. A. & Theorell, T. (1990). *Healthy Work: Stress, productivity, and the reconstruction of working life.* New York: Basic Books.

Katz, D. & Kahn, R. L. (1978). *The Social Psychology of Organizations* (2nd ed.). New York: Wiley.

Ketz de Vries, M. F. R. & Balazs, K. (1997). The downside of downsizing. *Human Relations, 50*, 11–50.

Kieselbach, T. (ed.). (2003). *Social Convoy in Occupational Transitions: Recommendations for a European framework in the context of enterprise restructuring.* Bremen: University of Bremen.

King, J. E. (2000). White-collar reactions to job insecurity and the role of the psychological contract: Implications for human service management. *Human Resource Management, 1*, 79–92.

Kinnunen, U. & Nätti, J. (1994). Job insecurity in Finland: Antecedents and consequences. *The European Work and Organizational Psychologist, 4*, 297–321.

Kinnunen, U., Mauno, S., Nätti, J. & Happonen, M. (1999). Perceived job insecurity: A longitudinal study among Finnish employees. *European Journal of Work and Organizational Psychology, 8*, 243–260.

Kinnunen, U., Mauno, S., Nätti, J. & Happonen, M. (2000). Organizational antecedents and outcomes of job insecurity: A longitudinal study in three organizations in Finland. *Journal of Organizational Behavior, 21*, 443–459.

Kjellberg, A. (1998). Sweden: Restoring the model. In A. Ferner & R. Hyman (eds.), *Changing Industrial Relations in Europe* (pp. 74–117). Oxford: Blackwell.

Kjellberg, A. (2000). The multitude of challenges facing Swedish trade unions. In J. Waddington & R. Hoffman (eds.), *Trade Unions in Europe: Facing challenges and searching for solutions* (pp. 529–573). Brussels: European Trade Union Institute.

Kjellberg, A. (2001). *Fackliga organisationer och medlemmar i dagens Sverige* [Union organizations and members in contemporary Sweden]. Lund: Arkiv.

Kjellberg, A. (2002). Ett fackligt landskap i omvandling [The changing union landscape]. In M. Sverke & J. Hellgren (eds.), *Medlemmen, facket och flexibiliteten: Svensk fackföreningsrörelse i det moderna arbetslivet* [The member, the union, and the flexibility: Swedish unionism in the modern working life] (pp. 27–51). Lund: Arkiv.

Klandermans, B. (1986). Psychology and trade union participation: Joining, acting, quitting. *Journal of Occupational Psychology, 59*, 189–204.

Klandermans, B. (1989). Union commitment: Replications and tests in the Dutch context. *Journal of Applied Psychology, 74*, 869–875.

Klandermans, B., Van Vuuren, T. & Jacobson, D. (1991). Employees and job insecurity. In J. Hartley, D. Jacobsson, B. Klandermans & T. Van Vuuren (eds.), *Job Insecurity* (pp. 41–64). London: Sage.

Klandermans, B. & van Vuuren, T. (1999). Job insecurity: Introduction. *European Journal of Work and Organizational Psychology, 8*, 145–153.

Klein Hesselink, D. & Van Vuuren, T. (1999). Job flexibility and job insecurity: The Dutch case. *European Journal of Work and Organizational Psychology, 8*, 273–293.

Kochan, T. A. (1980). Collective bargaining and organizational behavior research. *Research in Organizational Behavior, 2*, 129–176.

Korpi, W. (1978). *The Working Class in Welfare Capitalism: Work, unions and politics in Sweden.* London: Routledge and Kegan Paul.

Koukolaki, T. (2002). Stress prevention in Europe: Review of trade union activities – Obstacles and future strategies. *TUTB Newsletter, 19–20,* 4–11.

Kozlowski, S., Chao, G., Smith, E. & Hedlund, J. (1993). Organisational downsizing: Strategies, interventions and research. In C. L. Cooper & I. T. Robertson (eds.), *International Review of Industrial and Organizational Psychology* (Vol. 8, pp. 263–332). Chichester: Wiley.

Kuhnert, K. W., Sims, R. R. & Lahey, M. A. (1989). The relationship between job security and employee health. *Group and Organization Studies, 14,* 399–410.

Kuruvilla, S., Gallagher, D. G. & Wetzel, K. (1993). The development of members' attitudes toward their unions: Sweden and Canada. *Industrial and Labor Relations Review, 46,* 499–514.

LaRocco, J. M., House, J. S. & French, J. R. P. (1980). Social support, occupational stress, and health. *Journal of Health and Social Behavior, 21,* 202–218.

Latack, J. C. & Dozier, J. B. (1986). After the axe falls: Job loss on a career transition. *Academy of Management Review, 11,* 375–392.

Lazarus, R. S. & Folkman, S. (1984). *Stress, Appraisal, and Coping.* New York: Springer Publishing Company, Inc.

Lester, S. W., Turnley, J. M., Bloodgood, J. M. & Bolino, M. C. (2002). Not seeing eye to eye: Differences in supervisor and subordinate perceptions of and attributions for psychological contract breach. *Journal of Organizational Behavior, 23,* 39–56.

Letourneux, V. (1998). *Precarious Employment and Working Conditions in Europe.* Dublin: European Foundation for the Improvement of Living and Working Conditions.

Levanoni, E. & Sales, C. A. (1990). Differences in job attitudes between full-time and part-time Canadian employees. *Journal of Social Psychology, 130,* 231–237.

Levi, L. (1999). Empowerment, learning and social action during employment. In K. Isaksson, C. Hogstedt, C. Eriksson & T. Theorell (eds.), *Health Effects of the New Labour Market* (pp. 75–84). New York: Kluwer Academic / Plenum Publishers.

Lewis, P. & Murphy, L. (1991). A theory of trade union membership retention. *British Journal of Industrial Relations, 29,* 277–293.

Lim, V. K. G. (1996). Job insecurity and its ocutcomes: Moderating effects of work-based and nonwork-based social support. *Human Relations, 49,* 171–194.

Lind, J. (1996). Trade unions: Social movement or welfare apparatus? In P. Leisink, J. Van Leemput & J. Vilkrox (eds.), *The Challenged to Trade Unions in Europe: Innovation or adaptation.* Cheltenham: Edward Elgar.

Lindström, K., Leino, T., Seitsamo, J. & Torstila, I. (1997). A longitudinal study of work characteristics and health complaints among insurance employees in VDT work. *International Journal of Human-Computer Interaction, 9,* 343–368.

Locke, E. A. (1976). The nature and causes of job satisfaction. In M. Dunnette (ed.), *Handbook of Industrial and Organizational Psychology* (pp. 1297–1349). Chicago: Rand McNally.

Lovenduski, J. (1986). *Women in European Politics.* Brighton, UK: Wheatsheaf Books.

Lundberg, U. & Frankenhaeuser, M. (1978). Psychophysiological reactions to noise as modified by personal control over noise intensity. *Biological Psychology, 6,* 51–59.

Lyons, T. F. (1971). Role clarity, need for clarity, satisfaction, tension, and withdrawal. *Organizational Behavior and Human Performance, 6,* 99–110.

Martin, G., Staines, H. & Pate, J. (1998). Linking job security and career development in a new psychological contract. *Human Resource Management Journal, 8,* 20–40.

Mathieu, J. E. & Zajac, D. M. (1990). A review and meta-analysis of the antecedents, correlates, and consequences of organizational commitment. *Psychological Bulletin, 108,* 171–194.

Matteson, M. T. & Ivancevich, J. M. (1990). Merger and acquisition stress: Fear and uncertainty at mid-career. *Prevention in Human Sevices, 8,* 139–158.

Mattiasson, I., Lindgärde, F., Nilsson, J. A. & Theorell, T. (1990). Threat of unemployment and cardiovascular risk factors: Longitudinal study of quality of sleep and serum cholesterol concentration in men threatened with redundancy. *British Medical Journal, 301,* 461–466.

Mauno, S., Leskinen, E. & Kinnunen, U. (2001). Multi-wave, multi-variable models of job insecurity: Applying different scales in studying the stability of job insecurity. *Journal of Organizational Behavior, 22,* 919–937.

McDonough, P. (2000). Job insecurity and health. *International Journal of Health Services, 3,* 453–476.

McFarlane Shore, L. & Tetrick, L. (1991). A construct validity study of the survey of perceived organizational support. *Journal of Applied Psychology, 76,* 637–643.

McLean Parks, J., Kidder, D. L. & Gallagher, D. G. (1998). Fitting square pegs into round holes: Mapping the domain of contingent work arrangements onto the psychological contract. *Journal of Organizational Behavior, 19,* 697–730.

Mellor, S. (1992). The influence of layoff severity on postlayoff union commitment among survivors: The moderating effect of the perceived legitimacy of a layoff account. *Personnel Psychology, 45,* 579–600.

Messick, S. (1975). The standard problem: Meaning and values in measurement and evaluation. *American Psychologist, 30,* 955–966.

Messick, S. (1995). Validity of psychological assessment: Validation of inferences from persons' responses and performances as scientific inquiry score meaning. *Copyright 1995 by the American Psychological Association. Inc., 50,* 741–749.

Meyer, J. P., Allen, N. J. & Smith, C. A. (1993). Commitment to organizations and occupations: Extension and test of a three component conceptualization. *Journal of Applied Psychology, 78,* 538–551.

Meyer, J. P. (1997). Organizational commitment. In C. L. Cooper & I. T. Robertson (eds.), *International Review of Industrial and Organizational Psychology* (Vol. 12, pp. Chapter 5). New York: Wiley & Sons.

Mohr, G. B. (2000). The changing significance of different stressors after the announcement of bankruptcy: A longitudinal investigation with special emphasis on job insecurity. *Journal of Organizational Behavior, 21,* 337–359.

Morrisson, E. W. & Robinson, S. L. (1997). When employees feel betrayed: A model of how psychological contract violation develop. *Academy of Management Review, 22,* 226–256.

Morrow, P. C. (1983). Concept redundancy in organizational research: The case of work commitment. *Academy of Management Review, 8,* 486–500.

Mowday, R. T., Steers, R. M. & Porter, L. W. (1979). The measurement of organizational commitment. *Journal of Vocational Behavior, 14,* 224–247.

Mulaik, S. A. (1988). Confirmatory factor analysis. In J. R. Nesselroade & R. B. Cattell (eds.), *Handbook of Experimental Psychology* (pp. 259–288). New York: Plenum Press.

Nelson, D. D. (1985). Informal testing as a means of questionnaire development. *Journal of Official Statistics, 1,* 179–188.

Noer, D. (1993). *Healing the Wounds: Overcoming the trauma of layoffs and revitalizing downsized organizations.* San Francisco: Jossey-Bass.

Nunnally, J. C. (1978). *Psychometric Theory.* New York, NY: McGraw-Hill.

Näswall, K., Sverke, M. & Hellgren, J. (2001). Tryggare kan ingen vara? Metaanalys av relationen mellan anställningsotrygghet och välbefinnande [No one can be safer? Meta-analysis of the relationship between job insecurity and well-being]. *Arbetsmarknad & Arbetsliv, 7,* 179–195.

Näswall, K. & De Witte, H. (2003). Who feels insecure in Europe? Predicting job insecurity from background variables. *Economic and Industrial Democracy, 24,* 187–213.

OECD. (1997). Is job insecurity on the increase in OECD countries? *OECD Employment Outlook July* (pp. 129–153). Paris: Office for Economic Cooperation and Development.

OECD. (1999). *Employment Outlook*. Paris: Office for Economic Cooperation and Development.

OECD. (2002a). *Employment Outlook*. Paris: Office for Economic Cooperation and Development.

OECD. (2002b). *Labor Force Statistics 1981–2001*. Paris: Office for Economic Cooperation and Development.

Organ, D. W. (1988). *Organizational Citizenship Behavior: The good soldier syndrome*. Lexington, MA: Issues in organization and management series.

Parkes, K. R. (1994). Personality and coping as moderators of work stress processes: Models, methods and measures. *Work & Stress, 8*, 110–129.

Pearce, J. L. (1998). Job insecurity is important but not for the reasons you might think: The example of contingent workers. In C. L. Cooper & D. M. Rousseau (eds.), *Trends in Organizational Behavior* (Vol. 5, pp. 31–46). New York, NY: Wiley.

Peterson, C. & Stunkard, A. J. (1989). Personal control and health promotion. *Social Science and Medicine, 28*, 819–828.

Pfeffer, J. (1998). *The Human Equation*. Boston, Ma: Harvard Business School Press.

Podsakoff, P. M., MacKenzie, S., Moorman, R. H. & Fetter, R. (1990). Transformational leader behaviors and their effects on followers' trust in leader, satisfaction, and organizational citizenship behaviors. *Leadership Quarterly, 1*, 107–142.

Premack, S. L. & Hunter, J. E. (1988). Individual unionization decisions. *Psychological Bulletin, 103*, 223–234.

Probst, T. M. & Brubaker, T. L. (2001). The effects of job insecurity on employee safety outcomes: Cross-sectional and longitudinal explorations. *Journal of Occupational Health Psychology, 6*, 139–159.

Purcell, K. & Purcell, J. (1998). In-sourcing, outsourcing, and the growth of contingent labour as evidence of flexible employment strategies. *European Journal of Work and Organizational Psychology, 7*, 39–59.

Quick, J. C., Quick, J. D., Nelson, D. L. & Hurrell, J. J. (eds.). (1997). *Preventive Stress Management in Organizations*. Washington, DC: American Psychological Association.

Rajan, A. (1997). Employability in the finance sector: Rhetoric vs. reality. *Human Resource Management Journal, 7*, 67–78.

Regalia, I. & Regini, M. (1998). Italy: The dual character of industrial relations. In A. Ferner & R. Hyman (eds.), *Changing Industrial Relations in Europe* (pp. 459–503). Oxford: Blackwell.

Regini, M. & Regalia, I. (2000). Italy: The prospects for Italian trade unions in a phase of concertation. In J. Waddington & R. Hoffman (eds.), *Trade Unions in Europe: Facing challenges and searching for solutions* (pp. 365–392). Brussles: European Trade Union Institute.

Reilly, P. A. (1998). Balancing flexibility – meeting the interests of employer and employee. *European Journal of Work and Organization Psychology, 7*, 7–22.

Reisel, W. D. & Banai, M. (2002). Comparison of a multidimensional and a global measure of job insecurity: Predicting job attitudes and work behaviors. *Psychological Reports, 90*, 913–922.

Rifkin, J. (1995). *The End of Work: The decline of the global labor force and the dawn of the post-market era.* New York: Putnam.

Rizzo, J. R., House, R. J. & Lirtzman, S. I. (1970). Role conflict and ambiguity in complex organizations. *Administrative Science Quarterly, 15*, 150–163.

Robinson, S. L., Kraatz, M. S. & Rousseau, D. M. (1994). Changing obligations and the psychological contract: A longitudinal study. *Academy of Management Journal, 37*, 137–152.

Robinson, S. L. & Rosseau, D. M. (1994). Violating the psychological contract: Not the exception but the norm. *Journal of Organizational Behavior, 15*, 245–259.

Robinson, S. L. (1995). Violations of psychological contracts: Impact on employee attitudes. In L. E. Tetrick & J. Barling (eds.), *Changing Employment Relations: Behavioral and social perspectives* (pp. 91–108). Washington, DC: American Psychological Association.

Robinson, S. L. & Morrison, E. W. (1995). Psychological contracts and OCB: The effect of unfulfilled obligations on civic virtue behavior. *Journal of Organizational Behavior, 16*, 289–298.

Robinson, S. L. (1996). Trust and breach of the psychological contract. *Administrative Science Quarterly, 41*, 574–599.

Robinson, S. L. & Morrison, E. W. (2000). The development of psychological contract breach and violation: A longitudinal study. *Journal of Organizational Behavior, 21*, 525–546.

Rosenblatt, Z. & Ruvio, A. (1996). A test of a multidimensional model of job insecurity: The case of Israeli teachers. *Journal of Organizational Behavior, 17*, 587–605.

Rosenblatt, Z., Talmud, I. & Ruvio, A. (1999). A gender-based framework of the experience of job insecurity and its effects on work attitudes. *European Journal of Work and Organizational Psychology, 8*, 197–217.

Roskies, E. & Louis-Guerin, C. (1990). Job insecurity in managers: Antecedents and consequences. *Journal of Organizational Behavior, 11*, 345–359.

Roskies, E., Louis-Guerin, C. & Fournier, C. (1993). Coping with job insecurity: How does personality make a difference? *Journal of Organizational Behavior, 14*, 617–630.

Rothstein, B. (1992). Labour market institutions and working-class strength. In S. Steinmo, K. Thelen & F. Longstreth (eds.), *Structuring Politics: Historical institutionalism in comparative analysis* (pp. 33–56). Cambridge: Cambridge University Press.

Rotter, J. B. (1966). Generalized expectancies for internal versus external control of reinforcement. *Psychological Monographs, 80* (Whole No. 609).

Rousseau, D. M. (1989). Psychological and implied contracts in organizations. *Employee Responsibilities and Rights Journal, 2*, 121–139.

Rousseau, D. M. & McLean Parks, J. M. (1993). The contract of individuals and organizations. In B. M. Staw & L. L. Cummings (eds.), *Research in Organizational Behavior* (pp. 1–43). Greenwich, CT: JAI Press.

Rousseau, D. (1995). *Psychological Contracts in Organizations. Understanding written and unwritten agreements.* Thousand Oaks: Sage.

Schalk, R., Freese, C. & Van den Bosch, J. (1995). Het psychologisch contract van part-timers en full-timers. Een onderzoek naar de verwachtingen van werknemers [The psychological contract of part-time and full-time employees: An investigation into the expectations of employees]. *Gedrag en Organisatie, 8*, 307–317.

Schaubroeck, J., Ganster, D. C. & Fox, M. L. (1992). Dispositional affect and work-related stress. *Journal of Applied Psychology, 77*, 322–335.

Schaufeli, W. (1992). Unemployment and mental health in well and poorly educated school-leavers. In C. Verhaar & L. Jansma (eds.), *On the Mysteries of Unemployment: Causes, consequences and policies.* (pp. 253–271). Dordecht, the Netherlands: Kluwer Academic Publishers.

Scheck, C. L., Kinicki, A. J. & Davy, J. A. (1997). Testing the mediating processes between work stressors and subjective well-being. *Journal of Vocational Behavior, 50*, 96–123.

Shaw, J. B., Fields, W. M., Thacker, J. W. & Fisher, C. D. (1993). The availability of personal and external coping resources: Their impact on job stress and employee attitudes during organizational restructuring. *Work & Stress, 7*, 229–246.

Sherer, M., Maddux, J. E., Mercandante, B., Prentice-Dunn, S., Jacobs, B. & Rogers, R. W. (1982). The self-efficacy scale: Construction and validation. *Psychological Reports, 51*, 663–671.

Sherer, P. D. (1996). Toward an understanding of the variety in work arrangements: The organization and labor relationships framework. In C. L. Cooper & D. M. Rousseau (eds.), *Trends in Organizational Behavior* (Vol. 3, pp. 99–122). New York, NY: Wiley.

Shore, L. M., Tetrick, L. E., Sinclair, R. R. & Newton, L. A. (1994). Validation of a measure of perceived union support. *Journal of Applied Psychology, 70,* 971–977.

Siegrist, J., Peter, R., Junge, A., Cremer, P. & Siegel, D. (1990). Low status control, high effort at work and ischemic heart disease: Prospective evidence from blue-collar men. *Social Science and Medicine, 31,* 1127–1134.

Siegrist, J. (1996). Adverse health effects of high–effort/low–reward conditions. *Journal of Occupational Health Psychology, 1,* 27–41.

Siegrist, J. (2000). Adverse health effects of effort–reward imbalance at work: Theory, empirical support, and implications for prevention. In C. L. Cooper (ed.), *Theories of Organizational Stress* (pp. 190–204). Oxford: Oxford University Press.

Sinclair, R. R. & Tetrick, L. E. (1995). Social exchange and union commitment: A comparison of union instrumentality and union support perceptions. *Journal of Organizational Behavior, 16,* 669–680.

Sjöberg, A. & Sverke, M. (1996). Predicting turnover intentions among nurses: The role of work values. In V. V. Baba (ed.), *Work Values and Behaviour: Research and applications* (pp. 213–223). Montréal: International Society for the Study of Work and Organizational Values.

Sjöberg, A. & Sverke, M. (2000). The interactive effect of job involvement and organizational commitment on job turnover revisited: A note on the mediating role of turnover intention. *Scandinavian Journal of Psychology, 41,* 247–252.

Sjöberg, A. & Sverke, M. (2001). Instrumental and ideological union commitment: Longitudinal assessment of construct validity. *European Journal of Psychological Assessment, 2,* 98–111.

Smulders, P. G. W. & Klein Hesselink, D. J. (1997). Nederland lang geen koploper fexibilisering; how flexibel is Nederland vergeleken met andere landen van de Europese Unie? *Econonomisch Statistische Berichten, 82,* 888–890.

Sparrow, P. R. & Marchington, M. (1998). *Human Resource Management: The new agenda.* London: Pitman.

Sparrow, P. R. (2000). The new employment contract: Psychological implications of future work. In R. J. Burke & C. L. Cooper (eds.), *The Organization in Crisis; Downsizing, restructuring, and privatization* (pp. 165–187). Oxford: Blackwell.

Spector, P. E. (1982). Behavior in organizations as a function of employees locus of control. *Psychological Bulletin, 91,* 482–497.

Spector, P. E. (1986). Perceived control by employees: A meta-analysis of studies concerning autonomy and participation at work. *Human Relations, 39,* 1005–1016.

Spector, P. E. (1988). Development of the work locus of control scale. *Journal of Occupational Psychology, 61,* 335–340.

Spector, P. E. (1992). *Summated Rating Scale Construction* (Vol. No. 07–082). Newbury Park, CA: Sage.

Steel, R. P. & Ovalle, N. K. (1984). A review and meta-analysis of research on the relationship between behavioral intentions and employee turnover. *Journal of Applied Psychology, 69*, 673–686.

Still, L. W. (1983). Part-time versus full-time salespeople: Individual attributes, organizational commitment, and work attitudes. *Journal of Retailing, 59*, 55–79.

Storrie, D. (2002). *Temporary Agency Work in the European Union.* Dublin: European Foundation for the Improvement of Living and Working Conditions.

Sverke, M. & Kuruvilla, S. (1995). A new conceptualization of union commitment: Development and test of an integrated theory. *Journal of Organizational Behavior, 16*, 23–42.

Sverke, M. & Sjöberg, A. (1995). Union membership behavior: The influence of instrumental and value-based commitment. In L. E. Tetrick & J. Barling (eds.), *Changing Employment Relations: Behavioral and social perspectives* (pp. 229–254). Washington, DC: American Psychological Association.

Sverke, M. (1997). Emerging union structures: An introduction. In M. Sverke (ed.), *The Future of Trade Unionism: International perspectives on emerging union structures* (pp. 3–18). Aldershot: Ashgate.

Sverke, M. & Sjöberg, A. (1997). Ideological and instrumental union commitment. In M. Sverke (ed.), *The Future of Trade Unionism: International perspectives on emerging union structures* (pp. 277–294). Aldershot: Ashgate.

Sverke, M., Gallagher, D. G. & Hellgren, J. (2000). Alternative work arrangements: Job stress, well-being, and work attitudes among employees with different employment contracts. In K. Isaksson, C. Hogstedt, C. Eriksson & T. Theorell (eds.), *Health Effects of the New Labour Market* (pp. 145–167). New York: Kluwer Academic/Plenum Publishers.

Sverke, M. & Hellgren, J. (2001). Exit, voice, and loyalty reactions to job insecurity: Do unionized and non-unionized employees differ? *British Journal of Industrial Relations, 39*, 167–182.

Sverke, M., Hellgren, J. & Näswall, K. (2001). Vad vet vi om anställningsotrygghet och dess konsekvenser? Slutsatser från två decenniers forskning [What do we know about job insecurity and its consequences? Conclusions based on two decades of research] *Nordisk Psykologi, 53*, 91–108.

Sverke, M. & Hellgren, J. (2002). The nature of job insecurity: Understanding employment uncertainty on the brink of a new millennium. *Applied Psychology: An International Review, 51*, 23–42.

Sverke, M., Hellgren, J. & Näswall, K. (2002). No security: A meta-analysis and review of job insecurity and its consequences. *Journal of Occupational Health Psychology, 7*, 242–264.

179

Sverke, M. & Goslinga, S. (2003). The consequences of job insecurity for employers and unions: Exit, voice, and loyalty. *Economic and Industrial Democracy, 24*, 241–270.

Tetrick, L. E. & Barling, J. (eds.). (1995). *Changing Employment Relations: Behavioral and social perspectives.* Washington, DC: American Psychological Association.

Theorell, T. (2003). To be able to exert control over one's own situation: A necessary condition for coping with stressors. In J. C. Quick & L. E. Tetrick (eds.), *Handbook of Occupational Health Psychology* (pp. 201–219). Washington, DC: American Psychological Association.

Thompson, S. C. (1981). Will it hurt less if I can control it? A complex answer to a simple question. *Psychological Bulletin, 90*, 89–101.

Valkenburg, B. (1996). Individualization and solidarity: The challenge of modernization. In P. Leisink, J. Van Leemput & J. Vilrokx (eds.), *The Challenges to Trade Unions in Europe: Innovation and adaptation.* Cheltenham: Edward Elgar.

Valkenburg, B. & Coenen, H. (2000). Changing trade unionism in the Netherlands: A critical analysis. In J. Waddington & R. Hoffman (eds.), *Trade Unions in Europe: Facing challenges and searching for solutions* (pp. 393–415). Brussels: European Trade Union Institute.

Van Gyes, G., De Witte, H. & Van der Hallen, P. (2000). Belgian trade unions in the 1990s: Does strong today mean strong tomorrow? In J. Waddington & R. Hoffman (eds.), *Trade Unions in Europe: Facing challenges and searching for solutions* (pp. 105–141). Brussels: European Trade Union Institute.

Van Ruysseveldt, J. (1995). Growing cross-national diversity or diversity *tout court?* In J. Van Ruysseveldt, R. Huiskamp & J. van Hoof (eds.), *Comparative Industrial and Employment Relations* (pp. 1–15). London: Sage.

Van Ruysseveldt, J., Huiskamp, R. & van Hoof, J. (eds.). (1995). *Comparative Industrial and Employment Relations.* London: Sage.

Van Vuuren, T. (1990). *Met ontslag bedreigd: Werknemers in onzekerheid over hun arbeidsplaats bij veranderingen in de organisatie* [Threatened with dismissal. Job insecurity among workers during organizational change]. Amsterdam: VU: Uitgeverij.

Van Vuuren, T., Klandermans, B., Jacobson, D. & Hartley, J. (1991a). Predicting employees' perceptions of job insecurity. In J. Hartley, D. Jacobsson, B. Klandermans & T. Van Vuuren (eds.), *Job Insecurity* (pp. 65–78). London: Sage.

Van Vuuren, T., Klandermans, B., Jacobson, D. & Hartley, J. (1991b). Employees' reactions to job insecurity. In J. Hartley, D. Jacobsson, B. Klandermans & T. Van Vuuren (eds.), *Job Insecurity* (pp. 79–103). London: Sage.

Vandoorne, J. & De Witte, H. (2002). In het ongewisse. Over het voorkomen en de gevolgen van jobonzekerheid in Vlaandern [In a state of uncertainty. On the prevalence and consequences of job insecurity in Flanders]. In G. Vandenbroucke (ed.), *Arbeidsmarktonderzoekersdag 2001. Verslagsboek* [Proceedings of the bi-annual meeting of labour market researchers] (pp. 135–151). Leuven: Steunpunt WAV.

Vilrokx, J. & Van Leemput, J. (1998). Belgium: The great transformation. In A. Ferner & R. Hyman (eds.), *Changing Industrial Relations in Europe* (pp. 315–347). Oxford: Blackwell.

Visser, J. (1995). Trade unions from a comparative perspective. In J. Van Ruysseveldt, R. Huiskamp & J. van Hoof (eds.), *Comparative Industrial and Employment Relations* (pp. 37–67). London: Sage.

Visser, J. (1996). Traditions and transitions in industrial relations: A European view. In J. Van Ruysseveldt & J. Visser (eds.), *Industrial Relations in Europe: Traditions and transitions* (pp. 1–41). London: Sage.

Visser, J. (1998). The Netherlands: The return of responsive corporatism. In A. Ferner & R. Hyman (eds.), *Changing Industrial Relations in Europe* (pp. 283–314). Oxford: Blackwell.

Viswesvaran, C., Sanchez, J. I. & Fisher, J. (1999). The role of social support in the process of work stress: A meta-analysis. *Journal of Vocational Behavior, 54*, 314–334.

Waddington, J. & Whitston, C. (1997). Why do people join unions in a period of membership decline? *British Journal of Industrial Relations, 35*, 515–546.

Waddington, J. & Hoffmann, R. (2000). Trade unions in Europe: Reform, organization and restructuring. In J. Waddington & R. Hoffmann (eds.), *Trade Unions in Europe. Facing challenges and searching for solutions* (pp. 27–79). Brussels: European Trade Union Institute.

Warr, P. B. (1987). *Work, Unemployment, and Mental Health*. Oxford: Clarendon Press.

Watson, D. & Clark, L. A. (1997). Extraversion and its positive emotional core. In R. Hogan, J. Johnson & S. Briggs (eds.), *Handbook of Personality Psychology* (pp. 737–758). San Diego: Academic Press.

Western, B. (1997). *Between Capital and Class: Postwar unionization in the capitalist democracies*. Princeton: Princeton University Press.

Westman, M. (2000). Gender and job insecurity. In R. J. Burke & C. L. Cooper (eds.), *The Organization in Crisis; Downsizing, restructuring, and privatization* (pp. 119–131). Oxford: Blackwell.

Wheeler, H. N. & McClendon, J. A. (1991). The individual decision to unionize. In G. Strauss, D. G. Gallagher & J. Fiorito (eds.), *The State of the Unions*. Madison, WI: Industrial Relations Research Association.

Winefield, A. H. (1996). Unemployment: Its psychological costs. In C. L. Cooper & I. T. Robertson (eds.), *International Review of Industrial and Organizational Psychology* (Vol. 10, pp. 169–212). Chichester: Wiley.

World Bank. (2000). *Entering the 21st Century: World development report 1999/2000*. New York: Oxford University Press.

Zapf, D., Dormann, C. & Frese, M. (1996). Longitudinal studies in organizational stress research: A review of the literature with reference to methodological issues. *Journal of Occupational Health Psychology, 1*, 145–169.

Description of Measures

Job Insecurity

Table A.1. Means (and standard deviations) for job insecurity

Sources: Ashford, Lee, and Bobko (1989); De Witte (2000); Hellgren, Sverke, and Isaksson (1999)

Response scale: 1 (strongly disagree) – 5 (strongly agree), except for the alternative Belgian data set where responses ranged from 1 (unlikely or impossible to become unemployed) – 5 (very likely to become unemployed)

	Belgium	Belgium[a]	Italy	The Netherlands	Sweden	Sweden[a]
I am afraid I will get fired	2.10 (1.18)	–	2.30 (1.24)	1.76 (.76)	2.00 (1.30)	2.01 (1.39)
I worry about keeping my job	2.40 (1.09)	–	3.23 (1.29)	1.85 (.85)	2.03 (1.30)	–
I fear I will lose my job	2.27 (1.06)	–	2.51 (1.27)	1.83 (.83)	1.92 (1.24)	–
I think I might get fired in the near future	2.00 (.91)	–	2.36 (1.21)	1.75 (.73)	1.85 (1.20)	1.73 (1.14)
I am sure I can keep my job (R)	2.55 (1.09)	–	2.65 (1.13)	2.08 (.89)	2.63 (1.34)	1.67 (1.18)
What is the probability that you will become unemployed in the near future?	–	1.83 (.99)	–	–	–	–
N	1,103	1,482	451	611	1,904	1,451
Reliability (α)	.90	–	.76	.91	.89	.77
M (scale)	2.26	1.83	2.61	1.85	2.09	1.80
SD (scale)	.89	.99	.87	.69	1.06	1.03

[a] Alternative data set. Table reports insecurity scores for all samples used in the book.
– Not applicable.
(R) indicates reverse-scored item.

Individual Consequences

Table A.2. Means (and standard deviations)
for mental health complaints

Source: General Health Questionnaire (GHQ; Goldberg, 1979)
Response scale: 1 (never) – 4 (always), except for Belgium: 1 (no) – 2 (yes)

	Belgium[a]	Italy	The Netherlands	Sweden
Have you recently…				
…Been able to concentrate on whatever you're doing (R)	–	1.95 (.69)	1.56 (.68)	1.97 (.65)
…Lost much sleep over worry	–	1.99 (.80)	1.47 (.71)	1.93 (.86)
…Felt that you are playing a useful part in things (R)	–	2.93 (.82)	1.70 (.72)	2.42 (.77)
…Felt capable of making decisions about things (R)	–	2.40 (.78)	1.82 (.83)	2.11 (.67)
…Felt constantly under strain	–	2.59 (.83)	2.09 (.98)	2.25 (.76)
…Felt you could overcome your difficulties (R)	–	1.99 (.72)	1.45 (.66)	1.85 (.62)
…Been able to enjoy your normal day–to–day activities (R)	–	2.32 (.78)	1.70 (.70)	2.12 (.74)
…Felt you are unable to face up to your problems	–	1.84 (.68)	1.52 (.69)	1.82 (.80)
…Been feeling unhappy and depressed	–	1.84 (.66)	1.43 (.62)	1.85 (.73)
…Been losing confidence in yourself	–	1.50 (.66)	1.24 (.52)	1.70 (.86)
…Been thinking of yourself as a worthless person	–	1.43 (.66)	1.15 (.41)	1.58 (.89)
…Been feeling reasonable happy all things considered (R)	–	2.17 (.84)	1.65 (.68)	2.23 (.73)
Do you feel mentally exhausted by your work	1.28 (.45)	–	–	–
Do you feel empty at the end of a working day	1.41 (.49)	–	–	–

to be continued

Table A.2. Cont'd.

Do you feel tired when waking up in the morning, when there is another working day ahead of you	1.26 (.44)	–	–	–
Do you feel "burned out" by your work	1.17 (.38)	–	–	–
Do you feel frustrated by your job	1.16 (.37)	–	–	–
Do you think that you dedicate yourself too much to your work	1.41 (.49)	–	–	–
Do you feel at the end of your strengths	1.08 (.27)	–	–	–
N	1,093	451	799	1,890
Reliability (α)	.77	.74	.82	.84
M **(scale)**	1.25	2.08	1.58	1.99
SD **(scale)**	.27	.37	.42	.46

– Not applicable.

[a] The mean values for the Belgian data are based on a dichotomous item. The decimals indicate the proportion of the sample that responded "yes" on these items. (R) indicates reverse-scored item.

Table A.3. Means (and standard deviations)
for physical health complaints

Source: Anderson (1986), modified by Isaksson and Johansson (1997)
Response scale: 1 (never) – 5 (always)

	Belgium	Italy	The Netherlands	Sweden
Have you in the last 12 months suffered from…				
…Stomach problems	–	2.10 (1.14)	1.45 (.96)	2.02 (1.24)
…Problems from heart or chest	–	1.22 (.66)	1.23 (.66)	1.43 (.87)
…Muscular tension	–	2.13 (1.14)	2.08 (1.26)	2.92 (1.53)
…Mood problems	–	2.56 (1.12)	1.80 (1.01)	2.31 (1.13)
…Sleeping problems	–	2.03 (1.12)	1.71 (1.06)	2.25 (1.26)
…Headache	–	2.24 (1.06)	1.88 (1.02)	2.41 (1.17)
…Skin irritations or itching	–	1.71 (1.06)	1.40 (.83)	1.67 (1.14)
…Breathing problems	–	1.57 (.94)	1.31 (.86)	1.37 (.86)
…Tiredness	–	3.10 (1.12)	2.26 (1.19)	3.22 (1.31)
…Long–term colds	–	1.70 (1.08)	1.57 (.88)	1.72 (.93)
N	–	438	425	1,902
Reliability (α)	–	.81	.73	.81
M (scale)	–	2.04	1.67	2.13
SD (scale)	–	.65	.54	.71

– Not applicable.

Organizational Consequences

Table A.4. Means (and standard deviations) for job satisfaction

Sources: De Witte (2000); Hellgren, Sjöberg, and Sverke (1997), based on Brayfield and Rothe (1951)
Response scale: 1 (strongly disagree) – 5 (strongly agree)

	Belgium	Italy	The Netherlands	Sweden
I am (very) satisfied with my job	3.85 (.94)	3.55 (1.19)	3.85 (.81)	3.68 (1.13)
I enjoy being at my job	–	3.55 (1.11)	–	4.08 (.98)
I am content with the job I have/ in general	3.88 (.85)	3.71 (1.18)	–	3.57 (1.09)
I feel strong ties with my work	3.53 (.98)	3.94 (1.06)	3.85 (.74)	–
My job allows me to show what I'm worth	3.53 (1.11)	3.22 (1.24)	3.69 (.91)	3.41 (1.14)
N	1,108	443	611	1,899
Reliability (α)	.85	.87	.72	.82
M (scale)	3.70	3.60	3.79	3.68
SD (scale)	.80	.94	.63	.88

– Not applicable.

Table A.5. Means (and standard deviations)
for organizational commitment

Source: Allen and Meyer (1990)
Response scale: 1 (strongly disagree) – 5 (strongly agree)

	Belgium	Italy	The Netherlands	Sweden
I would be very happy spending the rest of my career with this organization	3.95 (1.07)	3.32 (1.29)	3.70 (.90)	2.80 (1.29)
I really feel as if this organization's problems are my own problems	3.02 (1.05)	3.03 (1.20)	3.22 (.98)	2.57 (1.13)
This organization has a great deal of personal meaning to me	3.52 (.99)	3.18 (1.23)	3.71 (.78)	2.57 (1.15)
I feel a strong sense of belonging to my organization	3.31 (1.04)	3.36 (1.21)	3.68 (.83)	2.56 (1.13)
I feel emotionally attached to my organization	3.14 (1.11)	3.10 (1.26)	3.28 (.96)	2.18 (1.14)
N	1,105	449	611	1,853
Reliability (α)	.86	.88	.78	.86
M (scale)	3.39	3.20	3.52	2.54
SD (scale)	.84	1.02	.65	.93

– Not applicable.

Table A.6. Means (and standard deviations) for turnover intention

Sources: Sjöberg and Sverke (1996, 2000), based on Camman, Fishman, Jenkins, and Klesh (1979) and Lyons (1971)
Response scale: 1 (strongly disagree) – 5 (strongly agree), except for Belgium: 1 (no) – 2 (yes)

	Belgium[a]	Italy	The Netherlands	Sweden
I feel that I could leave this job	–	3.11 (1.21)	2.85 (1.20)	2.25 (1.32)
I am actively looking for other jobs	–	1.95 (1.22)	–	1.94 (1.29)
If I was completely free to choose, independent of the current labor market, I would leave my present job	–	2.82 (1.40)	–	2.72 (1.52)
Did you think of looking for another job during the past months	1.35 (.48)	–	–	–
Did you do something during the past year in order to find a new job	1.23 (.42)	–	–	–
Would you still work in this organization if the choice was yours	1.27 (.45)	–	–	–
N	1,109	449	611	1,862
Reliability (α)	.73	.68	–	.78
M (scale)	1.28	2.63	2.85	2.30
SD (scale)	.36	1.01	1.20	1.15

– Not applicable.
[a] The mean values for the Belgian data are based on dichotomous items. The decimals indicate the proportion of the sample that responded "yes" on these items.

Union Related Attitudes

Table A.7. Means (and standard deviations) for union commitment

Sources: Meyer, Allen, and Smith (1993), adapted by Goslinga (1997); Sverke and Kuruvilla (1995)
Response scale: 1 (strongly disagree) – 5 (strongly agree)

	Belgium[a]	Italy	The Netherlands	Sweden
I believe in the goals of organ- ized labor	–	4.07 (1.05)	–	3.34 (1.16)
My union's problems are my problems	2.87 (1.42)	3.33 (1.22)	2.87 (.93)	2.72 (1.17)
My union means a great deal to me personally	2.82 (1.33)	3.52 (1.20)	3.03 (.92)	2.71 (1.22)
I feel a strong sense of belonging to my union	2.82 (1.39)	3.23 (1.28)	3.09 (.95)	2.83 (1.15)
I feel emotionally attached to my union	1.96 (1.25)	3.32 (1.33)	2.58 (.98)	2.14 1.15
N	868	423	799	1,860
Reliability (α)	.79	.86	.85	.86
M (scale)	2.62	3.50	2.89	2.75
SD (scale)	1.05	.92	.78	.94

– Not applicable.
[a] Alternative data set used.

Table A.8. Means (and standard deviations) for union satisfaction

Source: Sverke and Sjöberg (1997)
Response scale: 1 (very dissatisfied) – 5 (very satisfied)

	Belgium[a]	Italy	The Netherlands	Sweden
How satisfied/dissatisfied are you with your union	3.77 (.94)	–	–	–
How satisfied are you with...	–	–	–	–
...Your union	–	2.63 (.99)	3.66 (.74)	3.21 (.93)
...The union policies	–	2.44 (.97)	3.94 (.70)	3.28 (1.05)
...The provision of information by your union	–	2.60 (.96)	3.58 (.81)	3.07 (1.04)
...The services provided to individual members	–	–	3.68 (.78)	2.72 (1.09)
...The policies of the union federation	–	3.31 (1.17)	3.59 (.70)	–
...The provision of information by the union federation	–	3.39 (1.16)	3.73 (.69)	–
N	866	461	799	1,856
Reliability (α)	–	.87	.75	.87
M (scale)	3.77	2.86	3.70	3.07
SD (scale)	.94	.85	.49	.88

– Not applicable.
[a] Alternative data set used.

Table A.9. Means (and standard deviations)
for union turnover intention

Source: Sverke and Kuruvilla (1995)
Response scale: 1 (strongly disagree) – 5 (strongly agree)

	Belgium[a]	Italy	The Netherlands	Sweden
I would quit my union if I had a good alternative	2.98 (1.56)	2.70 (1.45)	2.73 (1.03)	1.39 (.49)
I sometimes consider quitting my membership	–	2.76 (1.50)	2.28 (.95)	–
I sometimes consider changing to a different union	–	2.22 (1.32)	2.03 (.75)	–
N	858	428	799	1,855
Reliability (α)	–	.75	.66	–
M (scale)	2.98	2.58	2.34	1.39
SD (scale)	1.56	1.20	.70	.49

– Not applicable.
[a] Alternative data set used.

Table A.10. Means (and standard deviations) for union support

Source: Shore, Tetrick, Sinclair, and Newton (1994), adapted by Goslinga (1996)
Response scale: 1 (strongly disagree) – 5 (strongly agree)

	Belgium[a]	Italy	The Netherlands	Sweden
I can always call upon my union with questions or problems	4.31 (1.06)	3.12 (1.29)	4.02 (.58)	3.52 (1.20)
My union hardly takes into account the things that are important for me	3.59 (1.32)	3.25 (1.17)	3.62 (.78)	3.41 (1.07)
My union appreciates my opinion	3.73 (1.21)	3.21 (1.05)	3.62 (.63)	2.63 (1.04)
If I have a complaint my union doesn't really care	3.70 (1.38)	3.44 (1.23)	3.58 (.74)	3.21 (1.15)
My union hardly has any concerns about my well–being	3.69 (1.35)	3.20 (1.18)	3.68 (.71)	–
N	864	434	799	1,862
Reliability (α)	.68	.61	.73	.71
M (scale)	3.80	3.24	3.70	3.19
SD (scale)	.84	.74	.48	.82

– Not applicable.
[a] Alternative data set used.

Personality Variables

Table A.11. Means (and standard deviations)
for general self-efficacy

Source: Sherer, Maddux, Mercandante, Prentice-Dunn, Jacobs, and Rogers (1982)
Response scale: 1 (strongly disagree) – 5 (strongly agree)

	Sweden[a]
When I make plans, I am certain I can make them work	3.76 (.93)
One of my problems is that I can not get down to work when I should (R)	3.96 (1.11)
If I can't do a job the first time, I keep trying until I can	4.03 (.89)
When I set important goals for myself, I rarely achieve them (R)	4.10 (.90)
I give up on things before completing them (R)	4.34 (.87)
I avoid facing difficulties (R)	3.43 (1.17)
If something looks too complicated, I will not even bother to try it (R)	4.26 (.92)
When I have something unpleasant to do, I stick to it until I finish it	3.77 (1.10)
When I decide to do something, I go right to work on it	3.71 (1.06)
When trying to learn something new, I soon give up if I am not initially successful (R)	4.31 (.94)
When unexpected problems occur, I don't handle them well (R)	4.09 (.93)
I avoid trying to learn new things when they look too difficult for me (R)	4.19 (1.01)
Failure just makes me try harder	3.60 (.96)
I feel insecure about my ability to do things (R)	4.09 (1.07)
I am a self–reliant person	4.41 (.71)
I give up easily (R)	4.38 (.87)
I do not seem capable of dealing with most problems that come up in life (R)	4.41 (.88)
N	1,443
Reliability (α)	.85
M **(scale)**	4.05
SD **(scale)**	.52

[a] Alternative data set used.
(R) indicates reverse-scored item.

Table A.12. Means (and standard deviations)
for internal locus of control

Source: Spector (1988)
Response scale: 1 (strongly disagree) – 5 (strongly agree)

	Sweden[a]
A job is what you make of it	3.66 (1.09)
On most jobs, people can pretty much accomplish whatever they set out to accomplish	3.30 (.98)
If you know what you want out of a job, you can find a job that gives it to you	3.38 (1.13)
If employees are unhappy with a decision made by their boss, they should do something about it	4.03 (1.10)
Getting the job you want is mostly a matter of luck(R)	3.61 (1.19)
Making money is primarily a matter of good fortune (R)	3.79 (1.20)
Most people are capable of doing their jobs well if they make the effort	3.96 (.95)
In order to get a really good job you need to have family members or friend in high places (R)	3.30 (1.25)
Promotions are usually a matter of good fortune (R)	3.88 (1.12)
When it comes to landing a really good job, who you know is more important than what you know (R)	3.40 (1.26)
Promotions are given to employees who perform well on the job	3.03 (1.15)
To make a lot of money you have to know the right people (R)	3.19 (1.42)
It takes a lot of luck to be an outstanding employee on most jobs (R)	3.95 (1.09)
People who perform their jobs well generally get rewarded for it	2.74 (1.19)
Most employees have more influence on their supervisors than the think they do	2.56 (1.04)
The main difference between people who make a lot of money and people who make a little money is luck (R)	3.99 (1.15)
N	1,495
Reliability (α)	.79
M (scale)	3.48
SD (scale)	.58

[a] Alternative data set used.
(R) indicates reverse-scored item.

Table A.13. Means (and standard deviations) for positive affectivity

Source: Agho, Price, and Mueller (1992)
Response scale: 1 (strongly disagree) – 5 (strongly agree)

	Sweden[a]
It is easy for me to become enthusiastic about things I am doing	3.97 (.85)
I live a very interesting life	3.50 (.98)
Every day I do things that are fun	3.53 (1.16)
I usually find ways to liven up my day	3.67 (.90)
Most days I have moments of real fun or joy	3.58 (1.13)
I often feel sort of lucky for no special reason	3.39 (1.00)
Every day interesting things happen to me	3.36 (1.12)
In my spare time I usually find something interesting to do	4.02 (.95)
For me life is a great adventure	2.93 (1.13)
I always seem to have something pleasant to look forward to	3.29 (1.05)
N	1,448
Reliability (α)	.89
M (scale)	3.52
SD (scale)	.70

[a] Alternative data set used.

196

Table A.14. Means (and standard deviations) for negative affectivity

Source: Agho, Price, and Mueller (1992)
Response scale: 1 (strongly disagree) – 5 (strongly agree)

	Sweden[a]
I often find myself worrying about something	2.60 (1.16)
My feelings are hurt rather easily	3.01 (1.13)
Often I get irritated at little annoyances	2.39 (1.11)
I suffer from nervousness	1.65 (.95)
My mood often goes up and down	2.41 (1.17)
I sometimes feel "just miserable" for no good reason	1.97 (1.06)
I am easily startled by things that happen unexpectedly	2.72 (1.11)
I often loose sleep over my worries	1.68 (.99)
Minor set–back sometimes irritate me too much	2.08 (1.06)
There are days when I'm "on edge" all of the time	2.23 (1.22)
I am too sensitive for my own good	2.24 (1.16)
N	1,448
Reliability (α)	.85
M **(scale)**	2.27
SD **(scale)**	.69

[a] Alternative data set used.

Index

About the Authors

Magnus Sverke, PhD, is Associate Professor at the Department of Psychology, Stockholm University. His research interests include organizational change and its effects on employees, job insecurity, employee attitudes and well-being, and union member attitudes and behavior. *E-mail*: mse@psychology.su.se

Johnny Hellgren, PhD, is a researcher and teacher at the Department of Psychology, Stockholm University. His main research interests concern organizational change, downsizing, job insecurity, health, work climate and attitudes, as well as the role of the union. *E-mail*: jhn@psychology.su.se

Katharina Näswall, PhD, is working as a researcher at the Department of Psychology, Stockholm University. Her main research interests concern job insecurity, employee well-being, and stress and coping. *E-mail*: knl@psychology.su.se

Antonio Chirumbolo, PhD, is Researcher at the University of Rome "La Sapienza". His dissertation focused on motivation and creativity. Other areas of interests are political psychology and job insecurity, as well as epistemic motivations and group creativity. *E-mail*: chirumbolo@uniroma1.it

Hans De Witte, Professor, is Lecturer in work psychology at the Catholic University of Leuven, Belgium. His research interests include job insecurity, attitudes towards work, trade unions, consequences of unemployment, working-class culture, and work related well-being. *E-mail*: hans.dewitte@psy.kuleuven.ac.be

Sjoerd Goslinga, PhD, was Researcher at the Department of Social Psychology and coordinator of the CNV/VU Research Program at the Free University Amsterdam at the time the studies for this book were conducted. He is now Researcher at the Dutch Criminal Investigation Service of the Tax and Customs Administration (FIOD-ECD). His research interests include organizational behavior, commitment, compliance and collective action. *E-mail*: sgoslinga@hotmail.com

From left: Johnny Hellgren, Antonio Chirumbolo, Sjoerd Goslinga, Katharina Näswall, Magnus Sverke, Hans De Witte

"Work & Society"

The series "Work & Society" analyses the development of employment and social policies, as well as the strategies of the different social actors, both at national and European levels. It puts forward a multi-disciplinary approach – political, sociological, economic, legal and historical – in a bid for dialogue and complementarity.
The series is not confined to the social field *stricto sensu*, but also aims to illustrate the indirect social impacts of economic and monetary policies. It endeavours to clarify social developments, from a comparative and a historical perspective, thus portraying the process of convergence and divergence in the diverse national societal contexts. The manner in which European integration impacts on employment and social policies constitutes the backbone of the analyses.

Series Editor: Philippe POCHET, Director of the Observatoire Social Européen (Brussels) and Digest Editor of the Journal of European Social Policy.

Recent Titles

No.43– *Wage and Welfare. New Perspectives on Employment and Social Rights in Europe*, Bernadette CLASQUIN, Nathalie MONCEL, Mark HARVEY & Bernard FRIOT (eds.) (2004), 206 p., ISBN 90-5201-214-8

No.42– *Job Insecurity and Union Membership. European Unions in the Wake of Flexible Production*, M. SVERKE, J. HELLGREN, K. NÄSWELL, A. CHIRUMBOLO, H. DE WITTE & S. GOSLINGA (eds.) (2004), 202 p., ISBN 90-5201-202-4

N°41– *L'aide au conditionnel. La contrepartie dans les mesures envers les personnes sans emploi en Europe et en Amérique du Nord*, Pascale DUFOUR, Gérard BOISMENU & Alain NOËL (2003) en coéd. avec les PUM, 248 p., ISBN 90-5201-198-2

N°40– *Protection sociale et fédéralisme*, Bruno THÉRET (2002) en coéd. avec les PUM, 2002, 495 p., ISBN 90-5201-107-9.

No.39– *The Impact of EU Law on Health Care Systems*, Martin MCKEE, Elias MOSSIALOS & Rita BAETEN (eds.) (2002, 2nd printing 2003), 314 p., ISBN 90-5201-106-0.

No.38– *EU Law and the Social Character of Health Care*, Elias MOSSIALOS & Martin MCKEE (2002, 2nd printing 2004), 259 p., ISBN 90-5201-110-9.

No.37– *Wage Policy in the Eurozone*, Philippe POCHET (ed.), Observatoire social européen, 2002, 286 p., ISBN 90-5201-101-X.

N°36– *Politique salariale dans la zone euro*, Philippe POCHET (dir.), Observatoire social européen, 2002, 308 p., ISBN 90-5201-100-1.

No.35– *Regulating Health and Safety Management in the European Union. A Study of the Dynamics of Change*, David WALTERS (ed.), SALTSA, 2002, 346 p., ISBN 90-5201-998-3.

No.34– *Building Social Europe through the Open Method of Co-ordination*, Caroline DE LA PORTE & Philippe POCHET (eds.), SALTSA – Observatoire social européen, 2002, 311 p., ISBN 90-5201-984-3.

N°33– *Des marchés du travail équitables?*, Christian BESSY, François EYMARD-DUVERNAY, Guillemette DE LARQUIER & Emmanuelle MARCHAL (dir.), Centre d'Études de l'Emploi, 2001, 308 p., ISBN 90-5201-960-6.

No.32– *Trade Unions in Europe: Meeting the Challenge*, Deborah FOSTER & Peter SCOTT (eds.), 2003, 200 p., ISBN 90-5201-959-2.

No.31– *Health and Safety in Small Enterprises. European Strategies for Managing Improvement*, David WALTERS, SALTSA, 2001, 404 p., ISBN 90-5201-952-5.

No.30– *Europe – One Labour Market?*, Lars MAGNUSSON & Jan OTTOSSON (eds.), SALTSA, 2002, 306 p., ISBN 90-5201-949-5.

No.29– *From the Werner Plan to the EMU. In Search of a Political Economy for Europe*, Lars MAGNUSSON & Bo STRÅTH (eds.), SALTSA, 2001, 526 p., ISBN 90-5201-948-7.

N°28– *Discriminations et marché du travail. Liberté et égalité dans les rapports d'emploi*, Olivier DE SCHUTTER, 2001, 234 p., ISBN 90-5201-941-X.

No.27– *At Your Service? Comparative Perspectives on Employment and Labour Relations in the European Private Sector Services*, Jon Erik DØLVIK (ed.), SALTSA, 2001, 556 p., ISBN 90-5201-940-1.

N°26– *La nouvelle dynamique des pactes sociaux*, Giuseppe FAJERTAG & Philippe POCHET (dir.), Observatoire social européen – European Trade Union Institute, 2001, 436 p., ISBN 90-5201-927-4.

No.25– *After Full Employment. European Discourses on Work and Flexibility*, Bo STRÅTH (ed.), 2000, 302 p., ISBN 90-5201-925-8.

N°24– *L'Europe syndicale au quotidien. La représentation des salariés dans les entreprises en France, Allemagne, Grande-Bretagne et Italie*, Christian DUFOUR et Adelheid HEGE, IRES, 2002, 256 p., ISBN 90-5201-918-5.

N°23– *Union monétaire et négociations collectives en Europe*, Philippe POCHET (ed.), SALTSA – Observatoire social européen, 1999, 284 p., ISBN 90-5201-916-9.

No.22– *Monetary Union and Collective Bargaining in Europe*, Philippe POCHET (ed.), SALTSA – Observatoire social européen, 1999, 284 p., ISBN 90-5201-915-0.

No.21– *The Regulation of Working Time in the European Union (Gender Approach) – La réglementation du temps de travail en Europe (Perspective selon le genre)*, Yota KRAVARITOU (ed.), European University Institute, 1999, 504 p., ISBN 90-5201-903-7.

P.I.E.-Peter Lang – The website

Discover the general website of the Peter Lang publishing group:

www.peterlang.net

You will find

- an online bookshop of currently about 21,000 titles from the entire publishing group, which allows quick and easy ordering
- all books published since 1992
- an overview of our journals and series
- contact forms for new authors and customers
- information about the activities of each publishing house

Come and browse! We look forward to your visit!